T0338086

Desert Dreamers

With the Warlpiri people of Australia

Barbara Glowczewski

Les Rêveurs du désert
by Barbara Glowczewski
(Plon 1989, pocket new edition Actes Sud 1996, 2000)

translated by Paul Buck and Catherine Petit as
Desert Dreamers

© Barbara Glowczewski

First Edition
Published by Univocal
123 North 3rd Street, #202
Minneapolis, MN 55401

Images © Barbara Glowczewski

Designed & Printed by Jason Wagner

Distributed by the University of Minnesota Press

ISBN 9781937561963
Library of Congress Control Number 2015958264

Table of Contents

PART FOUR (1984)

PART FIVE (1984)

PART SIX (1988)

ANNEX (2013)

Beryl Nakamarra Gibson, *Ngurlu Seed Dreaming for Miya Miya*,
acrylic on canvas, 130 x 100cm, 1989.

My thanks to the Warlpiri men and women of Lajamanu who have guided me, in particular the Barnes, Birrel, Blacksmith, Burns, Cooke, Fencer, Gibson, Gordon, Hargraves, Hector, Herbert, Hogan, Lawson, Long, Luther, Martin, Morrison, Patrick, Peters, Robertson, Rockman, Rosewood, Ross, Sampson, Simon, Tasman and Walker families.

For their support in the 1980s, I also thank the Central Land Council, the Centre National des Lettres, the Fyssen and Singer Polignac Foundations, the Maison des Sciences de l'Homme, and the research group ITSO (CNRS).

My heartleft gratitude to all the artists from Warnayaka Art, and their coordinator, Louisa Erglis, as well as all the Warlpiri Triangle team of yapa and kardiya teachers and linguists, especially Wanta Steve Patrick Jampijinpa and Mary Laughren, for sharing with me their struggle for the recognition of the Warlpiri language and stunning artistic creativity that sustain a cosmovision caring for the future of the planet.

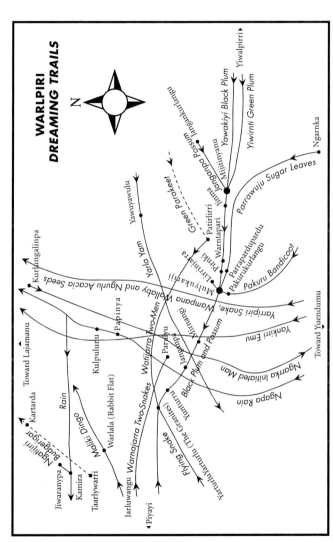

WARLPIRI _DREAMING TRAILS_ These diagrammatic tracings merely represent a small part of the Warlpiri mythological cartography.

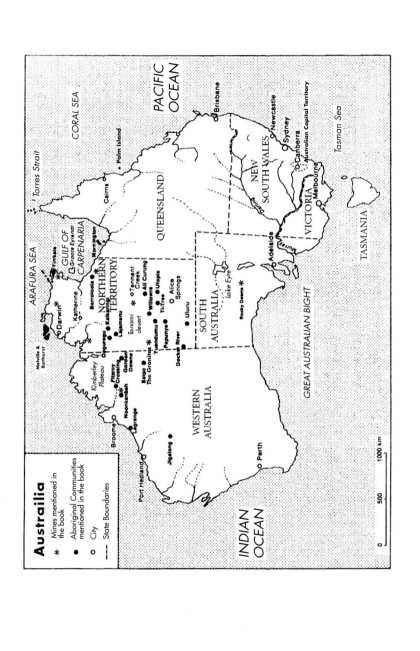

Australia

* Mines mentioned in the book
● Aboriginal Communities mentioned in the book
○ City
- - - State Boundaries

ARAFURA SEA

Torres Strait

CORAL SEA

GULF OF CARPENARIA

Groote Eylandt

· Palm Island

Melville & Bathurst

○ Darwin *

Tiwi *

Katherine

Borroloola ●

NORTHERN TERRITORY

Daguragu * Kalkaringi

Lajamanu

Tanami desert

Yuendumu ●

Papunya ●

Docker River ■

○ Tennant Creek

* Willowra

Ali Curung ●

● Utopia

Ti-Tree ●

Alice Springs ○

Uluru ■

Mornington

Cairns

QUEENSLAND

○ Brisbane

NEW SOUTH WALES

○ Newcastle

○ Sydney

○ Canberra
Australian Capital Territory

Darling

Murrumbidgee

Adelaide ●

SOUTH AUSTRALIA

Lake Eyre

Roxby Downs *

VICTORIA

○ Melbourne

Murray

Tasman Sea

TASMANIA

Kimberley Plateau

Fitzroy Crossing ●

Gordon Downs ●

Balgo ●
The Granites *

Noonkanbah ●

Lagrange

Broome ○

Port Hedland ○

Jigalong ●

WESTERN AUSTRALIA

○ Perth

GREAT AUSTRALIAN BIGHT

INDIAN OCEAN

PACIFIC OCEAN

0   500   1000 km

Nakakut Barbara Gibson Nakamarra painted *yawakiyi* Black Plum for Mulyukarriji, 1984

a journey in homage to
Nakakut Nakamarra Gibson, my Warlpiri mother

FUTURE DREAMING
Foreword to the American Edition, Univocal (2016)

When I arrived in the Central Desert of Australia in 1979, the Warlpiri had just won a land claim by gaining an inalienable freehold title. They traveled relentlessly by car and cattle trucks in order to rediscover their lands and visit their kin spread out throughout the central, western, and northern part of the continent. The four reservations where they had been forced to settle down in the 1950s had become self-governing communities with satellite encampments: Outstations that the Warlpiri created here and there across their lands. They used recent technological advances such as solar power for electricity and walk-in freezers for storing wild game and cold drinks. Water was pumped by way of wind energy and they built semi-precarious structures for camping. The government funds that allowed for this itinerant reappropriation of the desert were collectively managed as were the royalties provided from the mining companies in exchange for the right to mine the earth in search of gold. At the time, 24 years-old, I had the feeling I was living in a social utopia within a universe of invisible signs that called to mind Tarkovsky's film, *Stalker*. I learned to unlearn myself from myself, a new becoming woman among those women who painted my chest and made me dance upon the lines of their *Jukurrpa*, the Dreamings, totemic entities in becoming within everything that is named on the earth and in the sky.

In 1982, I received my PhD from the Department of Ethnology at University of Paris 7, founded by Robert Jaulin, an outspoken critic of the Amazonian ethnocide. One of his friends, the psychoanalyst, Félix Guattari, calls me on the phone out of the blue, excited about my thesis where I write of the relation between time and space for the Warlpiri. He invites me to his apartment to discuss it with him and we pass the whole afternoon talking up until his evening seminar. He proposes that we continue our discussion in public in front of 50 or so people who meet every week at his apartment in St. Germain-des-Prés. I accept the invitation. The seminar is recorded and will end up being published in the revue Chimères,[1] which Guattari will create later on. After my return from another trip into the field at Lajamanu toward the end of 1984, Félix offers me a room in his residence. For several months, we discuss the Warlpiri over breakfast. I write with abandon. Many of those pages will eventually become chapters of *Desert Dreamers*.

In 1988, a contract with the publisher, Plon, allows me to return to Lajamanu to complete *Desert Dreamers*. After two years, the movement of acrylic paintings on canvas initiated by the painters of Papunya has gone viral in the central desert.[2] Almost all the elders, men and women, begin painting: an explosion of art works find their way around the four corners of the earth and assures them a new revenue source. A satellite is installed in the desert that allows the Indigenous Australian communities to hold video conferences between themselves and city institutions as well as to broadcast images produced by the Warlpiri or other neighboring groups on local TV stations with Broadcasting for Remote Aboriginal Communities Scheme (BRACS). I was greatly impressed with what appeared to me as a vital survival strategy against Globalization, much more joyful than those perpetuated in current science fiction.

1. Glowczewski, Barbara. "Espaces de Rêve. Les Warlpiri discussion with Felix Guattari (1983 and 1985), *Chimères* 1: 4-37. (Engl. translation "Warlpiri Dreaming spaces 1 & 2" in B. Glowczewski *Totemic Becomings*, Sao Paulo: n-1 publications, 2015). See also Glowczewski, B. "Guattari and Anthropology." *The Guattari Effect*. Eds. Alliez, E. & Goffey A., New York: Continuum, 2011.
2. Myers, Fred. "Paintings, Publics, and Protocols: the early paintings from Papunya," in *Australian Aboriginal Anthropology Today: Critical Perspectives from Europe* ("Les actes"), Online. June 13, 2014. URL: http://actesbranly.revues.org/524.

In 1996, I write a postface for a paperback version of the present book in Broome, a pearling port in northern Australia where my two daughters are born, Milari and Nidala. The Internet offers a new space for "minor" forms of expression — in the strong sense of their alternative and transformative scope — for populations and peoples whose voices and experiences had become marginalized. I embark on a multimedia project with the elders and artists from the Lajamanu artistic co-operative, Warnayaka Art: our pioneering CD-ROM, *Dream Trackers* is installed on the first Macintosh computers in the school where a collective enthusiasm is shared by the students, parents, and teachers alike for the bilingual teaching of English and Warlpiri. *Dream Trackers* or *Yapa*, as the Warlpiri call it, originating from the term they have for Indigenous people and things, was constructed in concert with 50 artists in a rhizomatic manner, with an opening menu, a map of the Dreaming lines interspersed with hyperlinks. Bestowed with the special jury prize at Moebius, it is released in 2001 by UNESCO for the occasion of the first Indigenous Peoples book fair in Paris under the rubric of an international conference dedicated to the use of new technologies of communication for the promotion of Indigenous forms of knowledge.[3] The research participants who were invited included over 60 Indigenous publishers, artists, curators, writers, filmmakers, and activists from all over the world, including Jimmy Robertson Jampijinpa, a Warlpiri artist and coordinator of Warnayaka Art who explained to one delighted journalist, "The Yapa CD-ROM brings people to the mind…."[4]

Life at Lajamanu took a digital turn at the same time as it continued to rely on its ancestral rituals. Artists began to travel to accompany their painted canvases of multicolored acrylic and traced lines saturated with tiny dots that celebrated the pathways of the totemic becomings of their Dreamings,

3. International Symposium "Indigenous Identities, Cultural Diversity and Indigenous Peoples: Oral, Written Expressions and New Technologies" (UNESCO, Paris, 2001) was co-organized by B. Glowczewski for the CNRS; *Cultural diversity and indigenous peoples: Oral, written expressions and new technologies.* Eds. B. Glowczewski, L. Pourchez, J. Rostkowski, J. Stanton, and the Division of Cultural Policies and Intercultural Dialogue. Paris: UNESCO, 2004. CD-ROM.

4. Glowczewski, Barbara. *Rêves en colère. Avec les Aborigènes*, Plon: Terre Humaine. 2004.

Jukurrpa, through the flesh of the earth. During exhibitions, women painters danced with their chests covered with designs in red ochre referring back to the same sacred prints and cartographies, the *images-forces — kuruwarri —* of their Dreamings in becoming.

The decade of institutional recognition during the 1990s ended in a backlash which will see the specificity of the Indigenous Australians' rights brought into question under pretexts stemming from the Neoliberal ideology of Globalization whose logic and impact can be seen throughout the entirety of the Globe.[5] The Australia of the 21st century applies this ideology in a supposedly pacifistic manner but its effects are just as destructive as an armed conflict. In reality, the systematic negation of their differences affects the youth in the middle of their process of individuation itself. The results of this negation of differences can be seen in the suicides and depth of mourning within the communities not too mention the lethal effects of intoxication that are destroying men and women of all ages.

After the tragedy of the Twin Towers on September 11, 2001, Australian politics becomes engrossed in fighting anti-terrorism and the Indigenous Australians become the lateral victims of this fight. A minister affirms in 2005 that considering "the failure of collectivism throughout the world" since the fall of the Berlin wall, there is no reason for continuing to encourage Aboriginal collectivism. Of course the word "collectivism" here is then used to refer back to the communism of Eastern block countries during the Cold War and has nothing at all to do with the collective modes of assemblage that Indigenous Australians have re-elaborated in confronting colonization and the art market. But the forms of management and governance that they reinvent from one day to the next by way of the movement to re-appropriate their lands seems to play itself out by way of the norms of the State model. The federal government reduces the funding for a number of community programs such as the funding for the Outstations, but also for art centers, as well as the principle of a minimum wage for Community Development Employment Programs (CDEP) that allowed for

---

5. Biddle, Jennifer L. *Breasts, Bodies, Canvas: Central Desert Art as Experience.* Sydney: UNSW Press, 2006; Erin Manning. *Relationscapes: Movement, Art, Philosophy.* Cambridge: MIT Press, 2009.

numerous Indigenous Australians to responsibly assure municipal services for the community including public road upkeep, firewood, meals for the elderly, housing maintenance, etc. Living in Townsville on the northwest coast, as a professor invited by James Cook University, I followed the public hearings at the courthouse of the inquest into the violent death in custody of an Australian Aboriginal man from Palm Island in November 2004 which provoked an insurrection on the island during the reading of the autopsy one week after the death. I also attended the court proceedings of the committal hearing of the 27 Aboriginal men and women from the island arrested for "rioting." We published a book with one of them, Lex Wotton, prosecuted as the ring leader of the riot; condemned to 6 years of prison, he ended up getting out after two years, but on the condition that he couldn't speak in public (about anything) until the end of his sentence.[6]

In 2007, the government of the Northern Territory begins to suppress bilingual teaching and the elected councils in the 73 communities are placed under administrative supervision of the shires of several cities, such as Katherine for Lajamanu, the two of which are separated by 557 kilometers. At the same time, the federal government declares the Northern Territory Emergency Intervention that leads to sending the police and army into the 73 communities in order to search out cases of sexual abuse of children. In Lajamanu, when the police arrive, the men in the village are in the middle of initiating boys on sacred ground. This is a scandal for the Warlpiri people. A policewoman violates the taboo of any women approaching such sacred ground. Immediately a video appears on YouTube in Warlpiri and subtitled in English explaining their position "on this violation of a restricted ceremonial area."[7] Several months later, the police will make an official statement of apology. But anger still reigns. An Indigenous political party is created: First Nations. In Lajamanu, Andrew Johnson Japanangka is

---

6. Glowczewski, Barbara & L. Wotton. *Warriors for peace: The political situation of the Aboriginal people as viewed from Palm Island*, 2010 (updated translation of *Guerriers pour la Paix*, 2008, with a new foreword by Glowczewski & an afterword by Lise Garond). Free download: http://eprints.jcu.edu.au/7286.

7. "Lajamanu and the Law," uploaded Jan. 21, 2008: https://www.youtube.com/watch?v=aU4m3bRyRqU.

the first promoter of the party. The other political parties have their own Aboriginal candidates including a Warlpiri woman that switched from the Labor Party to the Country Party; this Western politics of representation runs counter to the traditional processes which, by way of negotiations, strive to find a common strategy, always based on the sacred forces of the cosmos, including when dealing with the mining companies.

A Warlpiri man from Lajamanu takes part in a new form of "cosmopolitics": Wanta Steve Patrick Jampijinpa is a visionary that allies himself with a theater troupe from Darwin, Tracks Dance, that for 20 years has regularly run workshops with the children and youth from the school in Lajamanu. Hip-hop has become a cultural tool for helping youth get their lives back on track after being in disarray. Wanta conceived of a festival that he named Milpirri where the youth dance hip-hop within a very well thought-out choreography along with the elders who interpret ritual dances in front of a gigantic decor of painted banners of their totemic paths. Each new edition of the festival, like the one in 2014, is a success that brings the people together in a community project.[8] Like elsewhere in the world, the art and dance of big festive group gatherings becomes a political response to recognition of cultures but also modes of alternative existence for thinking the world both in a molecular, microlocal manner as well as a molar, transversal, and transnational manner.[9]

In 2011, I decide to digitally archive my audio-visual Warlpiri data in order to place it at the disposal of not only researchers but of the Warlpiri themselves. It was a collaborative platform uniting the collection of 50 researchers working in Oceania. The Online Digital Sources and Annotation System (odsas.net) allows users to have different forms of access and ways of contribution to this archive. In 2011, I organize a workshop to show how to use the archive with the linguistic help of Mary Laughren who has been collectively developing a Warlpiri

8. "Milpirri: the Winds of change," by and with Wanta Jampijinpa. NITV, 2013: https://www.youtube.com/watch?v=vS4nxqxOqS0.
9. Glowczewski, B. "Between Spectacle and Politics: Indigenous Singularities." *The Challenge of Indigenous Peoples*. Eds. B. Glowczewski & R. Henry. Oxford: Bardwell Press, 2011; see also Introduction to Glowczewski B. "Totemic becomings / De-vires totemicos," Sao Paulo: n-1 publishing, 2015.

encyclopedia for the past 40 years. The elders rejoiced to see the images of days of old and to hear their stories and songs in Warlpiri. The youth were amazed and delighted to see this digital memory of their families and culture that they could annotate and share on their cell phones. We coordinate a new digital workshop in the art center and e-learning center in 2012, right before the meeting of the Warlpiri Triangle that unites the teachers and Warlpiri language aides of several communities in order to promote the teaching of the Warlpiri language despite the reduction of its course to only one hour a week at the school. The Warlpiri dream of a school in the bush with a digital classroom in order to teach in the Warlpiri language in an open-air setting. In 2014, there is a new meeting of the Warlpiri Triangle — the association mostly financed by the royalties that benefit the Warlpiri from mining explorations on their lands. The enthusiasm for the digital and a school outside the walls to learn the Warlpiri knowledge of the bush still excites those at the meeting, a majority of Warlpiri women, but digital development and access becomes more and more difficult: the shortage of funds and support, the time it takes for downloading, and the increasing costs for paying for a good Internet connection prevent the Warlpiri from surfing the web as they had grown accustomed to doing.[10]

The gap between the Indigenous, or First Australians, and the rest of the Australian population continues to grow. During my time in Lajamanu throughout the 1980s and 90s as well as elsewhere in Australia, large numbers of non-Aboriginal youth had invested time in Aboriginal communities with the hope of sharing and supporting new forms of existence as alternatives to neo-liberal and competitive models. Nowadays, these same communities became training grounds for the new technocratic elite who spend tax payers money on "fly in and fly out" investigations that only last a couple of days to distribute bureaucratic advice and supposed consultations where what the

---

10. See the Annex of the present publication, "We have a Dreaming: How to Translate Totemic Existential Territories Through Digital Tools"; Vaarzon-Morel, P. "Pointing the Phone: Transforming Technologies and Social Relations among Warlpiri." *The Australian Journal of Anthropology*, 25 (2014): 239-255.

Aboriginal residents have to say seems to never truly be heard or really taken into account.

I happen to witness and film a session for breast cancer prevention organized in the art center of Lajamanu, Warnayaka Art, by the employees of the Health Department who were sincerely devoted to their cause. They attempting to motivate the Warlpiri women that were present, by way of audiovisual explanations and by painting their nails pink, to convince the other members of their community to come get mammograms, but no one made the trip to receive the mammograms offered by the medical post during the two days it was stationed about 100 kilometers away. It wasn't that the women didn't want to get mammograms, but that their priorities were elsewhere. Two elders at the end of the workshop on cancer prevention sang two song lines from the Two Dreamings reminding everyone that traditionally health and well-being — of humans as well as the rest of the earth — came precisely from these kinds of singing rituals, *yawulyu*, where women paint their chests in order to fortify their health, as well as the health of all the living earth. Two younger women also sang a gospel hymn in order to insist on the fact that, without denying the force of the Dreamings, they also use the Baptist gospel in order to help care for their body and mind. But if none of them went to get a mammogram it's because everyone in the community had come together for the funeral ceremonies of an elder who had been an artist and a police officer. He had been taken to the hospital at Darwin and two days later was released and sent back by plane and he ended up dying midflight before landing. Everyone seemed to know in heading to the airport to wish him goodbye that he wouldn't be returning alive.

The Warlpiri from Lajamanu knew how to play the games of the White people, but they chose their own priorities. Up until that point many of the Warlpiri had benefited from mining royalties that came from searching for gold and even tore each other apart for thirty years regarding the distribution of their earnings. But when confronted with uranium prospecting, the concerned families now refused to grant the right to explore their land to the companies that proposed to pay them. In 2015, the government of Western Australia announced its project for closing Aboriginal communities in order to make them settle in the city. The Indigenous people mobilized themselves and a protest movement took place over the entire continent.[11] The Minister of Western Australia made a statement of withdrawal the day following the protests of the 1st of May, but the other states are just as seduced by the idea of doing away with the communities under the pretext that their maintenance costs too much. What will become of the Aboriginal communities of the Northern Territory such as that of Lajamanu if the families must exile themselves to the city? Numerous Warlpiri already live within the diaspora of northern towns and in cities located in the south as well. The question divides the politicians. Some of them are persuaded that it is necessary to do away with all the communities as if erasing their collective living areas will also erase the problem that the State perceives as a lack of "adapting" on the side of the inhabitants, a luxurious "lifestyle" that the government can no longer allow itself to enable. But other politicians know very well that when communities have been deprived of resources, the Indigenous populations have been forced into moving precariously into the cities in order to survive and where, without a proper system of integration and welcoming, they are left to a life of misery, discrimination, and racially motivated hate crimes.

Of course, there are many successful Indigenous Australians: students, social workers, health care workers, lawyers, not to mention artists that are invited all over world as well as film-makers and actors that are prized by the Cannes Festival, but they do not aim at being "assimilated." The Indigenous popu-lation, (that includes all people of mixed ancestry who declare themselves as Aboriginal) only make up 3% of the Australian population composed of diverse layers of migrants, but insists on its specificity: its role in the protection of Australian land. The maintenance of the conditions of existence of those who wish to stay within remote communities is essential. It is not a matter of reproducing a life on a reservation, based on refugee

---

11. Préaud, M., Glowczewski, B., De Largy, J., Le Roux, G., Castro-Koshy, E., McDue, M. co-signed by 17 French researchers working with Indigenous Australians "Non aux fermetures de communautés aborigènes en Australie." April 27, 2015. Trans., May 2, 2015: http://www.huffingtonpost.com/martin-preaud/australian-aboriginal-commu-nities-should-not-be-closed_b_7161392.html.

camp models where enclosure without any possibility for activities would force the Aboriginal people to "sit down," as they say, provoking self-destructive patterns oscillating between depression and violence against themselves. On the contrary, what is at stake is to promote an alternative for living that recognizes the Australian Aboriginal peoples' right to take care of humans as well as their environment. One of the reasons why some Australians are frustrated by the enclaves of Indigenous desert communities is not so much the violence — the problems with alcohol and domestic violence are much worse in the city — but rather the simple fact that Aboriginal people occupy the desert in order to live. One of the Australian economic fantasies is imagining the desert and the region to the north as devoid of inhabitants — as a never ending site for mining and energy resources, and a variety of experiments: fracking, burial sites for nuclear waste, military maneuvers of the Atlantic alliance, not to mention the nuclear testing that took place in the 1960s at Maralinga in the southern desert and along the west coast, around the Montebello Islands of the Indian Ocean. The First Australians, relying on their Ancestral cosmology, propose something else, another manner of inhabiting the world, which it is urgent to listen to in order to save the planet's ecosystem that we are part of.

This book is an invitation to embark on a journey into the time-space of the 1980s, not for remnants of a nostalgia for the past but rather to experience that which resists time: the difference within the repetition that produces new becomings. Behind the modes of life that are disappearing, there is a way for thinking a cosmopolitics in order to act with the earth that is not finished re-actualizing itself, not only for circumventing bureaucratic, political, of climatic constraints, but also for transforming all those, who like myself, are willing to accept letting themselves be contaminated a little bit by this manner of being in the world in order to better mutually live together.

Barbara Glowczewski, Paris, August 2015

PRELUDE

In the heart of Australia, across the red and crackled ground dotted with yellow prickly grass, bare bushes and dried-up creeks, hundreds of invisible trails intermingle. One such trail travels more than a thousand kilometers, marked out from north to south by a few hills, rocks and isolated trees, the sacred sites of that trail the Aboriginal people[12] of the Centre call Initiated Man or Stars Dreaming. All those landscape forms appeared with the passage of an ancestral people who, in the Dreaming time-space, crossed the desert before being transformed into stars.

When the earth was still flat, an immense windbreak floated in the sky. It settled on the ground and became a long hill of red rocks, which has since come to be called Kurlungalinpa. At the same time, a sidereal body that was not a shooting star but something bigger, more luminous and longer, similar to a comet, fell from the firmament. Its fall, in broad daylight, provoked a night that covered the whole earth. From that night emerged the Initiated Man people.

The sun rose again and the children of the stars began to dance, waving their arms and slapping their thighs. Then branches grew at their feet, forming poles several meters

---

12. In Australia, Aboriginal people (etymologically "originating from" a given country) is written with a capital "A" when referring to Indigenous Australians (in the 1980's French dictionaries have acknowledged the capital for the French word "Aborigènes" to designate all Australian First Nations).

high that rustled above their heads. They saw Orion and his daughters, the Pleiades, in the sky. They too had travelled across the earth, imprinting a trail marked by topographic signs: the Invincible Dreaming, the name of Orion who, on earth, married his daughters again and again, ordering them to kill the sons they gave birth to.

The men-trees of the Stars Dreaming had neither daughters nor wives. They walked and sang, the words that related their past and future journeys seeded the earth. They scattered images that transformed into eucalyptus or spirit-children.

They camped at the foot of the hill that fell from the sky and dreamed of the travel they were about to undertake toward the distant countries of the South. In dream they met the single dancing women of the Digging-Stick Dreaming. They too crossed the earth, scattering images of spirit-children and making acacias grow everywhere they dug in their sticks.

One day, having left the men of the Stars Dreaming to go hunting, they found a string and a headband made of threaded hair on their return. A hero of the Goanna Dreaming had made them by cutting the men's hair. The Digging-Stick Women, seduced by those new objects, agreed to reveal their knowledge in order to possess them. They made love to the men, relinquishing for them the prerogatives of spear-hunting and initiations.

There were no rules about marriage at the time, so they argued about the way they would divide up the men. Some wanted to share them, while others imposed the idea that each would have her own. Accordingly, in couples, men and women walked to Janyingki, where they gave birth to sons and daughters. Then, dancing and turning about, the women formed the cave that can still be found there.

The children grew up. Wearing headbands received from Goanna, the mothers danced the Shield ceremony so that their sons would become men and receive wives. Then they stretched out their arms and, hopping about, moved off, away toward the Eastern countries. Having crossed vast deserted plains, they disappeared beneath the earth, singing: "The power of the Voices of the Nights, the Yellow Ochre, the Digging-Stick has ceased to breath, it faded away, out of breath."

Underground and in the sky, the beings of the Dreaming time-space continue to dream. They dream the existence of dark-skinned men and women who have travelled the desert for thousands of years. By naming the sacred sites they had molded, the fabulous ancestors bequeathed to men and women a Law made of dances, songs and paintings. Ever since that time, the Aboriginal people have danced, sung and painted their bodies with sacred Images.

The spirit-children sown by the Initiated Men (ngarrka), the Digging-Stick Women (kana), Goanna (pilja), Invincible (wawulja) and all the other Dreamings, still live near the waterholes, rocks and trees. They catch women who come close and, generation after generation, enter them in order to give birth to the son and daughter custodians of this earth. That is why each Aboriginal person of the desert embodies the name and the song of the Dreaming that gives him or her the memory of the earth.

Ronnie Lawson Jakamarra and his wife Pupiya Louisa Napaljarri, Lajamanu 1984.

PART ONE

(1988)

A WARLPIRI FAMILY

With his shaggy beard and white hair tinged with red ochre, Paddy Gibson Japaljarri leaned across a big canvas spread on the sand. I was seated on the ground in the camp of a Warlpiri tribe watching with fascination the slow gestures of the old Aboriginal man in his jacket and turned-up trousers. He dipped a match into a pot and marked a series of small yellow dots, following the contours of the colored arabesques that blazed on the canvas.

Facing him was a very young Warlpiri woman, her legs folded under her miniskirt, marking other dots with a cotton bud. Arriving on all fours, her baby, Black with a blonde mop, crawled onto the dry part of the painting. Without interrupting her detailed work, the young painter grabbed hold of a tin with her free hand and shook it to make the baby change direction. It scratched at the canvas, hesitated and clambered onto its mother's lap to suck.

"Nungarrayi, look! The twins!"

A female voice was calling me by my *skin* name, the Aboriginal skin name attributed to me some years earlier on my first stay in Australia. I looked. A stout woman in a tight-fitting apron with a zip was pointing her long fine hand at two strapping fellows in Australian rules football jerseys.

"Remember?" she reiterated to me. "You danced for them to become men."

I barely recognized the twin boys of her husband Paddy whom she had raised after they lost their mother. They had only come up to my shoulders when the elders made the Shield (kurdiji) ceremony to initiate them. As custom required the sisters of the novices to dance during the ceremony, I was made to dance for them because they were two Jungarrayi, my skin *brothers*. Shy and reserved, as Aboriginal people often are, the twins shook my hand without raising their eyes, hidden beneath their heavy brow ridges, then rejoined a group of men and women seated in a circle on the ground.

Cards and dollars flew from hand to hand. Some pocketed crumpled notes while others added fresh stakes plucked from their boots or bras. A loser, with a vacant look, observed the game from atop a flour barrel that served as a seat. A second got to his feet and, one arm holding the elbow of the other behind his back, moved away, almost floating, toward the dusty horizon where the shells of a few abandoned cars shone in the setting sun.

Its red light highlighted the new arrivals, black silhouettes approaching with that same nonchalant step. The pack of dogs lolling in the sun started to bark. They jumped over each other and the fray found itself in the midst of a group of women in conversation. One old woman pushed them away with her stick, then replaced her head on the thighs of another to resume being deloused. Children covered in dust came running, laughing. They were called and cuddled. The eldest left again, disappearing behind bushes.

With a cap crammed down to his eyes, one kid rummaged through a pile of blankets rolled up against a piece of sheet metal stuck in the ground as protection from the wind. Finding a tin, he opened it with a knife, helped himself with his fingers and passed it to his father, Tony Gibson Japaljarri, a small man with a wise face who rested on a mattress. His first wife was lighting a fire by his side, while the second poured water from a billy can into a bucket, then placed it on the fire to make tea.

I felt tremendous pleasure rediscovering the strange serenity of these Warlpiri campers, called the Kurlungalinpa *mob*, the group of Kurlungalinpa, the name of two sacred hills formed by the Stars Dreaming that Paddy and Tony inherited from the ancestors of their clan. It was precisely that land and the Dreaming Ancestors that Paddy, helped by Tony's daughter, was painting on the canvas. The central arabesques in the shape of the double helix represented the Milky Way as well as the sacred trail, which linked Kurlungalinpa to Mirirrinyangu, another Dreaming site through which the mythical ancestors of the *ngarrka* people, Initiated Man, passed. Traditionally, such paintings acted both as geographic maps and symbolic identity cards.

In the past, the Warlpiri used to paint the sacred designs only on their bodies, the ground and ritual objects. I discovered that since my last stay they had followed the example of other Aboriginal communities. Almost everyone had started to paint their Dreamings on canvas. The demand in the national and international market was such that those acrylic paintings immediately sold for between 300 and 2,000 dollars, double or triple that amount when sold in contemporary art galleries.

Before earning money from their paintings, the Warlpiri did not live in destitution, some had full time or part time jobs, and others collected a family allowance, unemployment benefits, or retirement pensions.[13] The Kurlungalinpa group also benefitted from government aid for development financing decentralization from the reserve settlements, known in Australia as the Outstation Movement, in other words camps set up by the Aboriginal people on their traditional lands, equipped with windmill bores and sometimes houses.

Forced into a sedentary life on reserves in the Fifties, the Warlpiri had to wait more than twenty years before being able to settle down again on their respective lands. When the whole tribe, some 3,000 people, won a trial in 1978 allowing them to retrieve their territory, Paddy and Tony set up their Outstation in Mirirrinyangu, a paradisiac swamp inhabited by thousands of birds. It was at this time that I first made their acquaintance.

More than once I accompanied them on their tractor around their Outstation. Each week they would make the 120 kilometer trip that separated them from the old reserve in

---

13. A referendum in 1967 amended the Australian constitution to include Aboriginal people in the census and also enabled the Commonwealth to create laws for them such as the right to be paid an equal wage as other citizens. They had been given the right to vote in 1962.

order to fetch rations from the store and deposit those children attending school. Tony told me that, in the last three years, the government had sunk a windmill bore near the swamp, set up a few corrugated iron shelters, three prefabricated houses, two pit toilets, a radio and even a solar light and refrigeration system.

A few months before, a Japanese film director had turned up wanting to document survival in the bush. He enlisted Tony and his first wife, Barbara Nakakut Nakamarra, for filming. Over the course of a month, Tony and Nakakut re-enacted the life they had known in their childhood. Grandparents, aged, respectively, sixty and forty-five, they had both kept the slenderness and litheness of desert walkers. In the circumstances they abandoned their Western clothes to be naked again, except for a pubic apron woven from hair strings.

"It was exhausting," Nakakut related to me in Warlpiri. "We had to get up every morning with the sun and go hunting, me with my digging-stick and wooden dish, and Tony with his spear, spear-thrower and shield. We had to walk all day long to find goannas, yams, and kangaroos." Then Nakakut noted, with a mischievous look: "We didn't even have time to eat normally any more."

"I bin tell that Japanese man to send you that *yardwise* (film)," she added, in Aboriginal English.

Nakakut was my best Warlpiri friend and I could understand her irritation. Why that need for foreigners to deny contemporary life to the Aboriginal people in favor of an image of hunters untouched by White civilization? After all, they continue to hunt kangaroos and lizards, but with guns and crowbars instead of spears and digging-sticks. If they choose to integrate elements of our technology into their traditional culture, it still remains extremely subtle.

Without Nakakut, my skin *mother*, I would never have understood the life of the inhabitants of Lajamanu, the old reserve of the central desert that became a Warlpiri managed settlement. We became friends during my first stay in 1979, though it was in 1984 that Nakakut became both my privileged *informant* and my true confidant. For hours during the course of those months, we listened together to the narratives in Warlpiri I had recorded — myths and life stories — and she translated them into English for me, word by word, with additional enthusiastic comments.

This four year gap I had spent back in Paris, a part of my heart clung to the Australian desert, my spirit still immersed in the Aboriginal universe I was analyzing to write my State doctorate in Human Sciences. My thesis defended, I returned, this time with my partner, Bertrand.

"At least, my sister and Tony got paid for that film!" stated Beryl Nakamarra, the second wife of Tony. "Me, I didn't want to be in it."

With her long black hair and mischievous eyes, Beryl resembled her inseparable older sister, Nakakut. Some years before the two sisters had refused Tony permission to take a third wife, a lover from his youth, a widow at that point. Though they had also had affairs, nevertheless they were overprotective with the precious husband to whom they had been ritually promised even before their birth.

"Outsiders are really funny!" exclaimed Beryl. "Last year, while we were camping here, one Kardiya (White man) all face burned come pulling a trolley full of water cans. He walked from Warrego mine, 200 kilometers. He asked, is Lajamanu still far? We said, less far than Warrego. He slept one night with us and set off again."

The two sisters burst out laughing.

"We've had all kinds of stories at the Outstation," Beryl continued. "One day, I was washing my clothes near the swamp. Suddenly, I look up feeling the landscape swaying. I think I'm ill. But I see the others run and lie flat on the ground. The earth was shaking!"

"I straightaway thought the Warnayarra Snake Dreaming, who looks after the swamp, was angry," Tony commented, his look hidden by the rim of an old black felt hat. "At the Warrego mine the earth had cracked open, swallowing miners. All the machines had been destroyed. The earthquake lasted several days."

"We were very scared, but it's normal that Warnayarra gets nervous, White men dig much too much, they disturb the spirits," Beryl declared, turning to my partner.

Bertrand smiled, imagining all those White men who, without knowing it, tickled the belly of the Snake. A long time ago, he too was digging the earth, not in search of minerals, but uncovering old *marae* worship places in Polynesia. He unearthed dozens of them until one day his Tahitian assistants refused to work because they were afraid of the buried spirits. So Bertrand ceased his engagement with archeology. He then went to Africa to learn what people had to say about the remnants of their past. He told my Warlpiri friends an African story about a house fallen from the sky, and about rainmakers.

"It's a bit like here," Nakakut remarked. "The Stars Dreaming fell from the sky on an open shed turning into a big hill. It's my husband's *Jukurrpa*, Dreaming. His fathers still dream in the sky and in the sacred places like the Kurlungalinpa hill. We also have rainmakers, they come from the Rain Dreaming people who sleep in the clouds and in some waterholes."

I was very fond of those strange *Jukurrpa*, Dreaming stories that constitute for the Warlpiri and their neighbors both a religion and a Law, a means of knowledge linking them emotionally and by flesh to the cosmos and to the rules governing their society. Of course, today, they live with all the acquired knowledge of our technology, but they continue to celebrate through their rituals those splendid Dreamings that inhabit them and nourish their sleep.

Every natural or cultural phenomenon is in one way or another related to a Dreaming, a *Jukurrpa*. The Warlpiri say their tribe would not exist if the heroes of the Dreamings had not dreamed the Warlpiri language, and water would not exist if there was no Rain Dreaming. The trails of that Dreaming particularly follow the underground drainage. Ancestral sacred knowledge.

Nakakut told me that the houses at the Outstation flooded during the last rainy season. Although raised one meter from the ground, they proved to be poorly conceived for downpours. The surge of water prevented the campers from returning to Lajamanu. For one month they had to be supplied by helicopter. Later a youth had an accident with the Toyota allocated to the Outstation by the Department of Aboriginal Affairs. In the absence of a vehicle, the group dispersed, some resettled in the Aboriginal settlement of Lajamanu, while others went off for awhile to town, Katherine, 600 kilometers north.

The following year when they obtained a new Toyota, everybody met again at the Outstation, and the group was quickly besieged by Warlpiri visitors taking advantage of food rations bought by their hosts. They had to go back and forth continually to Lajamanu to replenish their supplies, and everyone put off responsibility for looking after the camp. Finally the windmill broke. It was no longer possible to water the vegetable garden made by the women. They had to wait months for a repairman to come and change the damaged piece.

Torn between domestic and technical worries, the people of the Kurlungalinpa group always roamed, sometimes living on their lands, other times in various Aboriginal communities or in town. Each time their means of transport broke down, they retired to Lajamanu. At this moment, the Toyota had been abandoned on a track, and the second-hand car Tony had bought, thanks to the cards, needed a new motor. However, they were already talking about leaving once more, for the government had promised them a new Toyota in a month.

The community in the Lajamanu reserve totaled around 500 members of the Warlpiri tribe.[14] While the Gibsons were one of the rare families that still continued to camp I had also noted, with some sadness, that with some of the Warlpiri having settled in prefab houses and others having departed for town, the camp which was once so animated had become empty. Between the high voltage masts that squared off the vast wasteland, only a few camps were left with their rows of corrugated iron used as open sheds, and their mattresses and blankets, wedged between two pieces of iron sheet, bags and suitcases. Only a few clothes, tools, and pots, as well as material for painting, were added to the rudimentary luggage, objects made out of wood and stone with which the Aboriginal people moved.

I quickly became accustomed to that precariousness, seeing there a form of resistance to Westernization. I had believed (along with the Warlpiri) in the Outstation Movement, in the

14. In the 1980s, the people who consider themselves Warlpiri number about 3,000. This figure regroups the Warnayaka of the North (the majority in Lajamanu), and the Ngaliya of the South (mostly in Yuendumu). Members of neighboring tribes married into the Warlpiri are partly assimilated. There are many more Warlpiri in the 21st century who live in diaspora throughout the continent.

possibility of once again returning to a more semi-nomadic life which would take advantage of the minimum of acquired technical knowledge. But the Kurlungalinpa group's old plan to set up a school in the Outstation to raise the children without dependence on the old reserve was no longer a reality. It appeared they were fed up with the land that was nevertheless so dear to their heart. In that Bicentenary year, which celebrated the arrival in 1788 of the first White settlers in Australia, the world was changing more painfully than I had thought.

Some Warlpiri asked if I had come back forever. I explained I could not stay more than a month.

"So you're back as a tourist?" one young woman shot back at me.

I would not answer. How could I explain the need to see this tribe again that haunted my memories? How could I admit my nostalgia for the complicity once shared with Nakakut and her sisters? I wanted to show the Warlpiri what I had written on them and to take account of possible changes. But the anthropological preoccupation suddenly seemed absurd when I realized neither they nor I were entirely the same as before. Nakakut understood. I was returning to see her as a friend.

LAJAMANU

Although the buildings in Lajamanu, mainly bungalows, often enclosed by barbed wire, had doubled in number in the previous ten years, they offered the same striking contrast: a mixture of refugee camps and holiday resorts. The enclosures of some, those mostly inhabited by Whites, screened a lawn, flowers and bushes sprayed by a garden hose all day long. The others, occupied by several families together, stood among hearths relit each evening, with large cans, empty tins and cardboard boxes strewn across the red sand, reminding everyone that we were well and truly at the edge of the desert.

Whether in concrete or corrugated iron, the most recent accommodations were aligned next to the dilapidated remains of abandoned buildings. Every square meter of ground seemed to be carved with the various stages of time elapsed since the creation of this bush settlement in the Fifties. So many scars marked out the recent history of a maltreated people.

Twenty Aboriginal people from the Warlpiri tribe had been taken there by force to prepare what was to become the Hooker Creek Reserve. Three years later, fifty families were transported there against their will. Subjected to a very strict discipline and mobilized to work on the maintenance of the settlement, they also had to eat together in a refectory and worship at the Baptist mission.

I was told by one old man with long white hair, held by a red headband: "When a man arrived badly shaved, he was deprived of his meal. We had to march in step, like the army. And as for going hunting, we didn't have the right to go beyond the limits of the reserve."

He related how, one night in 1951, they had decided to run away. In quite large groups, they traversed the desert some 600 kilometers south to return to Yuendumu, the first Warlpiri reserve created in the Forties. At least there they were on their traditional land. Hooker Creek was a land belonging to another tribe, the Kurintji, who had been pushed further north by the Whites. The Warlpiri did not want to live on a foreign land whose spirits could be maleficent to them. But the administrators put them back in trucks and returned them to Hooker Creek. Seven years later they made another attempt to escape, again without success.

Forced by Whites to stay on the land of the Kurintji, the Warlpiri established ritual exchanges with them in order to obtain from that custodian tribe the right to live there legitimately. As time passed they grew used to Hooker Creek, the name of a river that was dry most of the year, but which flooded the whole community around December, the hottest season.

Near the dry bed, bordered by a thick scrub, the remains of a mudhouse built in the Fifties was still to be found, built with a material that was quickly abandoned as it was unsuited to seasonal hazards. Also from that period, the broken wood fences of the cattle paddock remained, as well as the walls and corrugated iron roof of the old health clinic, and the ruins of the mission's kitchen and the baker's oven. Finally, the faint inscription, YMCA, on an open shed covered with graffiti showed how the old sports hall had been abandoned in favor of basketball and football grounds.

Some old buildings had been converted. The old colonial pavilion that sheltered the reserve manager had become the office of the Warlpiri Council. That Council was created even before the government gave back its land to the Warlpiri and Hooker Creek lost its reserve status to become the Lajamanu Aboriginal settlement from the name of a sacred site associated with the Mosquito Dreaming.

At the time when the Aboriginal people from the desert lived as hunters, they slept on the same ground and in the open air without ever building houses. They constructed bough shades from branches only to protect themselves from sun or rain, sometimes taking refuge in rock shelters. When such shade sources were absent, they used to follow the example of reptiles and small desert marsupials, digging the earth and burying their bodies to avoid dehydration. Though without villages, thousands of spots were named and culturally marked out. When an Aboriginal person died, the place of their last encampment became taboo and nobody could go there during the mourning period, which was at least two years.

With sedentarization, the Warlpiri have maintained that custom. They systematically shift their camp a dozen meters when one of them dies, and, if the deceased lived in a house, they temporarily vacate it, sometimes also abandoning the neighboring dwellings. Consequently, one could see in Lajamanu brand new houses that remained empty, avoided by everyone following a death.

A new building with a pointed roof had been erected on the camp's waste ground, bordering the barbed wire fence of the red mud floor landing strip where the clothes hung drying. From afar, the strange pistachio-colored construction did not seem to have windows. I came closer. In fact, the walls were made of metallic screens that could be opened anytime.

Some women sitting near the door invited me inside. On both sides of the huge entrance hall where electric cookers occupied the place of honor, a dozen rooms had been created, some of them locked with a padlock. A number of little girls, who had followed me, came racing into the open rooms and rummaged in the bundles of blankets and bags that constituted the only objects of those cells.

Constructed for the widows or single women of all ages, the building was in fact only inhabited by the youngest. The old women preferred to remain outdoors, sleeping in a line one against the other, warmed by a fire with their heads against a one meter high windbreak made from an old iron sheet and some bushes. Eventually they took refuge in the entrance hall in case of heavy rain. That hall also welcomed those who lived elsewhere and came to paint, sheltered from the wind.

There I found Peggy Rockman Napaljarri, a tall, mature woman with a young girl's smile. Four years earlier she was camping with her husband and her four sisters, two of them married to the same man, the other two widowed. Next to their shelter they had set up a paddock almost 2 kilometers long to raise a baby emu. I learned that following the death of their husband, the Napaljarri sisters had moved into a new house right in front of the women's building. Accustomed to open air life, they still slept on the veranda.

Peggy stretched her long legs on either side of an unfinished canvas. Over a black background, friezes of straight lines bordered with small arcs appeared. I thought I recognized the Budgerigar Dreaming in this design, which Peggy had painted upon her chest during certain rituals. Although different, it resembled other Budgerigar paintings on canvas I had seen. Each painter is free to choose her colors and improvise a composition. Only some recurring designs allow for the identification of the Dreaming, and in some cases correspond to one specific site of that Dreaming trail.

"Yes, these are the Dreaming birds sitting on branches and there, the small circles, are their eggs," Peggy confirmed in her soft voice. "With my sisters, we only paint that Dreaming, our Dreaming from our Karntawarranyungu land."

Beside Peggy, two other women painted their own Dreaming, *ngurlu* Acacia Seeds, a variety of Graminaceae that ants gather on the grass and pile in small heaps. Traditionally, women only had to collect those heaps in order to grind the seeds and make dampers. Nowadays they preferred to buy flour or a loaf of bread. The first painting on a red background was bursting with pink, yellow, and bright orange dots like a psychedelic mosaic. The second, more sober, intermixed a pointillistic camaieu of earth colors in inextricable spirals. The dots depicted both the seeds in their diverse states of ripening and the trail followed by the Acacia Seed beings, ancestors of the clans of the same name.

"Making all those dots is hurting my eyes," Peggy explained without letting go of the paintbrush she moved about almost like an automaton. "And that's too much work. One week I've been doing that painting and it's still not finished. I have to do cleaning at the school every day. It's time I stopped that job so I can do only painting."

The painters informed me that another new building, similar to the first one, fifty meters away, was restricted to men. It was occupied by youngsters still not married and little boys who chose to sleep and be taken care of by their older brothers and cousins rather than live with their parents. They had just finished setting up gleaming drums before the entrance, and armed with electric guitars they began to rehearse a mix of rock and country & western. Some kids jigged up and down, trying to dance like Michael Jackson.

I could not help thinking that this *men's house* was only modernizing the custom of separating boys from their mothers after their initiation, so that they would be looked after by the young initiated. Once, those men used to live in an isolated camp until they married around thirty. Even if they married earlier nowadays, the initiations are still practiced, as well as the custom of one age group being looked after by another.

In the Sixties, the last period of forcing semi-nomadic groups into reserves, it was stated that Aboriginal cultures were doomed to disappear. Indeed, the massacres, followed by the system of reserves have dismantled more than half of some 500 Australian tribes and, in so doing, destroyed the majority of the 200 languages and numerous dialects that differentiated them.[15] For the Aboriginal people, who have maintained a certain tribal cohesion like the Warlpiri, the effect of acculturation has proved entirely unpredictable.

Instead of being assimilated into White culture, the tribal communities have developed thus far unimaginable forms

---

15. Estimates of between 300,000 and 500,000 Aboriginal people were alive when the Europeans arrived. After a heavy demographic fall, Aboriginal people, represented more or less 2% of the 16 million Australians in the 1980s. Tindale, N.B. "Aboriginal Tribes of Australia," Canberra: Australia National University Press, 1974; Peterson, N. Ed., "Tribes and Boundaries in Australia," Canberra: Australian Institute of Aboriginal Studies, 1976. According to the 2011 census Indigenous Australians (Aboriginal people, Torres Strait Islanders, and all the descendants of mixed unions with non Indigenous settlers and migrants) represent 3% of the 21,507, 717 million Australians.

of affirmation of identity, traditional survival and renewal of their ritual life. In that respect, Lajamanu was still a cauldron used for cultural alchemy, of which the Warlpiri and outsiders, like the European migrants, became the sorcerer's apprentices. The forms that emerged had no more to do with traditional life than with the life of the Eighties in Europe and the States. The mixture of the two contributions suggested more of a science-fiction scenario.

For years Lajamanu has had a reputation for being violent. During my previous stays, when the Warlpiri were not busy with ceremonies, duals involving the whole community were not uncommon. The Warlpiri attributed those brawls to the fact they were too numerous, meaning nearly 700 living in the same place. In the past, when they were nomads, they rarely camped in groups of more than thirty. It was only for one month a year that several hundred would meet for the initiation ceremonies. If tensions caused opposition and degenerated into open conflict, they carried out ceremonies for settling disputes, smoothing out the disagreements until the next meeting.

I had the impression that with the multiplication of houses, quarrels were now confined to private matters.

"Anyway, the council has forbidden men to carry spears and boomerangs," Toby told me. "It is quiet now, we live in peace." Toby had been a Warlpiri *stockman* who had retained the composed look of the horse riders of the vast spaces. "Before it was enough for one man to see the footprints of his wife in the bush crossed with the footprints of another man to kick up a fuss. We were fighting, but we were also having fun. Today there's not much to do, only to receive *sitting-down money* (dole)."

Until recently the former cowboy drove the tractor used to pick up garbage with a sense of dignity. Now he devoted his time to the grand-children of Margaret Pampiriya Nungarrayi, a widow he had courted for years before marrying her. When I first made his acquaintance he was living with another woman and the little girl they had adopted. Pampiriya explained that the girl's mother, who lived in Katherine, had decided to take her back three years ago. For Toby it was a tragedy. His wife, equally desperate, left for Alice Springs where she married an Italian working in an Aboriginal art gallery.

There were always so few jobs in the Aboriginal communities, most of the services had to be carried out by Whites because the locals did not have the required competence. In Lajamanu, around a dozen Warlpiri were employed by the council, three in the health clinic, three in the school, three in the shop, two at the mechanics workshop, while a team of women took turns at the mission to prepare meals for pensioners who came daily at noon to fetch their meals. The others, if they were not painting, were walking about, having a nap, watching videos or playing cards.

I noticed that only a few men met each day like before to talk beneath the leaf shelter erected near the football pitch. The women did not have their shelter anymore, but took refuge in the shadow of a concrete box where two new washing machines worked without interruption. Facing it, the park, a vast parade with uprooted grass, remained the only meeting place between 10 a.m. and noon, and between 3 and 5 p.m., the opening hours of the shop.

Every day, small groups settled down on the ground amid cardboard boxes and loaded shopping bags. They chatted while eating chips, meat pies or fried chicken bought at the fast food restaurant. The children were allowed to leave school to meet the adults at playtime. They arrived in cheerful bands, running from one group to another begging for dollars or, failing that, for fruit, a packet of cookies, a drink or an ice cream.

Installed in an immense warehouse, the shop looked more and more like an urban supermarket with its two alleys of shelves loaded with tins, freezers with frozen foods, two checkouts and grocery carts. Everything the shop had on offer was consumed but, it seemed, more moderately than before. A few years previous, a consignment of bikes was sold out in a few days. Two months later, after scoring all the stony and rugged tracks around, the kids had abandoned their broken bikes without regrets or remonstrance from the adults. Young or old, nobody appeared to be attached to objects. Even having become

45

sedentary, the Warlpiri still lived as if they were always on the point of leaving.

Today, the houses, television, and video recorders held their attention a little longer. But nothing was made to last. When women bought flip flops or sneakers, the pair of shoes quickly became separated, carried off by the dogs. In order to protect their boots, the men often slept with them on. The children, one day dressed in brand-new clothes, the day after sported torn trousers, T-shirts in place of dresses, and adult-sized skirts tied-up with knots. Nevertheless, most wore those dusty red rags with an astonishing elegance.

More and more money entered Lajamanu only to leave it immediately. As before, card winnings were often the opportunity for a pub crawl, either by car to the two closest bars, 300 kilometers to the south or north from Lajamanu, or by plane to the town of Katherine, 600 kilometers north, and Alice Springs, 800 kilometers south.

Lajamanu, like most Aboriginal communities, was still a *dry area*, which meant it was forbidden to sell alcohol and to drink it. Whites as well as Aboriginal people could obtain exemption licenses to place orders, but only on the condition they drank at home and did not come out drunk. Very few Warlpiri succeeded in keeping their licenses, so they had to obtain a supply elsewhere. They often brought back loads of beer cans that they hid right at the edge of the *ten miles* forbidden zone, fifteen kilometers away. They went to these spots in large numbers to get drunk. From time to time a drunk came rolling into the community, and from there the manhunt would start. Five policemen from Lajamanu, three White officers and two Warlpiri police-aids would dash off in pursuit.

Wearing American-style uniforms, they constantly ploughed through the community in their Toyotas equipped with wire-mashed cages to cart off to prison those worse for drink. Situated apart, the police station was the most sophisticated of Lajamanu's buildings. In addition to the prison, there was also a courtroom. Once a month a judge and a lawyer arrived by plane and solemnly exercised the law, withdrawing alcohol licenses, issuing a series of fines to the recidivists and condemning the most incurable to a short stay in prison at Alice or Darwin.

I noticed the police had less motives to interfere than before. Some 200 Warlpiri had left over the previous two years to settle either in Katherine, or in two Outstations near Rabbit Flat, the southern gas station, isolated in the desert but selling alcohol. The consequence of this exodus was that, like the other Warlpiri, the police-aid, Japanangka, had started to paint in his leisure time.

Life in Lajamanu could seem surrealistic, oscillating continually between certain persistencies of tribal law and some graftings of technical or bureaucratic modernity. Geographically isolated, a victim of a fast transformation, the community evoked a small planet whose inhabitants would reinvent the rules from one day to the next in order to help them incorporate everything the outside world introduced into it. Far from provoking a headlong preoccupation with business deals, this sort of continual role-play gave the impression the Warlpiri were never in a hurry and lived in an aimless waiting and dawdling. One could become irritated by this, but if one could become more intimately immersed in their tribal stakes this type of life soon comes to look like an art.

YAPA AND KARDIYA

July 1988. About a hundred people were gathered in the enclosed space of Wulaign, the office of the Outstations, the bush satellite camps of Lajamanu. Looking like dark-skinned gypsies. Respecting tradition: the women on the west side, sitting on the ground, the men on the east, some on the ground, others stood leaning against the fence. The women had beckoned me to come and sit with them. They laughed at my partner who remained with the men. Between the two groups, on the steps leading to the house that had been transformed into an office, a young White woman in jeans, leaned against a stand, and struggled to make herself heard. For two years, Margaret devoted all her time, without a weekend or vacation, to the management of the Outstations.

"The Lajamanu Council has made clear that the cars of Wulaign cannot be repaired here any longer," she said. "The mechanic has too much work. From now on, you have to have them repaired in town, in Katherine, Darwin or Alice Springs."

Heavy silence, followed by asides. An old man in an anorak, the only one seated on a chair, straightened the large hat that hid his face and proclaimed:

"Us people of Taarlywarri, we always fix our transport at Warlala (Rabbit Flat), same for the Jiwaranypa mob."

The Outstations of Taarlywarri and Jiwaranypa, located near the gas station at Rabbit Flat, each comprised five prefab

49

houses in which a few families came and went. The man who had spoken, a retired police tracker, had steadily made his way into the tribal life of Lajamanu and finally earned the prestige of the elders, although he was not really initiated into the ceremonial affairs.

A man stood up. He was very smart in his turtleneck and tight-fitting suede jacket. He wore a headband on his gray hair. He spoke angrily.

"If the people of Lajamanu who have Outstations cannot make use of the services of the Lajamanu mechanic, it's like excluding us from the community. What does the Council mean by that?"

The Warlpiri Chairman of Lajamanu came forward to respond. In his forties, wearing a dark-green sweat-shirt and impeccable pants, he explained, half in English, half in Warlpiri, without relinquishing his politician's smile for a second:

"The people of the Outstations have their own problems, problems the Warlpiri with no Outstations don't have. But they also have advantages and their own organization. The DAA gives them cars. It's for them to manage their maintenance."

Representing the Department of Aboriginal Affairs (DAA), a young White man in a straw hat, with his notebook in hand, had arrived by plane for the meeting. He quickly seized his opportunity:

"I understand the Council mechanic is overwhelmed. You just need to see all the cars and trucks waiting in the garage. We, the DAA, are ready to consider financing a second mechanics workshop that will be managed by the shop. It will allow a young Warlpiri to be trained to become a mechanic."

My neighbors nodded. The government promised, but it took its time to act. More than one youth had already been trained to be a mechanic, but no one could take the pressure of that activity, constantly subjected to incessant solicitations by relatives, friends and others. One of them had become an excellent mechanic, assisting his White boss, but could never refrain from sneaking off work for a pub-crawl.

As arbitrator of the debate, Margaret decided to move on to another point on the agenda — an accountant was needed in Wulaign. The government had proposed to finance the training of a Warlpiri. The assembly was asked to vote to choose between two candidates.

The women looked concerned. They wanted to talk about the maintenance of the Outstations. None dared to stand and intervene. In the end, pushed by her companions, the wife of the man in the anorak rose. A scarf tied to her hair, wearing a low-cut T-shirt and a straight skirt, she explained in a soft but determined voice:

"We have a problem with the cesspits. The Taarlywarri one has been full for months now, and we are still waiting for it to be replaced. Anyway, that system doesn't suit us. The pit's the size of an oil-drum! We'd like toilets that flush."

Nakakut looked at me with a smile on her face. In Mirir-rinyangu they had resolved the problem. Having decided the cesspits were not functional, they had simply never used them.

"It's not possible to install toilets with water disposal," Margaret replied, "otherwise it will mix with the drinking water. Now we have to talk about the Wulaign truck?" she continued without stopping. "You know that it has been immobilized for six months at a scrap merchant in Alice Springs waiting to be sold at auction for a paltry sum. The DAA is ready to give us another truck, but only on certain terms. The vehicle can only be used for the needs of the Outstations. It is out of the question to lend or rent it for other uses. And a driver has to be appointed who must promise never to drink."

An uneasy feeling seized the audience. Her tone was too paternalistic, a tone often used by the administrators who treat Aboriginal people like children. The Warlpiri are extremely shy and sensitive to being shamed. "It's hopeless to have a discussion with the Kardiya (Whites), they don't understand anything about Yapa (Aboriginal people)," one of the women had once remarked.

Then the DAA officer tackled the problem of unemployment.

"We are willing to work, but what work?" asked a middle-aged man in a fluorescent blue shirt.

The officer replied that there were a lot of things to do in Lajamanu and the Outstations, like maintaining the houses and equipment, planning the gardens and fences, and setting up a new cattle station and bakery.

"Us people in charge of the Outstations, we are already working to look after them," replied a very beautiful woman dressed all in black. She lived at the Outstation of Lullju, 15 kilometers from Lajamanu. "To receive a wage, instead of money from the dole, won't change anything for us. But if the young people are forced to work in the Outstations, they will leave. And if they have to work here in Lajamanu, they will end up leaving Lajamanu and become stranded in the city."

The Chairman asked the officer for rapid and concrete measures for the community. After one proposed the idea of giving a wage to the painters, the meeting was adjourned, leaving the audience confused and worried.

In fact, the idea of paying a wage to painters had shocked everyone. Many paint and manage to sell their paintings by themselves. Some artists are in contact with galleries in Alice Springs, Darwin, Adelaide and even Melbourne or Perth. Others sell their productions to the Whites who live in Lajamanu, and if a painting is not sold after a week, they take it to a gas station where it has a greater chance to be sold to a passing tourist.

Before, the paintings from Lajamanu were systematically collected by a shop in Katherine. The manager stockpiled them and the artists were paid when the paintings sold. But misunderstandings quickly became glaring. The Warlpiri did not understand why some were paid and others were not, nor why they were not all paid the same amount.

A White man had tried to establish a co-operative based on the one existing in Yuendumu, a Southern Warlpiri community. The proposition was that a minimal sum would be advanced to the painters for all the paintings produced, who would later receive the remainder when the paintings were sold, in addition to assigning a percentage to be invested in the running of numerous communal needs. This idea did not satisfy everybody. In Lajamanu the project did not survive more than a couple of months. The person in charge, a Luritja woman married to a Warlpiri policeman, had a lot of trouble trying to manage the business and ended up leaving for town.

Autonomy has always been characteristic of the Warlpiri. Tribal life does not imply collectivism. Systems of obligation of exchange and solidarity are continually renegotiated, always with respect to each person's individual singularity. The Warlpiri had been obliged to elect a Council and they had become accustomed to it. But they contested its authority, especially since the sudden death of their first Chairman in his forties. Extremely bright, this Warlpiri Chairman had created the first Council to make the Kardiya respect the Yapa. He succeeded for more than ten years in leading all the negotiations with the governmental authorities, thus protecting the community from numerous administrative hazards. His body was buried in a sacred Warlpiri site, and the Prime Minister and other representatives of the Government had come for the funeral. The current Chairman had trouble facing many of the tensions of the community as well as the fresh pressures from the State.

It is important to add that the status of Chairman itself is completely foreign to the ancestral world of Aboriginal political organization. The notion of one chief for all was not conceivable before, only the authority of the elders worked. Each man and woman being the ritual custodian of certain lands, they negotiated their own systems of influence according to matrimonial alliances and respective ceremonial knowledge. That distribution of territorial rights had been recognized by the federal government and ritual exchanges had been maintained. But for a generation the Warlpiri have not needed to travel across the desert to feed themselves. Their new sedentary life increasingly disturbed the acquisition and traditional regulation of power.

ROYALTIES

A house made from iron sheets with boarded up windows, and in its yard, filled with rubbish, a four-wheel drive Toyota in perfect condition. Their owner, Victor Jupurrurla, a plump, middle-aged man, was seated on the sand, clean-shaven and stripped to the waist. At his side, his third wife, a gorgeous young woman helped him paint a huge canvas. He showed me the card of a gallery in Melbourne bearing one of his paintings.

"The owner of the gallery will soon be visiting me. She would like me to go to Melbourne for the next exhibition. But I won't go. I don't like big cities. It's too cold there and too crowded. I went to Sydney once and I got lost. It's enough to look at cities on TV."

Victor caught a chubby little boy in passing that he sat on his lap.

"My children belong to the Possum Dreaming, like my father and me," he said proudly. "But they also inherited from my step-father the *Kuruwarri*, Images of the Yarripiri Dreaming, the giant Snake the Wallaby people transported on their heads from the Pitjapitja (the Pitjantjarjara tribe). The story is secret but a Kardiya has written it down in a book.[16] South of our territory, more than 1,000 kilometers from it, there are lots of sites for that Dreaming, even paintings in caves. Near my Puyurru

---

16. Mountford, C.P. *Winbaraku and the Myth of Jarapiri.* Adelaide: Rigby, 1968.

Outstation, one can also see traces of the Yarripiri Snake — a spine similar to that of a man, but ten times bigger."

"The Kardiya could say it is a dragon, or another more complicated name the kids learn at school," his wife added, her eyes full of admiration for her husband.

"A dinosaur?" I ventured.

"That's it exactly," Victor replied. "You say these animals lived before the coming of men. But we say the Snake Dreaming travelled before the Yapa were born. But he is not dead. He sleeps underground. And his power is still alive in the tracks he left. One day, my elder son touched a piece of its petrified spine. It's dangerous, but nothing happened to him because his body has been fed with *Kuruwarri* Images of the Yarripiri Snake."

Victor, handling his English with perfection, smiled with an air of defiance rarely seen within the tribal Aboriginal people. I first knew him when he improvised himself as the spokesman for the Warlpiri confronted by a mining company that wished to prospect around The Granites, an old gold mine closed after the war. As that region was included in the territory given back to the Warlpiri in 1978, Victor succeeded once again in 1984 in negotiating agreements that brought in a lot of money, first in the form of compensation for the prospecting, then in the form of royalties for the exploitation of the eventual minerals. The company had since found important veins of gold. Victor had become the president of the Warlpiri Association administering the royalties, called *Janganpa*, Possum, the name of the trail of the main Dreaming which goes through the red rocks forming the sacred site of The Granites.

It was in the name of traditional land laws inherited from his father's grandfather and his father, both deceased, that Victor benefitted from the royalties. A hundred other Warlpiri had also been recognized as having rights, some because they were custodians of the region or the lands linked to The Granites by the same trails of Dreaming, others because they were born on the old mine or their parents had worked there. All these legal beneficiaries became prey to their relatives' requests, and every sum paid turned into a flash in the pan. Victor was the only one not to give his money away, tucking it away in a bank account, making him the *Lajamanu millionaire*. A strange millionaire who lived like everyone else, but who had the knack for rendering everything he undertook profitable.

"It's not normal that others break their cars all the time and abandon them," Victor explained to me, standing up straight again with a half-jolly, half-cunning air. "Me, I opened an account at a garage in Katherine. I go there regularly to have my car serviced, which is already three years old. And the repairs are paid for with the royalties money."

I asked him if the others could benefit like him from the account at the garage.

"There are already three of us signed up. Others just have to open their own account," Victor stated, with slight contempt.

"But most of them don't have any money in their accounts, since their royalty checks are paid in cash. I also heard a lot of them complaining about not receiving as much as you."

"That's because I'm organized, they can organize themselves too. I didn't have to apply to the DAA to obtain an Outstation. The mining company built it for me. And it's not a fake, six superb houses with electricity and not solar lighting!"

"But, Victor, you don't live there and nobody else has settled there."

"That's only temporary. We have to wait for the end of mourning for the old Jakamarra who raised me when I lost my father as a child. My father worked at the old goldmine and he was crushed by the wheel of a pump. So it's the old Jakamarra who taught me everything on The Granites region before I went to live at the Yuendumu Reserve then here, in Lajamanu."

Victor seemed to be in his element in this world between two universes. However, he was not always the happy man he was now. Four years earlier, he had taken a fourth wife against her will. The family of that young adolescent girl complained to the police that she had been raped, and the infernal judicial machine was set in motion. Victor was arrested, then released while awaiting trial. Several lawyers decided to work on the case, and the press followed the story for it was the first time such an Aboriginal problem was treated by the official justice system.

For the Warlpiri it was a shock. According to them, the affair should have been judged tribally by their Law and not in the Whites' law courts. Thus, in their dozens, they testified in favor of Victor, explaining that in their society the girls were promised in marriage to the men even before their birth. They tried to prove that Victor, having been initiated by the adolescent's father, had rights on her.

Victor was not cleared. But, because of the tribal consensus asking for his release, instead of going to prison, he was condemned to exile and assigned to live in Yuendumu, 600 kilometers south of Lajamanu. That exile was relative since Yuendumu is also a Warlpiri community, though Victor did not have any power there. At the end of a year, he moved back to Lajamanu, surrounded by the prestigious aura of the Prodigal Son. Instead of the reticent teenager, he inherited the consenting widow of the previous Chairman. Meanwhile, negotiations with the mining company had culminated in agreements that made Victor the master of the situation.

"Another meeting!" old Paddy announced plaintively. This time almost the whole community gathered on the lawn of the Council garden. For the occasion Paddy had washed his beard and hair, and also combed them with evident pleasure. I barely recognized him. All the men dressed smartly. Tony was clean-shaven and had put on his shoes. Victor in his freshly-ironed white shirt wore a superb hat trimmed with leopard fur. This meeting belonged to him, as the following hours would prove.

In front of the Council's fence six gleaming Toyotas were parked, vehicles of the CLC (Central Land Council) representatives who had come from Alice Springs for the occasion. Created in 1976 on the initiative of a White lawyer and an elder from the Aranda (Arrernte) tribe, the CLC had conducted the inquiries of the trial that permitted holding for the Warlpiri 94,694 square kilometers of their traditional land in a land trust. That Aboriginal organization, which employs legal experts and anthropologists, had since prepared many other land claims, and was used as an intermediary by all the tribal communities of the Centre to negotiate various affairs and, in particular, the mining contracts.

In Darwin, the NLC (Northern Land Council) was doing the same work for the Aboriginal people of Arnhem Land, where an important uranium deposit was located. It is important not to forget that Australia is, in effect, very rich in different minerals that are essentially exploited by multi-nationals. At the beginning, the Aboriginal people were systematically opposed to all exploitation for it destroyed the earth. However, after seeing the benefits they could gain from it, they accepted agreements provided that they would not be generalized across the whole continent. The Northern Territory alone, where the Warlpiri people live, is subjected to the federal law that permits the restitution of the lands to certain groups as well as the rights to underground resources. But in other states, compensation to the Aboriginal people varies according to the mining companies.

That day some unknown Whites in shorts, long socks and patent-leather shoes were busy setting up huge boards with photographs showing several mining installations against the building of the Lajamanu Council. A member of the CLC, microphone in hand, presented them:

"Here are the bosses of the mining company who have paid us the honor of coming to Lajamanu to explain the evolution of the mining exploitation at The Granites. They are ready to answer any question. Furthermore, they have addressed us with a new request for exploration. I have issued you a map of your territory on which appear three zones respectively marked in pink, yellow and green, the areas affected by the new drillings. It is for you to decide if you agree to consider the prospecting."

People seemed to know about it already. In the crowd I noticed new faces. Two days before, three trucks had deposited the Aboriginal people considered as traditional custodians of the affected lands. The delegations from Yuendumu, Willowra, Balgo, and Kalkaringi were gathered on the lawn.[17] The preceding day, in the absence of the mine's representatives, another meeting was held on the use of royalties. Hector had declared that rather than sharing the money between the beneficiaries they should invest it on a long-term basis so that everybody could benefit from it once the mine was exhausted. Some women had objected to the purchase of a house in Darwin for pupils from Lajamanu. They were unhappy to see the youth exiled like that

17. The Warlpiri from the East live in Willowra; the Walmajarri, the Kukatja and the Ngardi people live in Balgo, and other communities in Western Australia; and in Kalkaringi, situated to the north, live the Kurintji people.

59

without any guarantee of a successful education being given to them.

Disheartened by the discussions of the previous day, the assembly was a bit tense. If the mining company wanted to undertake new drillings, it also meant promises of new mining revenue; the fact that the company wanted to prospect with new drillings meant it would have to compensate the land owners. But the influx of money caused divisions and conflicts.

Old Paddy took the microphone and, without getting up, stated in Warlpiri:

"I have rights to the land exploited by the company, but I've never asked for anything because I've got my Outstation. If new explorations have to be made, we need to think together about the terms we'll accept from them."

Another man, woolen hat pulled down to his eyes, intervened in Warlpiri to say that people should not be divided and that everything should be discussed together. The leader of the meeting turned to the women. Peggy raised her arm to have the microphone. Having explained at length in Warlpiri her ancestral attachment to the land and her rights as a custodian to the sites of her Budgerigar Dreaming which should not be destroyed, she finished in English:

"Women are nothing, there are too many dangerous and secret things for us, it's for the men to decide all together."

"Four years ago, at the time of the signing of the contract," a Warlpiri said, "it was anticipated the mine would give us some work, then we never heard another word about that promise again. Will the new explorations give some work to the youth?"

A young go-getter male executive replied with a smile that the work in the mine was highly specialized, and the company had already employed two Aboriginal workers from another state. The memory of the Kardiya was short. Who remembered the time when the elders and their father's generation had helped prospectors lost in the desert and had themselves discovered some deposits from which only the Whites benefitted?

Then the participants divided themselves into two groups. The first gathered the representatives of a border region of Western Australia. It constituted a dozen women, among whom Peggy and her sisters, and a dozen men, of whom two originated from the Pintupi tribe and the delegation of Ngardi from Balgo. The second group, much more important, consisted of the representatives of a region to the east of The Granites, connected with the Yarripiri Giant Snake Dreaming, the Rain Dreaming and the Two Snakes Dreaming, where Victor's unoccupied Outstation was situated.

Nakakut explained to me that the Two Snakes Dreaming is one of her husband Tony's Dreamings. He was brought up there with his clan of the Stars Dreaming, whose mythical trail connects a site of the region in the sacred hills of Kurlungalinpa, a few hundred kilometers north. Indeed both were considering leaving those hills and their Mirirrinyangu Outstation to settle down more at the heart of the Warlpiri territory, in fact, to be precise, in Victor's Puyurru Outstation. Thus Tony would live again in his true native land and Nakakut and her sister would be closer to theirs, the sacred rocks of The Granites.

As elder daughter of the main custodian of that site, Nakakut was among the first women to receive mining compensations: 8,000 dollars that disappeared into the pockets of her sons and nephews as well as a Toyota that didn't survive a car crash. Since then, she hadn't received anything and complained about it. Victor had reassured her that if Tony settled down in Puyurru, he could benefit from the credit of the car repairs financed by the royalties. Seated among the women of that region, Nakakut led the discussion.

"The Kardiya are going to make holes until they reach our camps. They are already talking about pulling down the Puyurru Outstation to put it up somewhere else because there is possibly gold right underneath it!"

The audience burst into laughter. It was time to relax the atmosphere. All those stories of money created too many problems. The more money there was, the more alcohol and risks of car crashes in which husbands and sons were killed. But money was necessary too: the maintenance of the houses cost more and more; they had to pay rent; and there was talk about electricity and water being charged for. And the children wanted videos....

Victor's first wife, Napanangka, a tall woman in a bright pink T-shirt, with a sensuous mouth, stood up.

61

"All these home problems are our business, but we have to take the money from wherever it can come. The Granites mine won't be in operation for more than five years. What will we do after there are no more royalties? It is just as well the people from the mining company find other gold to continue. After all, the land has fed us before the Kardiya arrived, and it continues to feed us. Of course, our sacred sites can't be destroyed, but men are taking care of that."

I noticed over recent years that Napanangka had changed a lot. Reaching the status of a forty-year-old woman, she had become her husband's messenger beside her fellow sister-members, artfully pacifying those who had objections. Looking around for Victor who had just closed the men's meeting, she signaled him to come across. He explained the men had decided not to accept the proposal for prospecting, but that the CLC was granted a year to negotiate the best conditions for such an offer. Only at the end of that process would the definitive decision be taken.

The CLC representative thanked the audience for having delegated the CLC to undertake negotiations with the mining company. He announced food rations would be distributed to the participants. An engine roar drowned his voice. The bosses of the mining company had just taken off without waiting for the result of the deliberations that had lasted all day. Exhausted, the crowd dispersed. The youngest of Nakakut's six sisters, having located the ration bus, proudly brandished a plastic bag loaded with food:

"So, that's it. We talk about millions only to end up with a piece of meat!"

NOSTALGIA

When I arrived for the first time among the Warlpiri in 1979 I was 23 years old and believed I was escaping social pressures. A decade later, the complexity of the stakes causing fresh conflicts in Lajamanu went beyond me. I was having trouble accepting that the technocratic machinery had plunged its dangerous wheels into the heart of a people whose ancestors had maintained a different civilization for forty thousand years.

When Lajamanu was still a reserve, Whites almost never went there, except for a few officials verifying the work of the administrator or the missionaries. By becoming an autonomous settlement, Lajamanu witnessed its population of White residents, the Kardiya, rise to thirty: teachers, nurses, mechanics, electricians, shop managers and accountants for the Council. They were employed on two-year contracts and rarely stayed longer, though others replaced them immediately.

Since the wages in the Aboriginal communities were higher than elsewhere, in the beginning many *Europeans** volunteered through opportunism. They used to stay together, a bit frightened by the world that surrounded them, and were rarely eager to understand it. That was the type of people I met on my first visit. The image of my own culture thrown back at me was unbearable. I thought at the time that, faced with that antagonism, the Warlpiri would reinforce their autonomy.

A few years ago, a new wave of Kardiya arrived who were curious and devoted to the Aboriginal people. Respectful of all forms of cultural preservation, some even became knights of the development. In the past it used to annoy me. I imagined the Warlpiri caught in the trap of that solicitude. As a result, all signs of Aboriginal resistance, from the squandering of money to the children skipping school, appeared to me to indicate a healthy survival instinct.

In 1988 I found the Warlpiri to be sad and amused at the same time, a bit lost as strategist-apprentices in what they thought they grasped, some with a keen sense of the functioning of a world which they had entered less than a century before. They complained about the *too* numerous meetings and the *too* numerous *topmen*, officials and other representatives who were constantly making demands of them. Besides the DAA and the CLC, there were nearly twenty state, federal or private agencies whose employees changed all the time, and occasionally new acronyms popped up. The Aboriginal Development Commission (ADC), the Aborigines Benefits fund (ABTA), the Central Australian Aboriginal Media Association (CAAMA), and then Health, Welfare, Women's Protection, or the Aboriginal Cultural Foundation.... And that was without mentioning TV journalists, museum directors and art gallery owners.

Those incessant visits, the arrival of videos in 1983 and television in 1986, have made the Warlpiri and their neighbors discover a universe much more complex and confusing than even they had imagined. Despite their own journeys to town, they always lacked some facts to be able to organize the disparate information that reached them.

While we were having tea on the threshold of the clinic's studio, where I stayed with my partner, Nakakut explained that she had been very worried during the years of my absence:

"We have seen images of war on TV. You shouldn't stay *overseas*, it's too dangerous. You have to come and live here, in Lajamanu, you would be safer."

I discovered that Nakakut thought that Lebanon or Afghanistan were part of the same country as France, England or America, *overseas* being the native land of those who, even after two centuries of colonization in Australia, still describe themselves as *Europeans.[18]* I tried to explain to her the geopolitical configuration of the world. It was as difficult for her to grasp as it was for me when I was confronted with the social and mythical geography of the Aboriginal people.

She was probably right, France has much more in common with Lebanon and Afghanistan than with a community in the Australian bush! Nevertheless one language is common to contemporary international relations and the traditional policy of the Aboriginal people: residence rights. I made it clear to Nakakut that being French did not give me the right to settle down and work in Australia.

"Yes, I know," she replied. "There's a German woman who came here after you to learn the language. She wanted to work in the school, but was sent back to her country because she didn't have a permit to work. We wrote to the government to ask for her return. With that letter she will possibly obtain the required papers."

As soon as a new situation concerns them directly the Warlpiri immediately adapt themselves to the new conditions. The external world remains a vast magma for them, but they systematically interpret the elements that affect them according to their own interests. If the Western world was ethnocentric in its vision of the others, the Warlpiri was too, in its own way.

Ten years ago they did not use the word *tourist*. Recently, Australian tourism started to *sell* the Aboriginal people. And the word made its entry into the Warlpiri language, even if in Lajamanu itself there were still no tourists since, as with most of the Aboriginal communities, a permit was needed to venture there. In the Australian States that have not given back their lands to the Aboriginal people, authorization depends on governmental administrators. But in the Northern Territory, the demands have to be addressed to the Central Land Council (for the Centre) or to the Northern Land Council (for Arnhem Land) and the decision depends on the Council of the community concerned.

When I decided, as we anthropologists say, *to do fieldwork[19]* with Aboriginal people, I didn't know where to go. Having

---

18. *European* was, until the 1990s, a common expression used in Australia to refer to themselves as people of European ancestry.
19. *Faire un terrain* means "to make a field" in French.

written to the CLC, it was to Lajamanu that I was invited. Probably because the Warlpiri had just been given back their land and no female anthropologist seemed to have worked in that locality. That's what Beryl explained to my partner.

"Nungarrayi was the first woman to come here to learn about women *business*. The men have had two Kardiya before. Since then, other White women have taken part in our *yawulyu* ceremonies. But Nungarrayi lived with us like a Yapa. She slept at the camp of the Lajamanu women."

I was moved that Beryl took care to give him an account of what he didn't know about my past. I sometimes wondered if my affection for the Warlpiri was not merely a phantasy. I asked myself a thousand times if I had given something back to them in exchange for all the things they had taught me. Reality proved much more simple: having shared and participated in some of the events of their recent history, the time we spent together had in turn become part of some of their memories.

"She was travelling with us, crammed into a truck with the Yapa. And when there were conflicts, she cried. Once, she ran off into the bush and we had to find her. We looked after her," Nakakut said, adding with pride: "She was young and we grew her up."

Indeed, some Warlpiri perceived me at that time more clearly than I realized myself: on a quest for an identity. Born in Warsaw, I came to Paris when I was five, speaking not one word of French. Ironically, because of the Cold War, some children used to call me a Pole communist bastard. Spending vacations in Poland at sixteen, I was called a capitalist! At that time my parents considered emigration for the second time, this time to Australia, but that plan which I was very excited about, was dropped. When I was a student, and about to undertake a course at the Lodz school of cinema, my father was arrested in Warsaw, and I decided to leave for the Aboriginal people of Australia.

Why did I choose these people from that part of the world? Because of our failed emigration or because of my mother who, at the end of a war spent in a refugee camp in Algeria,[20] had

---

20. Established in El Biar (Alger) in 1940 by my grandfather, Jan Krygowski, who joined the Red Cross to lead a convoy of Jewish families from Poland, including his wife Jadwiga, my mother, Bozena and her younger brother, Zbyszek. The camp later became a base for the allies where my mother, who finished her secondary school at the French

hesitated between leaving for Australia or going back to Poland? I have no idea. The Aboriginal people looked strangely familiar to me. Their relation to time and space evoked in me the imaginary drifts that dwelt within.

The Warlpiri with whom I spoke of my father being in prison in Warsaw were very compassionate. They did not know that the Kardiya could be imprisoned unjustly like them, and adopted me with even more sympathy. In 1979, Lajamanu seemed to me like an enclosed world where, as in the Western and Eastern blocs, Yapa (Indigenous) and Kardiya (Whites) would have been represented by two opposing factions. And myself, remaining apart from the Whites, I was searching among the Warlpiri for another *way of being*. I do not mean as was suggested in the translation, that I wanted to be like a Warlpiri … but just find a new becoming … out of the opposition). At that time the community gathered regularly in the park to vote for each measure proposed by the Council. Whites did not participate in the vote, but attended and sometimes influenced it. One day, there was a vote to decide whether Lajamanu was to continue obtaining its supply by means of a private transport company based in Katherine, or if the Council should buy a truck that an employee could drive to Darwin where food was cheaper.

The Whites and many Warlpiri women did not appreciate the truck driver chosen by the Council, an old German who provided the men with alcohol despite the prohibition. Nevertheless, the idea of taking charge of the provision of supplies would make the community more autonomous. That was the argument maintained by the Council. Some teachers opposed to the project spread the rumor, via the children, that the truck would be bought by deducting from the child benefits given to the women. No one knew whom to believe anymore, and when the time to vote came the majority was opposed to purchasing the truck.

In the heat of the debate, the Chairman declared that if the Yapa did not trust the Council, there would be new elections. I had been invited by the women to sit among them and they asked for my advice. Without hesitation, I supported the Council. The missionary, who was standing a few feet away,

boarding school in Alger, was playing piano for the soldiers until 1946. The family hesitated for a year before returning Poland.

called me to account for interfering in the vote, arguing that the Kardiya did not have the right to do so. I stood up, angry, and replied violently that she had interfered in her own way over the previous days. Indignant, she left, but our altercation left the assembly stunned. I asked my neighbor if I had to leave. She ordered me to stay. The meeting was adjourned.

On the way back to the camp everything suddenly seemed vain to me. Heavy-hearted, I could not hold back my tears and fled toward the bush. Some women caught up with me and told me I did not have the right to cry. It was dangerous to go alone in that state of mind as it called forth the bad spirits. Later on, at the camp, I was told I had spoken "well," that the Council would buy the truck, but it was "not well" to argue with the missionary. In reality, the vote became a compromise. The Council bought the truck to obtain the supplies in Darwin and kept the contract with the transport company in Katherine to come only once a week instead of twice.

That story should have taught me that most Warlpiri do not want any antagonism with Whites and that, even if the converts are not the majority, the missionaries had their place among them. But, me, like a jealous child, I wanted the Warlpiri all for myself.

Yulyulu Lorna Fencer Napurrurla, leading the *kurdungurlu* line with *wurrpardi* spears, Lajamanu, 1984.

PART TWO

(1979)

WHAT IS YOUR SKIN?

May 1979: Alice Springs. For a week I've been sitting at a table in the offices of the Central Land Council feverishly consulting the archives: more than 2,000 pages of transcription from the two years of the Warlpiri territorial trial which had just ended. Throughout the pages I heard the faceless voices of men and women untiringly repeating the names of the Dreamings of their "clans" or local groups and sites. I discovered endless discussions of jurists and anthropologists aiming to define the status to give to the traditional relationship of the Aboriginal people with the land.

A map provided me with a thousand sites whose strange names were scattered across a huge desert. On a second map the approximate zones were drawn, partly overlapping each other. They indicated the respective lands of some thirty Warlpiri clans. A third map presented an example of some trails carving right through the tribal territory. Those trails, all named by the Dreamings — Rain, Emu, Kangaroo, Dingo... — corresponded to the respective ancestors of the clans who traditionally shared their custody.

On the basis of such mythic bonds linking the people to places and trails the Warlpiri have regained relative control of a vast portion of their territory. I learned that the judge and his assistants had made a special visit to certain sites to hear the Warlpiri explain how such a rock, or such a waterhole, was stamped by an ancestor of the Dreaming. On top of the enquiries and direct testimonies, the exhibition of sacred objects and the performance of rituals linking the groups to given lands counted as proof of traditional ownership.

Finally, for each trail of the Dreaming or portion of trail defining the land of a clan, I found a list of owners: their names, occasionally followed by an English surname, were all accompanied by another name that Europeans as well as Aboriginal people call *skin*. In each clan it was almost always the same two skin names that recurred, the children have a different name from their father, but the same name as their father's grandfather. As for their mothers, while being classified as part of their own father's clan, they had an altogether different skin name. But, from clan to clan, there were only four pairs of skin names for there are only eight altogether. All the Warlpiri, and their neighbors from the Centre, share between them only eight possible names.

Those eight skin names, called sub-sections by anthropologists, form a classifying kinship system. For example, all those who bear the same name consider themselves as skin *brothers*. And each name is associated with another single name as potential *spouse*. The non-Aboriginal people working with the Aboriginal people systematically receive one of the names that register them in this kinship classification. In the Central Land Council, I heard employees having fun interpreting the relationships among themselves:

"You are called Nakamarra? Me, I am Jungarrayi. So you are my *mother*!"

Those types of games played by the Whites annoyed me somewhat. Why are they acting as if they were Aboriginal people? It took me a very short time to realize that to understand the relationships between those names, and to learn to find my way in their classification, was the *sine qua non* condition to any interaction with the Warlpiri.

A few days later I set off for the first time along the desert tracks, driven in a Toyota 4x4 by an Aboriginal man of mixed ancestry, Stanley, employed as liaison officer by the CLC. His mission was to drop me off in Lajamanu. Recalling the films on Aboriginal people seen in France, I remembered that I had already seen him on the screen. He took part in a documentary on the Coniston cattle station where thirty-one Warlpiri were massacred by the Whites in 1928.[21]

We stopped to fill up at a gas station. In the bar my driver introduced me to one of his Aboriginal friends.

"What is your skin?" he asked me.

At the time I felt uneasy. Obviously I was White and, even if I sympathized with the conflicts that set Aboriginal people against Whites, I would never be Black. I quickly thought again. His question was not a provocation, he was only asking to be informed on my eventual kinship classification.

When we were driving once again along the red sand track capped by a Neapolitan ice cream sky that disappeared into a horizon of fluorescent grasses, my guide informed me with an amused tone in his voice:

"You already have a skin name. The president of the CLC called you Nungarrayi."

"Why Nungarrayi?" I asked, intrigued.

"Probably because the first Aboriginal person you met, Gary, whom we sent to meet you in Darwin, belongs to the same skin. He's a Jungarrayi, and thus you become his skin *sister*. As for me, I'm a Jangala, so you are my potential *spouse*," he explained, then burst into laughter.

Gary Williams, the descendant of a New South Wales tribe, had been involved in the creation of the CLC. Later he would leave that agency to return to Sydney and meet the film director Werner Herzog, appearing in "*Where the Green Ants Dream*" as the fair skin Aboriginal pilot of the green war plane given to the Indigenous elders who asked for that "giant flying green ant." I was happy to become Gary's *sister*, but could not help but wonder if my potential *spouse* had not made up that relationship

---

21. Cribbin, J. *The Killing Times — The Coniston Massacre 1928*. Sydney: Fontana/Collins, 1984; see also *Coniston*, documentary by David Batty and Francis Jupurrula Kelly, (2012) where it is stated that a hundred Warlpiri were killed. Rosie Napangardi's testimony who witnessed the killing of her parents was recorded by B. Glowczewski in 1984 and can be heard on the author's Warlpiri audiovisual archive (www.odsas.net) with a an English transcript of the Warlpiri translation (also published on the CD-ROM *Dream Trackers*, Unesco Publishings, 2000, section "history" in "field notes").

to try to seduce me. In a most serious tone he stated he would present me as Nungarrayi to the Warlpiri of Lajamanu.

I was left to revise the relationships of kinship classification between the eight names. First they divide into gender: the same name begins with a "N" for the women and a "J" for the men. One can illustrate that relationship with a cube:

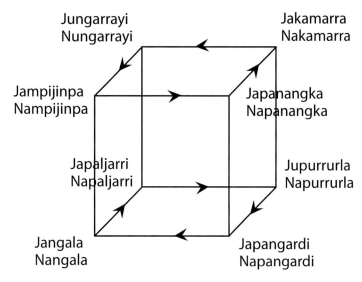

Eight sub-sections of the Warlpiri *skin* names

On that cube, the vertical lines represent the relationship between an individual and his *fathers* or *father's sisters*: for example, the Jungarrayi and Nungarrayi are respectively *fathers* and *father's sisters* of the Japaljarri and Napaljarri, but inversely these last ones are *fathers* and *father's sisters* of the firsts. Thus it occurs that a child is called equally *son/daughter* or *father/father's sister* by an adult whose skin name is the same as the child's real father. People also consider themselves as skin *brothers* of their *father's fathers* and their *father's father's sisters*, for they have the same name.

By another route, the arrowed lines of the cube represent the relationship between an individual and his *mothers* or *mother's brothers:* for instance the Nungarrayi are *mothers* and the Jungarrayi are *mother's brothers* of the Nampijinpa and Jampijinpa. These last ones are respectively *mothers* and *mother's brothers* of the Napananka and Japanangka who in their turn play the same roles for the Nakamarra and Jakamarra, themselves being in that relationship with the Nungarrayi and Jungarrayi. Thus, contrary to the paternal cycle which comes full circle in two generations, the maternal cycle does it in four generations. A woman and her great-grand-daughter consider themselves skin *sisters* for they have the same skin name.

Finally, in order to determine pairs of potential *spouses*, one has to look for the name vertically associated with the child of a woman and obtain the skin of the man she has to marry. Thus there are four couples divided according to gender:

Jungarrayi	marries	Nangala	and	Jangala	marries	Nungarrayi
Japaljarri	marries	Nakamarra	and	Jakamarra	marries	Napaljarri
Japanangka	marries	Napurrurla	and	Jupurrurla	marries	Napanangka
Japangardi	marries	Nampijinpa	and	Jampijinpa	marries	Napangardi

The Aboriginal people do not always respect these regulations and sometimes marry into an incorrect skin. In that case, the relationships of real kinship no longer coincide with the classifying relationships.

For example, if a Jungarrayi married a Napurrurla woman, a problem arises because their children will have different skin names if they *follow*, as the Aboriginal people say, their father or their mother. It is for the family to decide which name to attribute to them. If they are named *following* their father, thus Japaljarri for a boy and Napaljarri for a girl, they will find themselves in classifying relationships of *mother's brother* and *mother* with their own mother. Inversely, if they are named *following* the mother, thus Japangardi and Napangardi, they will be in relationships of *mother-in-law* (or *brother of the mother-in-law*) with their father.

In fact, as I was soon to discover, these parental classifications, rather than systematically constraining marriages, have above all an importance in ritual life. Thus, when a Dreaming is celebrated, each man or woman receives a role according to the skin name he or she bears.

In theory all Dreaming is in the custody of the clans whose members have one or the other of the two skin names associated as *father/father's sister* and *son/daughter* (the four vertical lines of the cube):

Stars, Budgerigar Dreamings...	*Rain, Emu Dreamings...*
Jungarrayi/Nungarrayi	Jampijinpa/Nampijinpa
Japaljarri/Napaljarri	Jangala/Nangala
Digging-Stick, Goanna Dreamings...	*Acacia Seeds, Possum Dreamings…*
Japanangka/Napanangka	Jakamarra/ Nakamarra
Japangardi/Napangardi	Jupurrurla/Napurrurla

Those who have the same two names as the custodians of the celebrated Dreaming act like them in the ritual and are assisted by all the people who have the two other skin names of the same column. The total of the people of that column are then called *kirda*, (*boss, owner*), masters *owning* the Dreaming and the ritual in question.

Inversely, all the people whose skin names are found in the other column are called *kurdungurlu*, (*worker, policeman, lawyer, manager*), thus assistants *managing* that same Dreaming and ritual.[22] Their role is to prepare the ground and the ceremonial objects. They also direct the choreography of the dances executed by the *kirda*. By definition, each Warlpiri is induced to play one or the other role according to the celebrated Dreaming.

When they lived in the bush, the Warlpiri carried out rituals on the sites of the Dreamings, without being necessarily numerous. But every *kirda* land owner had to be assisted by his/her *kurdungurlu* managers, not only to be able to celebrate his Dreaming but also to accomplish certain tasks like fetching water or wood in his/her sacred site. Each man had his own particular *kurdungurlu*, as they are his sisters' sons, themselves

---

22. Laughren, M. "Warlpiri Kinship Structure"; Nash, D. "An Etymological Note on Warlpiri kurdungurlu"; Eds. J. Heath, F. Merlan & A. Rumsey, "The Languages of Kinship in Aboriginal Australia." *Oceania Linguistic Monograph* 24, 1982.

kirda of the Dreaming and lands associated to other clans, for it is forbidden to marry into one's own clan.

For decades anthropologists have underestimated the role played by women in traditional societies. During the inquiries for the restitution of the land to the Warlpiri, it was confirmed that women have not only rights and ritual responsibilities on the land, but also that they are organized as *kirda* and *kurdungurlu* like the men: *kirda* owners of their father's land, they are *kurdungurlu* managers of their mother's land.

Through contact with the Warlpiri, I would soon discover the importance of those female rituals. Moreover, I would have the surprise of ascertaining that the role of *kurdungurlu* manager, for the women as well as the men, is not restricted only to the Dreaming and the mother's land, but applies equally to the Dreaming and land of the spouses. That way a man has to manage the ceremonies of his wife's brothers and, traditionally, that is the way he earned the right to camp and use the resources and lands of his brothers-in-laws. In the same way, a woman has to manage the ceremonies of her husband's sisters, which allowed her in the past to ritually watch over his land when they were camping there, and to teach their children not only the sacred knowledge of her own clan but also that of their father.

I found it amusing that as a French student landing in a society of which I knew almost nothing, I had placed my finger on the importance, both ritual and social, of a marriage relationship. In reality, the systems of kinship in traditional societies, and particularly in the Australian Aboriginal people, have generated a lot of debate in the history of anthropology. To summarize those debates, we could say that the major conflict contrasted the defenders of filiation, mostly Anglo-Saxons, with the French school of structuralism inaugurated by Claude Lévi-Strauss, which insisted on alliance.

Ironically, having completed my studies at the University of Paris VII at Jussieu, I was steeped in the post-68 anti-structuralism that characterized the anthropology department directed by Robert Jaulin. The result: Lévi-Strauss was contested and we did not have a course on Kinship studies! It was only when working in the field that I realized all of that was lacking in my education. I even wrote a letter of reproach to the director of my M.A. thesis, Michel de Certeau, who was extremely amused by it. Marked by Lacan, his work was in fact impregnated with structuralism. It would take me a few years before deciding to read Lévi-Strauss and admit that his work deserved the glorious raising of one's hat to it.

THE *BUSINESSWOMEN*

Amid the stifling heat and wind whipping up the red dust. Cawing crows hovering above a few scrawny dogs wandering among the corrugated iron strewn on the ground.

"There you are! Your destination! Look, that's the police station," Stanley, my Aboriginal driver from the CLC, announced.

In the dazzling light, I could discern the barbed wire and a large concrete construction. Further away, an iron water tank made me think of a watchtower in a military camp. We rolled slowly between the sheds daubed with graffiti. On one the inscription LAJAMANU was writ in big letters. From another emitted the infernal humming of an electricity generator. Passing along twenty bungalows in a line, we arrived at a vast desolate expanse with a gas pump where a group of Black men stood in their crumpled clothes, covered in dust.

My guide explained my presence. One went away and returned with a sturdy Aboriginal man: Lajamanu's Chairman, Maurice Luther Jupurrula. I had seen him for a few minutes in Darwin on the street where he was talking to a Warlpiri delegation after a meeting. With a piercing look he eyed me from head to toe, shook my hand and exclaimed:

"So you're the one coming to study us?"

The others burst into laughter and I smiled stupidly. The imposing Chairman led me to the mission. The missionary, a stern woman in her forties, told me in a dry tone that I could stay in the visitors' bungalow for 30 dollars a week.

I had not expected to pay rent, imagining to sleep at someone's house, or camp if necessary. My budget for five months, 7,000 French francs,[23] saved while working in an animation studio, would not hold out and I replied that it was too expensive. The Chairman looked at me, intrigued. He was not used to penniless Whites, nor to my accent. I also had the impression that he and the missionary did not get on that well.

"We'll arrange that. You can live in a Council studio for 5 dollars like the Warlpiri," he declared with a determined voice.

The studio was adjacent to five others, their sliding glass doors opening onto a shared yard that was filled with rubbish and a fire where the families cooked. My studio was provided with an electric cooker and even heating. There was also a shower, a big table, a small bed and a cupboard. Pure luxury!

Two hours later the Chairman returned with his young and attractive wife, long legs beneath her bright green miniskirt. She held the hand of their small daughter whose long blonde locks were characteristic of the Black desert children. We climbed into a Holden and the Chairman dropped us in a kind of shanty town whose corrugated iron shelters scattered here and there were no bigger than one and a half meter. Rows of mattresses and rolled blankets were spread out as far as the eye could see.

"This is the *top camp*, the East camp, where most of the Lajamanu Yapa live," the Chairman explained before disappearing.

I could not help but feel uneasy facing what appeared as a caricature of consumer society. On my right, card players were putting down and picking up dollars from the ground. Littered around us were plastic wrappers, empty cans and other refuse in which rather mangy and half-starved dogs rummaged.

The Chairman's young wife, Agnes Napanangka, indicated with a nod of her head a group of women seated in the distance. Entrusting me to a woman with an emaciated face who looked to be around fifty, she whispered:

"*Business*, they are the *businesswomen* … like Lily Nungarrayi, your *sister*."

More card players? My *sister* Lily pushed me toward them and indicated that I sit down on a blanket. Their chests were naked and they were singing a very repetitive chant. Some were

---

23. 1,560 Australian dollars, or 1,650 American dollars, at that time.

rubbing white, red or yellow rocks on a stone palette. Pouring a few drops of cooking oil from a bottle onto the powder obtained from the process, they dipped in their index fingers and painted wooden boards.

A few feet away, three painted poles were planted in the ground, placed approximately two meters apart and connected with red ropes. An old woman, quite small, with bright eyes, drew me by the hand and forced me to rub my palm upon the extremity of each pole where the ropes hung, topped by white feathers. My hand became tinged with red ochre and the old woman, delighted, repeated several times:

"*Jukurrpa, Jukurrpa....*"

That word, pronounced "tchookoorrpa," I knew already, for it was used by the Warlpiri as well as by Western tribes who translate it into English as *Dreaming* or *Dreamtime*. Everything I had read on the *Dreaming* before coming to Australia had fascinated me, making me hungry for more.[24] Why do Aboriginal people call the "Dreamings" their mythical ancestors and their travelling trails that link different groups to different lands? It was the answer to that question that I had come to look for here. I was not disappointed. The *business* proved to have something to do with the Dreaming.

I had already forgotten about the rubbish and looked astounded at the singers sitting close to each other who now placed their ochre covered fingers on the torso, breasts, and shoulders of their neighbors. The painted women let themselves be drawn in every sense by the painters who traced strange patterns. Some used little sticks to widen the thick marks with finer lines and different colors.

24. Elkin, A.P. *The Australian Aborigines: how to understand them,* Sydney: Angus & Robertson, 1976 (1938); Maddock, K. *The Australian Aborigines,* Melbourne: Penguin Books, 1970; Roheim, *The Eternal Ones of the Dream,* International University Press, 1945; B. Spencer & F.J. Gillen, *The Native Tribes of Central Australia,* London: Macmillan & Co. Ltd., 1899 (revised, *The Arunta,* 1927); Stanner, W.H. *Aboriginal Religion,* Sydney: Oceania Monograph 11, 1963; Tonkinson, R. *The Mardudjara Aborigines: Leaving the Dream in Australia's Desert,* New York: Holt Rinehardt & Winston, 1978.

A fat woman arrived wearing a long chain around her neck from which keys hung. She introduced herself, Annie Nungar-rayi, another of my *sisters*. She showed me two finished body paintings, one, then the other, and stated clearly in two languages:

"*Yankirri Jukurrpa*, Emu Dreaming … *Ngatijirri Jukurrpa*, Budgerigar Dreaming…."

Those two Dreamings had been indexed in the list of clans reclaiming the Warlpiri territory. I wondered if the women belonged to these clans or were painted with the Dreaming of another clan. Another *businesswoman* in a pink dress talked to me at length in Warlpiri. Despite the few language classes I had taken at the Institute for Aboriginal Development in Alice Springs, I only understood that she was my Napurrurla skin *cousin* and that she called herself *kurdungurlu*, "*policeman*," like other women she pointed out to me when giving me their respective skin names. In return, the women painted with the Budgerigar Dreaming, Nungarrayi and Napaljarri skin, were *kirda,* "*boss*."

After two hours twenty *businesswomen* were painted. They donned hairbands on which white feathers in the shape of peaks were sown and received the painted boards from other women. Then, separating into two lines, they started to dance. Hopping on their slightly parted legs, they shook the boards with both hands or placed them under their arm. The two lines turned around the three poles and crossed each other in complicated meanders, imprinting on the sand a system of overlapping lines. Some non-painted women surrounded them, and some hopped intermittently in order to shout orders in Warlpiri, as if they were directing the movements of the dancers. As one explained:

"These are the *kurdungurlu*, '*policemen*.'"

All of a sudden the company stopped singing. The dancers laid down their boards. It was finished. They asked if I appreciated it. I assented enthusiastically.

"Do you have a tape recorder?"

I said I did, a film camera too. I was invited to return the next day with my equipment for another *business*, but on one condition. "You will only show the film to women in your country, the women *business*, the *yawulyu*, is not for men."

A very attractive dancer pulled a T-shirt over her Budgerigar Dreaming painting and, hoisting her four-year-old daughter onto her hip, proposed to accompany me back.

"Nungarrayi, me Peggy Napaljarri, your *auntie*. Napaljarri and Nungarrayi always dance their Dreamings together. They're not all from the same country and the same Dreaming as me, but all are *kirda*, *boss* for my Budgerigar Dreaming."

She had answered the question I had asked myself. A woman is not necessarily painted with the Dreaming of her clan, but she tends to be painted with the Dreamings for which she is classified boss *kirda* by her skin name.

I spent the night reflecting on it all. I learned by heart the names of the twenty or so Dreamings listed in the book of the Warlpiri land claims,[25] the pairs of skin names associated with each, as well as a few named sites characterizing them.

The day after, at the camp of the *businesswomen,* after I was introduced to an old Nungarrayi wearing a red and green woolen hat, I unloaded word for word the name of each Dreaming followed by a pair of skin names and a toponym. The inquisitive eye of my interlocutress immediately turned vacant and she nodded without saying a word. A young woman looked on, rather startled, and told me reproachfully, in English:

"She is distressed because you know too much!"

I had made a monumental gaffe. I thought that by showing I knew that Dreamings were associated with places, I would win the trust of these women more quickly. Had I transgressed the taboo which forbade talking about what was restricted to men? And yet were the women I had seen dancing not celebrating their land? I did not dare ask this question. Besides, my young interpreter had left and the *businesswomen*, most of them old, did not speak English, with the exception of a few words in pidgin. It was advisable that I become capable of expressing myself in Warlpiri. Failing that, I decided that in the future I would keep silent and, instead, open wide my ears and eyes.

And so the days and the weeks passed. I learned nothing new by asking questions. But, always unexpectedly, a woman would tell me something with a knowing look, half in English, half in Warlpiri, punctuated by an inevitable "*you know,*" signaling

25. Peterson, N., McConvell, P., Wild, S. & Hagen, R. *A Claim to Areas of Traditional Land by the Warlpiri and Kartangarurru-Kurintji.* Alice Springs: Central Land Council, 1978.

that with what I had seen, I should already know what her precise details were telling me.

I discovered that this was the method of learning among the women themselves. The young could not ask questions of the elders but, by means of participating in the rituals, of repeating what they saw and listening silently to the discussions of the initiated, each constructed, little by little, her knowledge. Later, when growing older, the women entered another process that consisted in *exchanging* what they had learned for secrets held by others.

In reality, the *businesswomen* referred to the land in their *yawulyu* dances and painting sessions, but each only talked publicly about the particular site that characterized her clan, the one in which are condensed the *Kuruwarri*, Images, and ancestral marks that give life to human beings and to the phenomena named by her Dreaming.

They could spend years singing, painting, and dancing the Dreamings without knowing the exact story of the corresponding mythical heroes or the succession of sites of their journey's trail. Generally, however, once past forty, they knew an impressive number of sung verses they could associate with narrative episodes and places. Each was in some way specialized in the Dreamings of which they were directly the ritual depositary, master or manager. And that was by her paternal or maternal affiliation and her marriage, and not by her skin name, which gave her a role in the celebration of any Dreaming.

Nowhere else did I have the sensation of *being woman* with as much clarity as when I was with the Warlpiri. A sensation both organic and mental, located in the depths of my body and far beyond, an extreme bliss and panicking pain. It was the gradual experience of the breaking-up of my identity which made me lose that feeling of being individually a woman and even simply an individual.

Day after day, nothing which I used to identify with in the past found an echo. The aesthetic, intellectual or emotional criteria to which I was accustomed did not seem to make much sense when pitted against those of the Warlpiri, which I had trouble pinning down. The image they threw back at me of myself was monstrous. Ugly for being White, stupid for being incapable of communicating in their language, I was made to feel as if I was living in the vegetable-like state of an object manipulated or ignored, for all my efforts seemed to pass unnoticed.

In a way I would have liked to have charmed them, but lacking the knowledge of how to, I thought I would never succeed in being accepted. However, I was adopted and even with a certain sympathy. It baffled me for I had no privileged relationship with any individual to make heads or tails of that acceptance. It was the body of the community itself that was integrating me and, more particularly, the group of women responsible for the rituals.

I soon became a *businesswoman* in the eyes of the community as I spent all my time with those designated as such, even though I was much younger and more ignorant than them. Such was the status which gave me a place in the tribe. And because of that, the men rarely talked to me, and the young women of my own age avoided me.

KAJIRRI

Access to the *jilimi,* the camp where the *businesswomen* gathered, was forbidden to men. Widows and single women slept there as well as married women when their husbands spent the night at the men's ritual camp, went pub-crawling or had an argument with them. At the edge of the *jilimi* Tony Gibson, a Japaljarri, camped with four Nakamarra sisters who were bringing up their children together. Only two of the sisters were his spouses and attended the rituals. As they were still young women, they were painted, and they only painted, sung or danced when the elders invited them. They were also not allowed to take part in discussions. The younger women was named Beryl and the older women was named Barbara, like me. For two days I had the feeling that my namesake was looking at me in a pleasant and pensive way. I did not yet know the name by which I was going to call her, Nakakut. Finally she approached.

"My eldest son Jungarrayi is in the bush with other boys," she said in almost perfect English. "I won't be able to see him for several months, when the Kajirri *business* is over and he is *malyarra.* Until then we have to dance every day to help the *punyunyu* become men."

I learned we were at the height of the initiation cycle. I had read an account of the Kajirri ceremony by Mervyn Meggitt, an American anthropologist who worked here around 1952 and

1953, just after the creation of the Hooker Creek Reserve.[26] He insisted women were excluded from ritual life.

If the young novices are kept in seclusion away from the women, I was about to discover that during the four months of the initiation cycle, parallel to the male rituals, the women celebrate it in their own way. Regularly, one or two women elders worked together with a man elder at the edge of the *jilimi* to decide on the stages of the ceremony. This consisted partly in retracing, site by site, the long epic of the Kajirri heroes, as well as by celebrating all the trails of the Dreamings which those heroes crossed on their journey.

It is said that the Warlpiri received the Kajirri ceremony from their northern neighbors, the Kurintji, a hundred years ago. In order to integrate it, they had extended a trail which crossed the territory of that tribe, making it cross the Warlpiri territory, and thus laying claim on the new journey as a local Dreaming. That innovation was interpreted as a *remembrance:* the men said to have *remembered* what was from the beginning in *Jukurrpa*, the time-space of the Dreaming.

At the time of the American anthropologist, the Kajirri Dreaming did not seem to identify any clan. All the men of Japangardi, Japanangka, Japaljarri, and Jungarrayi skin, in other words more or less half of the men, were considered *kirda* bosses or masters of the ceremony. The other half were *kurdungurlu* managers.

Almost thirty years later, the men were still divided that way for their ritual roles. Peter Blacksmith Japanangka, the last survivor of the Kartangarurru tribe, was referred to as the *boss* of *bosses:* Kajirri was the name of his clan itself.

His daughter Maggy, a blind Napangardi approaching forty, gave me Warlpiri lessons.

"My Dreaming is Kajirri." She spoke in whispers. "My *kurruwalpa* was sown on that Dreaming road. My spirit child chose my mother in Parnta, my father's land, to enter her and be born (palkajarri "become body") as me."

While having Kajirri for clan Dreaming and conception Dreaming, the blind Napangardi was not old enough to be the *boss* of the female Kajirri rituals. The *boss* was another

26. Meggitt, M. *Desert People*. London: Angus & Robertson, 1962, and "Gadgeri among the Warlpiri Aborigines of Central Australia." Sydney: Oceania Monograph 14, 1966.

Napangardi, Rosie, who, as a young mother, still lived a traditional life in the bush, hiding from the Whites. Today, considering her old age, which obliged her to walk with a stick, it was one of her nieces by classification, Betty Napanangka, belonging to the clan of the Goanna Dreaming and approaching fifty, who directed operations.

Like the men, the women considered *kirda* masters of Kajirri were all the Napangardi, Napanangka, Napaljarri, and Nungarrayi, whatever their clans or conceptual affiliation may be. And, in the same way, the *kurdungurlu* managers of the ceremony were all the bearers of the four other skin names. That way, the whole community was involved in the celebration.

Although *Warlpirized*, the Kajirri ceremony is connected with some fertility cults of the northern tribes, such as the Big Sunday among the Kurintji and the Kunapipi from Arnhem Land. The Big Sunday refers to a maternal entity properly called Kajirri, while Kunapipi celebrates the two Wawilak sisters who scattered numerous Dreamings and spirit-children, and inaugurated the Kunapipi rituals they transmitted to the men.[27] According to Meggitt, by contrast, the Warlpiri would have elaborated for Kajirri a myth-trail having two men for heroes.

I learned during the first week that the women identified the Kajirri Dreaming not with the journey of two men, but with two sisters having Nampijinpa for their skin name. Thus, those were classified as *mothers* and *spouses* of the Japanangka and Japangardi men of the Kajirri clan, which confirmed the maternal symbol of the Northern cults.

I discovered that two of the poles I was made to touch on the women's dancing ground on the day of my arrival *materialized* the presence of the two ancestral sisters. Those poles placed the participants in the ritual in contact with the time-space of the Dreaming. An Australian musicologist, who was in Lajamanu during the first month of my stay, pointed out that the male rituals sometimes referred to two men, but more often also to the two Nampijinpa sisters.[28] What had happened in thirty years? In the Fifties were the women really excluded from

27. Berndt, R.M. *Kunapipi*. Melbourne: Cheshire, 1951; Warner, W.L. *A Black Civilization*. Chicago: Harper & Brothers, 1958 (1937).
28. Wild, S. "Men as Women: Female Dance Symbolism in Warlpiri Men's Rituals." *Dance Research Journal* 10:14-22, 1977.

Kajirri and were there no female heroines? Or else, had Meggitt not seen that aspect of the celebration? The question remained unanswered because, for the Warlpiri, the two Nampijinpa have *always* existed in the Dreaming, and the women have *always* danced. The only thing one could say was that while the discourse about the ceremony had evolved, the participation of women and the two mythical sisters still have a prominent place today.

What was most surprising was that as I steadily gathered the toponyms defining the trail of the two Nampijinpa and the name of the Dreamings they had encountered on their way, it confirmed they coincided with those reported by Meggitt for the journey of the male heroes. In other words, men and women told two different stories that were secret, but which had the same partly public geographic structure.

One day when I was setting off for a walk alone on a bush track, a woman caught up with me.

"You cannot go in the South-West direction because of Kajirri, the *punyunyu* from Yuendumu arrive that way."

The *punyunyu* were the twenty or so novices, among them a Jungarrayi from the Gibson family, who had been taken by the elders for an initiation journey into the other Warlpiri community 600 kilometers away. For two weeks their return was announced as imminent. During their initiation the boys could not be seen by, nor see, the women, who had to avoid being in the vicinity of the track along which they had a chance of arriving.

I was surprised the rule applied to me too. I even started to feel a bit like a prisoner, for I did not have the right either to go out by the other track to the North-East, on the pretext that the men's ritual camp was there, inaccessible to women. I was told time and again:

"If you had a car, you could take us into the bush as far as the *free* zone."

In the end, two women invited me to accompany them hunting. We crossed the dry riverbed that marked the southern border of Lajamanu and passed across undergrowth. I admired

92

the agility of those two rather stout women whose very thin legs slid barefoot through the thicket. On the red plain, with its bare vegetation, they peered carefully at the ground in search of an animal print, testing the earth here and there with the tips of their crowbars.

Abruptly they sat down, one with her legs stretched out, the other with hers tucked under her thighs, the usual manner of Aboriginal women who rarely sat up crossed-legged. Finding a place to dig, they bored the hard ground with a crowbar. Then they took turns to empty the hole, first with their hands, then with a *billy can*, a tin bucket used to make tea. They regularly studied the lumps of earth they dug out.

"You see, those little prints indicate the direction in which the Goanna's nose is pointing. And there, that soft earth is mixed with its excrement."

All of a sudden, in a flash, one woman caught the tail of a lizard the size of an arm and violently smashed its head against a rock. Then she emptied its guts through a little hole while her companion lit a fire on which to grill it. I received a piece of the tail, the best bit. Lined with fat, the juicy and slightly elastic white flesh was quite tasty.

"*Pilja* Goanna is my Dreaming," specified one of the two hunters.

We set off again. My guides showed me the wild food growing on the bushes, particularly the *kanta* insect galls, edible parasites of some eucalypti. With a crack of a stone, one opened the shell which contained an insect and pink fibers she made me taste. A delicious sweet liquid tickled my palate. They looked delighted and explained:

"*Kanta*, it's *Kuruwarri*, Kajirri *Kuruwarri*."

Kuruwarri, a word with multiple meanings, literally *image*, designates any painting made by men or women, but also the mythical narratives and everything that gives its name to a Dreaming. *Kuruwarri* are also the marks left by the heroes in the landscape: cave paintings whose origin was attributed to them; depressions in the ground they would have made when sitting; beds of sand dug out under their steps; springs that sprung from their urine, sperm or milk; ochre deposits brought to light from their coagulated blood. Most of the landscape features are thus imprints of the passage of the Dreaming heroes or the metamorphosis of their bodies. A swamp or a cave mark their disappearance into the earth. Rocks testify to their petrified organs. Trees reveal their underground forces.

Dreaming Images are not simple images. A painting made on an object or an individual is reputed to nourish its support both physically and spiritually with the total power of the represented Dreaming. In the same way, prints left by the heroes are animated with their eternal powers. Thus, to paint a Dreaming is at the same time to regenerate its powers and to bind the object or the person to the land and the time-space of the heroes who *dream* the life of men and their environment.

Almost everything that had been given a name in Warlpiri had its Dreaming and Images. But only certain things expressly designated clans and trails. Anthropologists call such names *totems*.[29] I discovered that each totem or Dreaming characterizing a clan was connected with other totems that together formed a constellation, in other words, the elements of a mythical narrative.

For example, *Kanta* Gall was the name given to certain painted designs of the Kajirri Dreaming because the two Kajirri heroines had scattered on their path the galls, from which bushes with new galls had grown. Because of that, *Kanta* Gall is a Dreaming-totem synonym of Kajirri, as well as other foods eaten by the two heroines, such as *panyapanya* leaves on which sugar crystals form that dissolve beneath the tongue leaving a sweet fresh taste. In short, to eat in the bush was already to begin to *dream*.

29. Lévi-Strauss, C. *Totemism.* London: Merlin Press, 1964 (*Le Totémisme aujourd'hui*, PUF, 1962) and *The Savage Mind.* London: Weidenfeld & Nicolson, 1966 (*La Pensée sauvage*, Librairie Plon, 1962).

TOTEMS AND TABOOS

At noon a hundred women were gathered at the camp, among them strangers from Areyonga, an Aboriginal community located more than a 1,000 kilometers south of Lajamanu. They had followed the convoy that brought back the novices of Yuendumu that night. Three rows of dancers painted respectively with the Insect Gall Dreaming, Honey Bee Dreaming, and *wampana* Wallaby Dream, were hopping around the two usual sacred poles bound together with ropes. Then three old women from the audience were laid face down on the ground and their backs violently rubbed with other ropes coated in red ochre.

Shouts overlaid the chants and before long a Warlpiri woman started to cry in that singular way that characterizes mourning, the sound coming from the chest and modulating itself to the rhythm of a restrained breathing. Each time her voice died away, and before starting again, another woman joined the intoning. My blood ran cold, and yet I was carried along by that lament which, amplified by the whole assembly, reached us like waves from the horizon.

I was told the three old women stretched out on the ground were the relatives of a custodian of Kajirri who passed away six months ago. They had just been subjected to one of the funeral rituals that punctuate the mourning, a mourning that can sometimes last for years. Still in tears, all the women made their way to a camp-less space where they sat in two groups corresponding to the master/manager division of their skin names. Then they fell silent. The silence was almost apocalyptic.

Some elders armed with spears formed a row and, vibrating their hands before their mouths, let out a curious howling. Women replied with a "yu yu" sound, and all of them lowered their heads. My neighbors bent mine down. I had just enough time to glimpse a group of men brandishing foliage with which they hid four naked adolescent boys. Once they had passed between the two groups of women, those who were the mothers of Kajirri novices stood and danced with their arms stretched out in the direction they had taken, toward the men's camp, where the other novices were already secluded.

Some members of the Council built a new bough shed for the *businesswomen*: a flat roof of branches and sheet iron fixed on four thin tree trunks. One could not stand up straight beneath it, but that was not its purpose. The roof was used to hide, among its branches, sacred objects and food, keeping them out of reach of dogs and children. A kangaroo leg, as well as an emu leg, occupied a place of honor, offered to women by their sons, brothers or cousins.

In turns they took a bite of the cooked meat and replaced it in the roof of the shelter when they were full. It was very rare for the Warlpiri to have a meal together. In the shadow of the shed, shifting in relation to the sun, the women stretched out to delouse each other. As always, a little girl inspected my head and wanted to rub her hair against mine so that I could be deloused as well.

Suddenly a cry in the distance tore the silence. My neighbors sat up straight immediately and started intoning the same insistent sound. Without prompting, they set about covering their foreheads, cheeks, arms and chests with a white powder mixed with water, the mourning paint. Rising, they went to meet another group of women coated in a similar fashion. They sat on the ground in a circle, heads lowered, still issuing their cries, and drew close together holding one another with their arms outstretched. All around us other little groups began to form. Men approached and joined the women one by one. The groups came apart and re-formed each time differently to accommodate new comforting embraces.

One woman took hold of a billy can with which she bashed her head. Another seized a crowbar to do the same, blood running down her face. Some women tried to stop her. Several others were bleeding already, the tops of their heads open. I understood why most of the elders have a scar and not hair at that place. At each mourning, depending on their kinship with the dead, they mutilate themselves in that way. Some men had started to slash themselves across the thighs with knives. It was a *sorry business*, a ritual of affliction. I was asked to leave the camp, which I did, shaken by the contagious emotion of the sorrow of those people.

During the night I was awoken by a knocking on my studio door. A young woman asked me to go to the health clinic to fetch a nurse and take her over to the Gibson's camp. There a Japanangka was lying on the ground, his skin already purple. The nurse looked at me in dismay:

"I was warned during my training," she said, "that when Aboriginal people decide to let themselves die, medically speaking, there's nothing one can do."

The man was the stepfather of the young man whose death in a car crash had been announced that day. According to custom, from sorrow and pain, he had set himself in a sort of catatonic state that could make him die. Only his relatives and friends, by talking to him and massaging him, could halt this process. After a few hours of moving solicitude, men and women taking turns by his side as he lay upon the ground, speaking softly to him, he came back to life.

The next day all the women, coated in white once again, walked in procession through the community sweeping the ground with leafy branches. They went in all the houses and public places, the shop, school, health clinic, repair shop, church, and then crossed all the camps. That procession aimed to drive the spirit of the dead man away from the community, to help him to become detached from his relatives in order for him to go back, by following the trail of his Dreaming, to the site where he had to merge with the ancestors of his clan.

In the following weeks, regularly, the cries resumed and the women coated themselves with white and kaolin offered impressive quantities of sugar, flour and tea to the men having the same *mother's brother* skin name as that of the deceased — in this case, Jupurrurla, for the young man was a Japangardi.

A new camp was also established for a group of Nampijinpa women, the skin name having a *spouse* relation to the one of the deceased. Although he was not married, they fulfilled the role of widows. With their hair cut short, for several weeks they remained there without speaking, communicating with hand sign language, as elaborate as our *deaf and dumb* sign language.[30] They did not have the right to cook and received food prepared by other women, with the exception of the big game, which was taboo for them. True widows would have been subjected to that diet for two years.

"Don't utter the name of your country any longer," several Warlpiri warned me. "It has become *kumanjayi.*"

I learned that the term *kumanjayi* was a sort of *thingamabob*, a synonym of *no name* which takes the place of all the words made taboo because of a mourning, and that remain taboo for at least two years. Those words correspond to the name of the dead person and to everything that, by their sonority, evoke his or her name. France had become taboo because the deceased young man was called Francis.

Thus there were many adults and children whose English names became temporarily unspeakable. The teachers had to respect the rule and refer to the pupils by the term *kumanjayi* or by their skin name only. Some of the current expressions in the language had also become taboo due to the fact that they sounded similar to Warlpiri names. For example, because of an old man's death, the Warlpiri word for milk, *lampunu*, became unspeakable and was referred to by the term *kumanjayi*.

A synonym sometimes replaced the taboo word. A few years later, I noticed that after the death of a certain Lawurrpa, the word for saying "no," *lawa*, had completely disappeared from the language to be substituted by *walku*. One can imagine the

---

30. Kendon, A. "Iconicity in Warlpiri Sign Language." *Iconicity: Essays on the Nature of Culture.* Eds. Bouisac, P., Herzfeld, M., Posner, R. Tübingen: Stauenburg Verlag, 1985; Eds. Umiker-Sebeok, J. & Sebeok, T.A. *Aboriginal Sign Language in the Americas and Australia.* New York: Plenium Press, 1978 (2 vol.).

impressive mental gymnastics prohibiting the use of such a general term supposes. More than a simple rule, it is more of an emotional relation that the Warlpiri have with language. To utter a taboo word means to cause pain or insult those touched by the loss. It also risks holding back the deceased in the world of the living instead of helping them merge into the land and time-space of the Dreaming.

Although their origin is often lost, it is said that the Warlpiri names correspond to condensed verses of song, a form under which the heroes of the Dreaming would have scattered the *spirit-children* who became embodied in human beings. Traditionally, everyone personified chanted words generated by the name of a Dreaming, their totem of conception.

The verses symbolically or homophonically linked to the deceased thus became equally taboo. I often witnessed women breaking off in the course of a song and, with a few signs of gestural language, signal what had to be skipped before restarting the cycle of the trail of the Dreaming. A marvelous work of mourning that inscribes the dead into memory through holes in the language, spoken or sung.

Another hole created by death is the one of the space taboo, which forces the vacating and avoidance of the camp or house of the deceased. For months following the death of the young man, I saw adults and children by-passing the forsaken zone of his camp, located only a few feet from zones of activity. In time, whole families ended up moving in turn as new deaths arose.

The space and language taboos characterized not only mourning but also the relationship between a man and his mother-in-law. They must never talk to each other or come close to one another. In the past, this avoidance behavior was common to all Australian tribes. I noticed that, with the Warlpiri, practically all men and women whose two skin names were a *mother-in-law/son-in-law* relationship had to avoid each other, even if the men were not the actual sons-in-law of those women.

They were considered as potential sons-in-law, except if they were too closely related by blood to the women in question. In that case, the prohibitions did not apply. Otherwise, when a Nakamarra woman saw a Jangala man coming, she immediately turned away from his path, and it was the same between a Nungarrayi and a Japangardi and the other pairs in that relationship.[31] Even in order to talk about one another to a third party, mothers-in-law and sons-in-law had to use a special language, *yikirrinji*. If a woman or a young girl was in the company of her mother or a classifying mother, a man who through his skin name could normally court her could not come close and refrained from doing so, for to come close to a potential mother-in-law was *kuntangka*, shameful.

When two men clashed, if a mother-in-law, real or classificatory, of one of the men interfered, the shame was such that he had to flee and thus to detach himself from his adversary. In reality, the women only took recourse to that method of pacification as a last resort, usually letting the conflicts run, sometimes until a spear pierced the thigh of one participant.

I had been warned there were brawls in Lajamanu. Or rather, every dispute gave way to an emotional demonstration, a strange play whose actors obey precise rules. As soon as an altercation grew acrimonious, one would hear from every direction, "*kulu*! *kulu*!", which means anger and conflict. Everybody rushed to that place of confrontation, the gathering quickly reaching more than a hundred people. The women threw themselves on the children to protect them from the spears or boomerangs expected to be seen flying, though hours of commotion could pass without any flying object being launched.

The opponents, although armed and threatening, turned in circles, hurling abuse at each other while making gestures as if to raise their weapons. Their relatives, according to their kinship relation, had to take part or to play the role of mediator. They were themselves shouting so loudly the scene was in fact dramatic. The audience encircling the actors regularly moved away only to come back again immediately. That continued until exhaustion and resumed the following day, for as long as the opponents had not reached an agreement.

If the women interfered in the male duals, in return the men abstained from doing the same in female quarrels. It often happened that in the course of a dispute, two women brandished

---

31. Glowczewski, B. & Pradelles de Latour, C.H. "La diagonale de la belle-mère." *L'Homme* 104: 27-53, 1987. Also see Glowczewski, B. *Totemic becomings*. Ibid 2015: 26-27.

their fighting sticks *kuturu*, the same type as the sacred poles. They served as swords. Some of their relatives or allies would automatically intervene to calm them down.

Generally, the combatants rapidly stopped shouting and used sign language to abuse each other silently, playing with their sticks as if to strike. Sometimes they jumped in the air, lifting their legs high and holding horizontally their weapon by the two ends. Then they adopted a stance with a threatening look, and made their thighs shake. That erotic *dance* signifying anger was also performed during the funeral rituals to underline the sorrow of the mourners.

All those manifestations of silent (but very explicit) anger, gradually gave way to a reconciliation as the audience started laughing. Due to such confrontations, the men took to calling the bough shed under which the women gathered by the name for sign language itself, *rdaka-rdaka*, the hands.

I was struck by the fact that, in their childhood, boys and girls seem protected from all frustrations — the adults who are very indulgent satisfy almost all their desires. When they reach adolescence, to make up for it, they are supposed to learn to submit their desires and emotions to what the Warlpiri call the Law of the Dreaming. They have to share food, for if they are mean their relatives ridicule them. They also have to respect the marriage promises arranged for them by the elders, as to court or seduce partners reserved for others provokes a public scandal which discredits the culprits. Moreover, they are not allowed to go into forbidden places or reveal the secrets into which they are initiated by the elders, under pain of death.

Despite those rules, the young men did not wait to be fully initiated to freely co-habit with girls of their choice. The elders could not oppose them unless the couple was not in a *spouse* relationship through their skin names. If this was the case, they were strongly pressured to separate. If, despite the discredit, the lovers succeeded in staying together and had children, they ended up being integrated. In the past, young lovers who were not promised to each other had to run off into the bush, far away from everybody. If they survived that exile for a season or more, they could join their tribe again.

One day a crowd was gathered at the camp around a humpy (hut). I was told that a Jampijinpa in his forties and a Napangardi married to another man had taken refuge there. For two days they did not leave, waiting for the community to accept their liaison. They won their case. Adultery was quite common, and, though practiced secretly, was quickly discovered. If the lovers wanted to live together, the spouse had to agree to a divorce and the custody of the children had to be amicably resolved. In the past, the woman generally returned to her husband after a beating or a collective rape carried out in a ceremony, while the lover was subjected to a wound inflicted on his leg in order to *shed blood*, a ritual practice supposed to obliterate the offense. But under some circumstances it could degenerate.

In the Fifties, a man and a woman, both married and parents of several children, ran away together and were pursued by the husband who killed them. It was legitimate from the Warlpiri point of view that the husband should try to catch up with the culprits, but he had no right to kill them. Thus the clan of the unfaithful spouse and the one of the lover decided to avenge them by attacking the clan of the murderer. Rather than form an alliance for vengeance, they accused each other of being the offenders, one for having let the woman seduce her lover, the other for having permitted the lover to involve the woman. A cycle of vendetta broke out between the three clans who clashed for so many years that this old story was still brought up for discussion and opposition each time there was talk of celebrating the Dreaming of one or the other.

At all times the Warlpiri have been haunted by such conflicts. I was told the case of a well-known old man who, when his wife left him, asked to be killed to prevent the troubles that could follow. He was sacrificed according to his wish. An extreme situation, nevertheless a decision that was considered wise by the elders. For lack of an embodied authority, each person introverted in his own way the incompatibility of his desires with the desires of others. It is by way of this perpetual confrontation that the system of obligations that makes the Law was woven.

At the turn of the century a gang of young Warlpiri formed to attack groups of people they met, killing men and children, raping the women and eventually forcing the women to follow them. The clans of the victims retaliated with an armed conflict and a witchcraft practice that consisted in killing at distance by *singing a person* and *pointing a bone* in his/her direction. Those retaliations proved to be effective as there is no longer a trace of the *wingki*, the transgressors, who, according to the Warlpiri, by not respecting territorial rights and the rule of alliance, had *forgotten their Dreamings.*

Did all the Warlpiri still remember their Dreamings? I did not want to know, preferring to spend my time with those who still did.

THE TRUCK

Yellow grass as far as the eye could see, a few dry shrubs, and emptiness. That was Parnta, a Dreaming site crossed by the trail of the two Kajirri heroines. The Warlpiri men who had dropped me off here with ten *businesswomen* and three little girls had to come back to collect us in two days. Before leaving Lajamanu, my companions had danced to unearth the two Kajirri poles erected on the ceremonial field and then entrusted them to the women who remained behind. But they had brought with them two other non-painted poles.

After discussions about who would be part of the journey, four Napangardi skin *sisters* were chosen first. The oldest was Rosy, the little widow *boss* of Kajirri who walked with a stick almost as tall as herself. She always seemed to have the air of enjoying herself beneath the woolly hat pulled down to her eyes. Younger and with a seductive smile, the second was Maggy the blind, who incarnated a spirit-child of that site. Her old husband, also blind, made a scene when we left, reproaching her for not staying to cook for him. It was said she lost her sight beneath the effects of a punitive magic, for she had seduced too many men.

The two last Napangardi, Kungariya and Kajingarra, despite being in their forties, had the status of spinsters, *single girls*, since, having lost their husbands when very young, they refused to remarry. Always happy, they slept permanently at the

105

women's camp to look after the sacred objects. They were always in demand to dance in duo and be painted, their buxom breasts rousing the admiration of the other women.

Four Napanangka, *kirda* masters of Kajirri, had also joined us: two widows, one still covered in the white paint of a recent mourning, who only communicated through sign language; and two married women. The first, Betty, was a stout and authoritative woman who rarely smiled. She was the deputy of the *boss* of Kajirri. A gigantic scar went right across her hip, the trace of a wound made by a spear thrown by her husband when she was young, following an affair. Betty usually lived with him, but for the duration of the Kajirri cycle each settled down at their respective ritual camps.

Nganjiljiya, the fourth Napanangka, was considered the *number one* singer, inimitable for her high voice and her memory of songs was unrivaled. She camped with her husband, but came every day for the rituals during which she related all sorts of funny stories that she punctuated with a short laugh and an odd twist of the mouth, much to the amusement of the others.

Finally, the journey would have been inconceivable without the *kurdungurlu* managers of Kajirri, two sisters of Napurrurla skin. The elder, Rosie Tasman, a very thin widow, with a hatchet face and a pouting expression that rarely left her, always led a busy life. Her frantic activity was in sharp contrast to the slowed-down rhythm of the other women, particularly her younger sister who always looked as if she was on another planet. The latter slept apart from the other campers of Lajamanu, alone with her husband, a highly esteemed elder whom she pampered lovingly.

The two Napurrurla sisters and Maggy the blind took me to visit the place. To begin with I was shown the precise place in the dry bed of the river where Maggy's mother would have been entered by a spirit-child. The blind woman was very moved:

"The Insect Gall Dreaming, that's where I come from."

Then we stopped before two twin trees that seemed to mirror one another. The women came to a standstill, as if in trance, and whispered:

"Kajirri *Jukurrpa.*"

The two trees were the trace of a secret episode of the myth of the two Kajirri heroines. I was not allowed to film. A bit further on, two other gigantic trees formed a match. This time I was allowed to film. They belonged to a public episode of the Emu Dreaming, a couple of emus in love had rested there before resuming their journey to the *salt water*, the sea.

I went back to the sand bed with the two little girls to dig at the spot where the women had indicated the existence of a waterhole. One meter down the sand became wet and then, slowly, a limpid water rose to the surface. Filling our buckets, we brought them back to the camp to make tea.

At nightfall all of the women underwent metamorphosis. Hair flattened with oil, made up with a white line across the nose, face and chest gleaming with red ochre, their eyes became metallic. In the heavy silence, Rosie Napurrurla stood and, turning her back on us, began to talk in a strong, staccato voice. My neighbor whispered in my ear: "*Kuuku.*"

It was the tutelary spirits of the earth who live by night and sleep by day, benevolent toward those who have the right to occupy the land they inhabit and malevolent toward strangers. Rosie, as required of a *kurdungurlu* manager, explained to the *kuuku* who we were and asked them to leave us in peace. The women pointed to the different places where those spirits moved about while they talked to them. They could hear a spirit-baby crying and the mother trying unsuccessfully to find it again. I could hear nothing.

Rosie's sister had knelt down. She was holding a coolamon (a ritual dish) on which lay two poles, beneath her arm in the way one lays down a new-born baby on that type of container to carry it or set it down. She undertook a strange pantomime, coming and going, crouching or kneeling, over a 5 meter stretch. Disappearing into the dark and reappearing in the firelight, looking to her right and left, as if searching for something or as if being followed, she put down her dish several times and shook the two poles.

I learned she was playing the role of one of the two Kajirri heroines who was supposed to inhabit her during the dance. It did not suggest a behavior of possession at all, but rather the behavior of a puppet animated by invisible threads which

107

enclosed us in a kind of bubble. The eyes of the spectators were completely blank, as if they saw something other than me. They were on their journey.

The following day we went hunting, and in the afternoon the women had a thorough wash with plenty of water and soap before painting themselves with red, white and yellow patterns. I too was called upon to take off my clothes and be painted with the design of the Insect Gall Dreaming, a thick line joining the clavicles and small circles on the breasts. I thoroughly enjoyed being painted, seeing in it the sign of my integration into the universe of the desert dreamers.

My companions danced with the two poles, passing them from hand to hand. Then Betty Napanangka who, until that moment, had never spoken to me in English, said slowly, searching for her words:

"Nungarrayi, now you are a *businesswoman*, you have to find a way to get us a car and take us to the other Dreaming places. When you go to Canberra, you will ask the *topmen* for a truck for the *business* of the Lajamanu women."

All that remained for me was to try to obtain what they requested.

A few days later the whole community crammed into cars and cattle trucks and went down to Yuendumu for the inter-tribal meeting held there every August. While the elders continued with their palavers, the youth of the neighboring tribes measured their strength through diverse sports: football, basketball, softball (a female version of baseball), running, long jump and high jump. The sight was unexpected. The teams in sportswear removed their sneakers to run faster. The girls kept their skirts on, even for jumping. And in contrast to the Whites that organized the competitions and looked completely exhausted, the Aboriginal participants arrived late, would leave a race when a friend called them, or did not even respond when summoned to the podium with the winners.

During the evening, there was another surprise: Aboriginal rock groups and country-western bands followed each other onto the stage. Seated on the ground amid the youth, the elders watched without appearing perturbed. Only the children danced, and in an astonishing fashion. They took turns standing and shaking for a few seconds in a very sexy manner, then ducked back down quickly, and the whole process started over again. The game consisted of amazing their friends without ever giving the impression of showing off.

The second day, the men organized a competition of spear throwing (with their spear-throwers) at a plastic kangaroo. Meanwhile, near the building where the *businesswomen* of Yuendumu kept their sacred objects, the women from several communities assembled. In small groups, one after another, they painted their chests and danced.

Instead of going back to Lajamanu, I took advantage of the proximity to Alice Springs to take the plane for Canberra, the federal capital, with the hope of obtaining a vehicle for the women. The musicologist, who had just ended his stay in Lajamanu, had advised me to make a report on my first months in the field and submit it to the AIAS (Australian Institute of Aboriginal Studies),[32] the Institute that centralized the data on the Aboriginal people and financed professional researchers and students. Perhaps I would benefit from the Toyota of the Institute that the musicologist had used and left in Alice Springs.

Waiting for a response to the report I had given, I spent my days at the Institute in Canberra between the book and film libraries consulting an enormous number of archives unobtainable in France. These were coded into *public* and *restricted*, presupposing several degrees of restriction: forbidden either to the non-specialists, men, or women, or else necessitating the permission either of the director, or their author. These rules had been recently instituted since the Aboriginal people were reticent to divulge their secret ritual life. The irony was that some urban Aboriginal people then complained the Whites deprived them of their history by hiding the archives relative to the massacres and other violence they had endured, which was true in some other institutions.

Ten days later I was back in Alice Springs. I had been refused permission to use the Toyota, and at the same time it was pointed out to me that, coming from France, I should be glad to have

32. The AIAS later became the Australian Institute of Aboriginal and Torres Strait Islander studies, AIATSIS.

managed to find somewhere to do my research so quickly, and on the top of that, to be there at the right moment, at the peak of the ritual period. It seemed a lot of Australian students did not have that chance.

In search of another solution, I learned of a Yanmadjeri community North-East of Alice called Utopia, where a young Australian lived who had taught women how to drive. I decided to pay her a visit and discovered a place very different from Lajamanu. A few young Whites employed on contract by the Health and Education Department had set up genuine structures of self-management after discussions with the Yanmadjeri people. There were no houses and people were scattered in small camps. Men bred cattle and women did batik on silk and string bags that they sold in Alice. With the income they bought gas for the truck obtained from the ABTA, the Aboriginal trust fund financed by the mining companies.

Encouraged by what I had seen, I hitchhiked up the motorway as far as Katherine, and from there I took advantage of the *road train*, the heavy diesel truck that supplied Lajamanu's shop. Only one gas station on the way, Top Springs, the North bar where the Warlpiri came to drink. As soon as I climbed down from the cabin I caught sight of Nganjiljiya, the Napanangka who sang so beautifully and whose stories were so funny. She jumped up and led me into the shade to tell me everything that had happened during my absence. I was very moved and felt indebted for I was returning empty-handed.

The reception in Lajamanu was such that I really experienced a feeling of coming home. The women with whom I had camped in Parnta decided to organize a reunion in my studio. A Napaljarri, Yiripanta, who was almost as imposing as her son the Chairman, accompanied them. They asked me to connect the tape recorder and record a declaration that would be the starting point of the letter I was to write to the Aboriginal trust fund for them to obtain a vehicle like the women from Utopia. A fair skin young woman, the daughter of an adventurer who lived in the bush with a group of Warlpiri, helped me translate. Now it was time to find some money because the fund only granted its help if the Aboriginal people concerned provided 10% of the vehicle's price.

The women sent me to Lajamanu to sell their traditional necklaces — made of berries pierced to be threaded on a string made of human hair — to the Kardiya. The process was difficult. Most of those Whites assumed the Warlpiri already had enough money. Moreover, they did not appreciate the fact that I spent all my days at the camp. A few charitable souls, who believed the women to be ill-treated by the men, agreed to buy a necklace or gave a few dollars. But the capital raised remained insufficient.

Having only recently arrived, the shop manager and his wife, a Maori from New Zealand, had an idea. As they also managed the open-air cinema, they decided the profits from the tickets and drinks of every third show would be placed on the account opened for the women's truck. In two months, it was estimated that the necessary sum would be collected and sent to the trust fund.

Meanwhile excitement was growing. The *businesswomen* had already named the truck Parnta-Kanta, after the name of the site and the Insect Gall Dreaming. This also became the name given to the account. Betty Napanangka dreamed one night that she was driving it. In everybody's opinion, that was a good omen.

IN SEARCH OF THE DREAMING

Upon announcing that the first images I had shot of the women's rituals had been processed, fifty or so *businesswomen* huddled together in the school's projection hall. I showed them the images, which flooded past as if in accelerated motion with faces and bodies overlapping each other. The room became agitated.

I had filmed frame by frame to economize the stock, recording a maximum of different paintings and dances. I also wanted to ascertain the reaction of the Warlpiri faced with such images which, by not unfolding in real time, seemed to me to evoke the process of compression characteristic of some dreams.

"It is not nice to make us look like fools," reproached the women.

I was disappointed. Upset by my visual effects, the women did not speak about their dream visions.

One night, in my studio, I was woken by the distant echoes of a rock concert. I thought I heard a delirious crowd. Knowing that there was a rock band in Lajamanu, I went out in search of the concert. There was no concert, everyone seemed to be sleeping. Back in bed, I could not sleep. I was sweating, I had fever.

The following day, going to the women's camp, situated some ten minutes away from the houses, I mentioned I had not slept. The women started laughing:

"You know, last night, we were singing very loud here, thinking you might hear us and come here."

I was bewildered. In my sleep, had I transformed these women's songs that I could not possibly hear from that distance into a rock concert?

"If you want, you can camp here in the *jilimi*. The nights are warm now and we are going to dance and sing late at night. Anyway, it's not good for you to stay by yourself like that."

That evening I went to the *jilimi* carrying my *swag*, a blanket and a waterproof canvas that bush campers use to lie on the ground and cover themselves. But, to honor my coming, a Napangardi gave up her *bed* — iron sheets placed on jerry cans.

For a month I slept at the camp of the Kajirri custodians, living under their orders, carrying their food containers and fetching water. Almost daily, at the end of the afternoon, women painted their bodies and danced. At that point I took down two little bags suspended under their shelter, in the shade, and removed the tape recorder and movie camera. It was out of the question now to shoot frame by frame. Mingling among the women, I cranked the handle of my old Pathé Webo and allowed the images to run at the rhythm of their movements. Between shots, systematically, I wrote down in a notebook all the body paintings. Those *yawulyu* rituals enchanted me. Sometimes I danced.

Barefoot, body and face covered with dust or ochre, hair tangled under a scarf and wearing crumpled clothes, each morning I sought refuge in my studio to store the roll shot the night before, take a shower, change my clothes and write. The children called me Jungle Girl.

One morning, a group of *businesswomen* sent me to the Council to ask for a car. They wanted to go to another Aboriginal community to buy materials for there was nothing left at the shop. I obeyed their instructions and before long a Toyota 4x4, with a dozen women crammed in the open truck bed, sped off down the track.

After 100 kilometers we arrived at Kalkaringi, the reserve of the Wave Hill cattle station where one of the first strikes by the Aboriginal people known as the Gurindji walk off had taken place. That was in 1966, before an Australian referendum guaranteed them wages equal to those of Whites. Until then they often worked for food rations, clothes or blankets only. The Kurintji (Gurindji) pastoral workers had left Wave Hill to set up their own station in Wattie Creek: Daguragu.[33] Some had returned since, especially to send the children to school.

We picked up a woman on the way. Thirty kilometers further, the buildings of Daguragu appeared. The shop was closed and nobody knew who had the key. My *businesswomen* did not seem that disappointed. The woman from Wave Hill climbed out of the Toyota to whisper something in the ears of a Kurintji man. Another man invited us to settle ourselves on the ground and some women offered us a bit of meat.

The *businesswomen* unwrapped a sacred object rolled in hair ropes smeared with red ochre. Twenty or so men came closer and, in turns, filed past and touched the object, then smeared their arms with the ochre that had rubbed off on their fingers. A few elders showed the very shy youngsters what to do.

An old sick man was lain on a blanket. The *businesswomen* stood and surrounded him, singing. With the help of two Kurintji women, they massaged him, smeared him with ochre, painted a Snake Dreaming design around his navel on which they placed the sacred object disentangled from its strings. It was a very flat and smooth oval stone. Some poured water into their mouths to spray the torso, neck and hair of the old man. Then, in single file, hanging onto a long hair rope, they walked with their legs spread above the old man and slowly moved away. I was told it was a healing ritual allowing the disease to be evacuated.

The healers sat again and around twenty Kurintji women arrived carrying fabrics. After touching the sacred stone, each placed her parcel before the healers. We left with the Toyota full of fabric I settled on the roof and felt like laughing. It was business

33. Hardy, Frank. *The Unlucky Australians.* One Day Hill, 2006. (1st published,1967: http://www.theage.com.au/news/book-reviews/the-unlucky-australians/2006/09/08/1157222319244.html).

in the proper sense, a ritual settled with a payment. But had they not said they wanted *to buy* materials? Then I heard the women laughing behind me and I could not hold myself back. Had they planned to receive materials in exchange for their therapeutic intervention or was it a welcome coincidence?

My companions regularly pointed out to me that the men were happy because "I was taking care of the women." I rather had the impression that it was them who were taking care of me. Thinking I was too skinny, they painted my chest to fatten me up, the Images of the Dreaming being reputed to *nourish* children as well as adults. They were also concerned that I did not talk enough. Eventually, Maggy the blind diagnosed that "I missed my Jangala."

She indicated by that skin name — the *son* of hers and *spouse* of mine — my boyfriend who remained behind in France. My *mother-in-law* had decided I needed a *jarada* love magic. And so I found myself in the bush, my head covered with a white headband I had to put on again to seduce my man when I saw him next. The headband was *sung* by three women who added our two names to the seduction formula. Then they told me to speak French to it. A bird of the Dreaming would transmit the message so that he would think about me. A week later I received a letter from France. Maggy announced proudly:

"You see, it worked!"

One morning I awoke in sweat. The day before I had been asked to clean a ritual wooden board *yukurrukurru*. For each new *yawulyu* ritual, the women erase the designs of the previous ritual in order to paint the boards anew. The one I was given was encrusted with sand and I had not managed to scrape it all off. I had had a dream and the women asked me to recount it. Helped by Nakakut, who translated, I explained I had seen a mother in a sad state dropping her baby for a man. It fell in the water and I cried out that it was about to drown. But I rescued the small body which was covered with pustules. I rubbed it and its skin once again became smooth.

The women glanced at each other with a knowing look and told me, one after another, that it was a "good" dream. One

116

added that the boards were "like" spirit-children and that it was the Kajirri heroines who had given me that dream. All of them seemed amused.

The day after, Maggy the blind asked me to follow her into the undergrowth where she cut a trunk down with an axe and brought it back to the camp. In the afternoon Nakakut escorted me to her husband. He was busy carving a dish from the log.

"Your *father* Japaljarri is making a baby-carrier for you. You will take it back to your country to bring us back a little Jampijinpa or Nampijinpa."

Longing for a child. That was the interpretation the women had given to my dream. I was very moved.

One day, the *businesswomen* started to lament. They were showing their sorrow at having to be separated from the two Kajirri Dreaming sisters, materialized in the two sacred poles they had planted and dug out a hundred times in order to paint them afresh. After five months of celebrations, the end of the ceremony was taking place and with it the end of the seclusion of the young initiated. Sadness gave way to joy for the mothers were excited at the idea of seeing their sons again. They did not sleep anymore but sung and danced. For the occasion, other women, who usually did not participate in the rituals, had settled in the ceremonial camp to assist them.

On the third sleepless night I was exhausted and started to tremble. My companions panicked. I explained it would soon pass. I knew the symptoms, it was an attack of spasmophilia. They massaged me vigorously. Then Lily Nungarrayi shook a piece of paper pulled from her bundle before my eyes. I recognized a page of the catechism showing Jesus holding his hand out to Lazarus. Soon after my spasms stopped. My *sister* Nungarrayi was delighted. She explained she had cured me with the Bible, the Kardiya Law. Everything was back to normal. Even if I did not go to the Baptist church of Lajamanu, Christianity was my Law, in spite of everything.

A strange return to my origins. Brought up a good Polish Catholic, I came to anthropology precisely because I was not satisfied with that religion. At fifteen, talking with a chaplain, I realized that my taste for the sacred did not have a lot to do with Christianity. Thus I started to devour everything I could find on the beliefs of other peoples. Coming across the Aboriginal people, I was immediately seduced. Their religion did not separate man from the rest of the world. Each man, and each woman, was linked to the cosmos by a mythical story, a people of fantastic ancestors, a Dreaming. Later on, living in Lajamanu, I noticed that the whole life of the Warlpiri was impregnated with the sacred for all that constituted their surroundings was a sign of the Dreaming. Their paintings, their songs and dances immersed them in a parallel dimension.

The dances had started again. At the break of day, Betty Napanangka dug out the two sacred poles and threw them to other dancers. They left the camp, hopping about and juggling with the poles. Meanwhile, some two hundred women accompanied by their children had gathered and, guided by the *businesswomen*, set off in the direction of the men's camp in the bush. Betty vanished from the crowd with the two poles and reappeared empty-handed. She had buried them secretly. They would be kept hidden until the next Kajirri cycle.

We arrived at a cleared field where all the women and children sat and lowered their heads until they received the order to look up. Twenty meters away stood a group of men, some wearing only a loin cloth, majestically holding their spears high. They raised a canvas cover placed on the ground before them, from which emerged the young initiated. Some men lifted them to their feet and covered them entirely with printed fabric and hair ropes. I was authorized to film.

Two of the boys were brought to us and all the Nampijinpa stood and pressed closely around them. These were their skin *mothers*, for the two boys were Japanangka. One by one, their real mothers removed the materials and the ropes, the ritual presents meant for them. In exchange they gave their sons a bucket of tea and bread that they took back with them to sit among the men. The same stratagem occurred seven times, for each of the eight skin names.

Immediately after we left the men's camp, running. From that day on it would change place and be inaccessible to women again. The secluded *punyunyu* became initiated *malyarra*, reintegrated into their families in the afternoon. Heroes of the day, they provoked gentle jokes that spread loudly between the camps.

The next day I noticed a strange atmosphere. I was summoned from beneath the shelter in the shade where the men usually gathered to hold endless conversations, and I saw twenty people lying on the ground in a line.

"They are *prisoners*, as you know they must sleep."

I knew without really knowing. For weeks now a new cult had been secretly announced. I had participated in a few rehearsal sessions of songs and dances, although many Warlpiri had been excluded. A curious combination of circumstances gave me that privilege.

At the beginning of my stay, I had accompanied the musicologist, Steven Wild, and his Warlpiri informant to Gordon Downs, a cattle station in Western Australia, right on the other side of the border with the Northern Territory. We had only stayed a couple of days to listen to the claims that the group of Nyining people who were camping there, had to make on the lands adjacent to the station. After I had localized a few Dreamings with the women, they said that since I came from Lajamanu, they would sing something special for me. I recorded them. They asked me to play the tape to the two men who accompanied me and to inform them they would return in the evening to sing with their companions. As soon as I played the first verses, the Warlpiri man roared in dismay:

"But it's secret!"

He explained it concerned songs from a ceremony that came from Broome, the town of the West Coast where an Aboriginal woman had dreamed it in the Forties. Its name being secret, it was referred to as Balgo *business*, the Walmaljarri from Balgo being the last depositaries of that cult which travels from tribe to tribe. It was there that some Warlpiri from Lajamanu had been initiated into the corresponding rites. He added that in the following months, other Warlpiri would be initiated into that very *hard* business which scared the non-initiated. I was allowed to keep the tape on the condition I would not play it to anyone. On our return to Lajamanu, I did not speak about it, but a few young women came to tell me they were initiated into the new *business*. They invited me to the rehearsals taking place in the bush, near the camp of a Pintupi group who had settled a kilometer to the west of the community.

It was the famous Balgo *business* that had just started. Maggy the blind was among the *prisoners*, the novices. Some Warlpiri hid, scared stiff. The missionaries, according to rumor, had accused the cult of being devil's business. At Fitzroy Crossing, a Western mission, that same cult is said to have taken the form of a religious syncretism. What I was about to witness and hear for ten days, without permission to film or record, would be overwhelming. An extraordinary collective organization for a journey, in the proper and figurative senses. Hundreds of people would camp together, moving around following a ritual circuit. There a new Law would be played, a new *Dreaming* whose aim was to reconcile traditional and modern ways of life.[34] After that fantastic lesson of survival in the bush, I was so *Warlpirized* that I slightly lost my footing. When the time came to leave Lajamanu to return to France, I had a lump in my throat.

"Do not stay too long in your country. Now you have two ways, Kardiya way and Yapa way," said Maggy the blind.

I replied I would like to take with me a *yukurrukurru* painted board as a memento. Betty went to fetch one for me wrapping it in an old cloth.

"Send me some shoes in exchange!"

34. Glowczewski, B. "Manifestations symboliques d'une transition économique." *L'Homme* 23 (2): 7-35, 1983. See also: "From academic heritage to Aboriginal priorities: anthropological responsibilities." 2013: http://actesbranly.revues.org/526.

Sally-Anne Nampjinpa Burns (Two Feathers) and other Warlpiri girls dancing a *yawulyu* led by Lily Hargraves Nungarrayi (holding a dish), 1984.

PART THREE

(1979-1983)

THE FILM

November 1979. A difficult return to France. Like a roll of film, I had been exposed to the Warlpiri people and now, like a film negative, I had to be developed in order for the print to emerge on paper. I was obsessed with sharing what I had just lived with others. I started writing and organized a film projection to show my new images of female rituals.

Respecting the wish of the Warlpiri women, I only invited women. Around a hundred came, crowding into a large apartment lent for the occasion. Some were my friends, others simply professional acquaintances, and the rest strangers flocking in as feminists for a women-only event. Personally I did not seek a discourse on liberation, I only hoped to find in the female audience that same complicity I had experienced with the women of the desert. What a mistake!

At the moment the film engaged in the projector I had that sudden feeling of indulging in a lewd act. The image the Warlpiri women presented would be incomplete and risked betraying them. When they appeared on screen, I experienced an unexpected pain as I realized how much I missed their presence. I was torn by a feeling of guilt. I did not know what I was guilty of, but the fault seemed irreparable.

The agony lasted two hours. The silent images of the body paintings and the dances unfolded to the sound of a tape of songs that someone turned systematically every half-hour.

I had brought other tapes but I could not move any longer, stuck in a corner, paralyzed. Gradually I discovered all the things the images did not tell, that would have had to be told for the spectators simply to *see* them.

I realized clearly that my encounter with the Aboriginal people had, without my knowing, deeply transformed me. That discovery sent me into such a deep feeling of loneliness I was unable to articulate the slightest commentary. The task seemed insurmountable. I wished only to cry out: "No, all of what you think you're seeing is false!" I could not bear rediscovering on that screen those corrugated metal shelters or the piles of rubbish that irrevocably reminded all of us of shanty towns. I recalled my dread and repulsion during my first days, then my feeling of detachment toward that environment that I learned from the Warlpiri people.

Searching for new words to talk about my experience, that sensorial symbiosis with the women of the desert, all I heard in return was hysterical laughter and half-embarrassed, half-mocking exclamations. Why that uneasiness? The absence of a commentary had undoubtedly encouraged all sorts of phantasms.

There was flesh, naked, touched, marked ... too much flesh. Especially breasts, huge and floppy mammaries, hanging down to the waist and bouncing to the rhythm of dances. And all those eyes, impassive, deep, shifty, distant ... so distant, penetrating ... too penetrating. And there were the sacred poles, those smooth sticks, gleaming with ochre, tapered slightly at both ends, rubbed and painted, handed from one to another, raised to the sky, pointed toward the horizon, erected in the ground, unearthed, held at arm's length, slid between legs, thrown, caught again, replanted, bound again with ropes, touched with the hollow of the palm, shaken, massaged with joined hands, in short, manipulated like objects and treated like living beings.

At the end of the projection, the inevitable question, of course, was asked:

"What are those phallic objects?"

"They are the most sacred objects of the women."

126

Laughter and grins. This time the betrayal of the *business-women* was complete. Their rituals seemed to add up to no more than a phallic cult, while my experience with the Walpiri people had consisted in living in a female world autonomous from the male one. However hard I tried to explain that female rituals are a descent into the woman's body, a transformation of the body into earth, a passage to the Dreaming, a universe of metamorphosis where sexual differentiation is no longer a reference because the process of becoming plays with the infinity of terrestrial and cosmic forms, I came up against a question that seemed stupidly reductive:

"Thus the woman is identified with Mother Earth?"

I became agitated, incapable of explaining the relationship of the Aboriginal people to the earth, which is for them, depending on the places, *mother, father, spouse, etc.*, that is, as many relatives as there are in the society of relationships differentiated by the Dreamings. In reality, Warlpiri men and women are both on the side of nature and on the side of culture. Being perceived as a succession of trails of the bodies of metamorphosed ancestors, the earth is not just a biological metaphor but also a memory support for the Law which rules society.

I explained the cartography of mythical trails linking the earth to the Dreamings, and I added that women inherited from their father the Dreaming and the vital force with which they became identified. The responses I received were psychoanalytical comments on the Oedipus Complex.

The malaise became heavier and heavier. Some spectators finally admitted they could not bear the constant presence of flesh, that they felt denigrated in their femininity, unable to identify with women so *primitive*. Others did not say anything.

It was true the body of the Aboriginal women conveyed the power of reproduction. A body damaged by pregnancies and old age, bloated or hollowed by a sedentary life and junk food, shaped by wind, rain and sun, etched by illnesses, ritual wounds or accidents. A body polished by time which reflected a certain image of the mother, undoubtedly universal but from which, often, we protect ourselves. It is the mother who changes into an ogress, mouth that swallows, vagina that consumes, belly that digests, womb that transforms, that mother from which we come and which is virtually there inside us as a destiny, the one we do not want to look like and who haunts us like a fatal repetition, the one from which we would like to detach ourselves but who hurts, pains and aches us.

Some spectators recounted later their emotions on seeing the transfiguration of the painted bodies. They had felt a power that seemed to come from the beginning of time which called them, seduced them, looked familiar. Behind the bodies they had seen the substance carved as a rock, resistant for eternity, full and alive. They had tasted something secret. Whether modesty or an impotence of words, they could not speak, or they did not want to. They had perceived that body which can become all of nature's kingdoms, animal, vegetable, or mineral. Perhaps they had felt like me, in the heart of the substance, the earth and the stars, where there is nothing left but the force of fullness which opens onto the void, the force of the inside where all forms are suspended. The dreams of women or the dreams of men.

The essential point of female rituals and, it appears, also of male rituals, is to refer to the Dreaming as a surpassing of dualisms. The Dreaming is the actual experience of the paradoxes, the setting of the inversions, the way to overcome sexual identity and find oneself elsewhere, in the heart of the secret of life, in the heart of the power of metamorphosis.

When I said I had felt "like" a woman with the Warlpiri, I was saying that I was on the path that leads right to the edge of the human where sexual identity vanishes. Whether ecstatic or nightmarish, all those impressions and sensations seem then to melt into the collective reality of that female being, a "becoming-woman", on its way to dissolution. What happens then I cannot say. I stopped on the path for, not knowing where I was going, I was overwhelmed by terror. The Warlpiri women have the ancestral references of the Dreamings to find their way.[35]

---

35. This chapter was first published in English in Glowczewski, B. "Beyond the frames of film and Aboriginal fieldwork." *Experimental film and Anthropology*. Eds. Arnd Schneider and Caterina Pasqualino. London: Bloomsbury, 2014: 147-164.

EVERYTHING COLLAPSES

June 1980. Ali Curung, an Aboriginal settlement where Warlpiri, Kaytej, Alyawarra, and Warrumungu-Warlmanpa live together. In a huge warehouse full of men, seated on chairs or on the floor, was a stage with a table and microphones. The Black Chairman of the meeting, a fair skin Aboriginal vice-Chairman, and a White administrator sat behind the microphones. A meeting of the CLC gathering delegates from most of the Aboriginal communities of the Northern Territory was held that day.

An Aboriginal man stood up. A red headband held back his long black hair. He firmly requested for a car to settle on his land with his family. The response was that the CLC's job was to reclaim the land, and as for a car, he would have to enquire elsewhere.

The first question on the agenda was the project for an artificial lake in Alice Springs that would flood the sacred sites. The Chairman explained at length why he did not want the territory of his tribe, the Aranda (Arrernte), to be violated. It was agreed to undertake an action to change the place of the lake. Then someone denounced the use of barbed wire to protect the sacred sites. In fact, it was doing the opposite and prompted people to come closer. The administrator promised to study the question.

An official from the Forestry Commission congratulated the Aboriginal people on having maintained their land so well for a thousand years by lighting bush fires. Did they want equipment to continue or would they accept the Europeans taking charge now? The audience replied that if the rangers wanted to do it, the Aboriginal people would assist them.

I took advantage of the *smoko*, the tea-break, to locate the delegates from Lajamanu: two Jangala, superb elders, custodians of the Rain Dreaming. They were tall, slightly gangly, their hair in a tangle, but with piercing eyes. Abe had guided the army through the desert to map out the roads of the Northern Territory, then he had built the old Hooker Creek Reserve at Hooker Creek. Jimmy, a seasonal cowboy before going into a reserve, had known all the cattle stations from north to west. Looking as moved as I was, they shook hands with me and my friend Michel:

"So, here is Jangala, our *brother*."

They automatically called the man who lived with me Jangala, since this skin name was in a *spouse* relationship with mine. Jimmy took a postcard folded in four from his pocket. I was touched when I recognized the view of Paris I had sent to his family some months before. Abe nodded his head and talked about his wife.

"Annie worries for you. We don't know why the Council doesn't want you to come back. For us it's all right. You are busy with the women's *business*, that's all. And your Jangala can stay with us, no problem."

A thrill of relief ran through me. A month before when we had arrived in Australia, I had telephoned Lajamanu by radio to announce my return, and a White administrator told me the permit to stay in the community had been refused. The ground had collapsed under my feet. For seven months I had worked in Paris at the Maison des Sciences de l'Homme, coding genealogies from New Guinea for the director of my thesis,[36] with the

---

36. Maurice Godelier was then Professor at the School of Advanced Studies in Social Sciences (EHESS) and a member of the Laboratoire d'Anthropologie Sociale founded by Lévi-Strauss at the Collège de France. He supervised my PHD for the Paris 7-Jussieu University ethnology department (which was created by Robert Jaulin) despite the conflict between Jaulin and Lévi-Strauss: on the politics of French anthropology in the 1970's, see B. Glowczewski, "Guattari and Anthropology," Ibid, 2011.

sole aim of paying for another stay in the field. Everything was losing its meaning, the previous stay, the thesis to be written, and, above all, the stupid idea that the Warlpiri had accepted me.

In Alice Springs the CLC confirmed that a month earlier, before the election of the Lajamanu Council, they had received confirmation for another stay of five months. Phoning back, I managed to talk with the Chairman Maurice Luther Jupurrula.

"Sorry, Barbara, the missionaries were displeased with an article you wrote in a French newspaper. They explained to the Christian members of the Council that you didn't understand the community and could only do harm. That's why the Council has decided to forbid you from returning. I don't agree with that decision, but I have no power in the new Council."

Everything sunk. I did not understand what I was guilty of. A sob choked away my voice. The Chairman agreed to discuss the possibility of me coming to explain myself to the Council. I had, of course, published an article in *Le Monde* in which I spoke of Lajamanu as an example of a community which, having succeeded in retrieving its tribal lands, was successfully marrying the attainments of modern life and its traditional ritual life. In one paragraph the Christians were mentioned:

"Those who regularly go to church don't forgo their traditional sacred life as a consequence. They just dream the songs, relating in Warlpiri the life of Christ, as they dream those of their mythical ancestors. When the missionaries denounce their rituals as devil business, they reply that there's no good or bad business since all business is God's."[37]

Was it the suggestion of internal tensions within the community that had displeased the Warlpiri Council? Or had I offended the Christians and under-estimated their importance? Faced by my warm meeting with the two Jangala rainmakers, I began to hope everything could still turn out alright. They promised to intervene at the Lajamanu Council to gain permission for me to come with my partner.

At the resumption of the meeting, the White administrator invited us onto the stage. He explained the situation in a few words and suggested the refusal for the permit came

37. Glowczewski, B. "Les Aborigènes sortent de leurs réserves." *Le Monde du dimanche.* 17 février 1980 ("Out of reserves and into tribal lands." *The Guardian*, March 1980).

from the Whites of Lajamanu, not the Warlpiri people. The Aranda (Arrernte) Chairman from the CLC agreed loudly, seizing the opportunity to harangue the assembly in order to not let themselves be manipulated by the Whites. The Aboriginal people had to manage themselves and intervene in the decisions of the Councils of the Communities they elected. Each, being the owner of his land, had a right to speak. It was up to them to summon the courage to confront the decisions of the Whites that did not suit them.

Planted on stage, we felt rather uneasy. These Aboriginal people had better things to do than support two Whites against other Whites. Fortunately, we had only been a pretext to raise a totally different debate. Two Aboriginal men from Ti-Tree, a cattle station belonging to a White, had risen to denounce the abuses going on there. They asked the Chairman to make a similar speech there, like the one he was making here. He replied it was up to them to do it and they could have the assistance of a lawyer from the Aboriginal legal aid.

Lunchtime arrived. A bullock was killed and everybody received a piece of grilled meat and tea. Afterwards, various propositions were voted upon. The government wanted to know if the Aboriginal people would accept an amendment to the recent federal law on territorial rights (Northern Territory Land Rights Act, 1976), to authorize the army to make their way across their lands in case of war.[38] Some old men shook their heads in disapproval. Some remembered the American soldiers who made them build roads, while others had seen the Japanese bombings on the North coast.

Only two yes votes were forthcoming, but the amendment was considered as accepted. A strange consultation. No matter, with or without the agreement of the Aboriginal people, the army has priority. New vote: was it necessary to set in place a system of *rangers*, bush keepers, to prevent vandalism by the tourists who have already damaged the paintings of two Aboriginal caves? Since nobody was the sole custodian of those two sites, the assembly did not make a decision.

---

38. www.clc.org.au/articles/cat/land-rights-act.

The administrator finally drew attention to the existence of a new law of the Northern Territory requiring every owner of a gun to register it and pay 12 dollars to obtain a shooting license, otherwise they risked six months in prison and a 1,000 dollar fine. A general burst of laughter echoes all around. Fines and prison, most knew all about them. Any pretext was good enough to shut an Aboriginal person in jail.[39] The best thing to do was to laugh. The meeting ended. All were invited to queue. Beneath the eye of the vice-Chairman's video camera, each delegate received 20 dollars, a remuneration for his participation in the meeting.

Taking refuge in an Alice Springs hotel for two weeks, Michel and I awaited a reply from Lajamanu. Our budget flew out the window. Painter, artist, occasional actor and singer, Michel accepted the job of painting and refreshing the buildings of the CLC. He was finishing when the telegram arrived from Lajamanu saying that my request to go and explain myself would not be discussed for three weeks, the date of the Council's next meeting.

We decided to go to Western Australia. In the back of the old Holden bought second-hand in Darwin, we carried rudimentary camping equipment, swag, camping-gas and tins, plus the gun on which our heads rested as we slept. We were told not to venture onto the tracks without protection. In gas stations there were posters advertising for bounty hunters. We had heard that bush delinquents used to simulate accidents to steal the gas of passing travellers. We were primed, in that semi-Western, semi-Mad Max atmosphere, to shoot at jerry cans, without ever daring to shoot at wild game! Several times we had to finish off kangaroos or bullocks agonizing at the edge of the road. Trucks never stop when they hit animals, the impact is so strong that they fly far way.

We stayed for sometime in Broome, a small town on the West Coast offering vast beaches and living off the culture of pearls. In the center of Broome there was a pub where Whites, Asians,

---

39. The scale and conditions under which the Aboriginal people are imprisoned led to the creation of a Royal Commission into Deaths in Custody, in 1987. Since 1980, 108 deaths of imprisoned Aboriginal people have been registered, some found hanged in their cells. See the report, *Indigenous Deaths in Custody, 1989-1996*: https://www.humanrights.gov.au/publications/indigenous-deaths-custody-report-summary.

and Aboriginal people got heartily drunk, and a bit further on, a museum of traditional art set up by an Aboriginal man of lighter skin named Paddy Roe.[40] His mother, from the Nyigina tribe, hid him from the Whites when he was little and he was raised by the Karajarri. Now he had his own tribe, dozens of children, grandchildren and great-grandchildren who lived together in Coconut Well, a land for which he had obtained a ninety-nine years lease. Entry was inaccessible to foreign Whites.

I asked Paddy if he had heard of the Aboriginal woman from Broome who, according to some Warlpiri people, would have dreamed in the Forties the famous Balgo *business*, the secret cult I had witnessed at the end of my previous stay. Paddy knew the *business* but, according to him, the dream was older and came from a man in Port Hedland, a town situated further south, some 1,000 kilometers from the Western Coast.

The revelation of the cult would have followed the wreck of the *Koombana*, a boat which left that town and never arrived in Broome, its destination. Paddy narrated the ritual he had witnessed in the Twenties, when he was at the Lagrange mission, halfway between the two towns. His description resembled much of what I had seen in Lajamanu. In the maritime library in Sydney I later found a newspaper cutting of the disappearance of a boat with that name. The wreck had happened in 1913. The cult was at least seventy years old.

At the end of three weeks I phoned the CLC to enquire if we had permission to visit Lajamanu. No news. I was disappointed but hardly surprised. The Warlpiri people had other things to think about besides my desire to go there. They were perhaps involved in the event that was on the front page of all Australian newspapers, the Noonkanbah dispute, a community gathering members of several western tribes who had risen against the project of an oil drilling on one of their sacred sites.

The government had given the green light to AMAX (an American mining company) and a convoy of sixteen gigantic road train trucks carrying drilling equipment had just left Perth, flanked by a police escort. All along its route of nearly 2,000 kilometers Aboriginal people, as well as White militants,

40. Roe, P., *Gularabulu*. Fremantle Arts Centre Press, 1983; Benterak, K., Muecke, S. and Roe, P. *Reading the Country — Introduction to Nomadology.* Fremantle Arts Centre Press, 1984.

among them priests and ministers, organized sit-ins to show their solidarity with Noonkanbah and prevent the convoy from passing. Michel and I attended the Broome sit-in. Hundreds of people waited hours on the road for the arrival of the convoy. They brandished the Aboriginal flag, created in 1972, a yellow circle superimposed across two horizontal bands, the bottom half red, the top black, symbolizing: "We Blacks on the red earth and beneath the sun."

The crowd sung along to various country-western tunes[41] about the disappointments of the government with regard to the multi-national mining companies. In that affair the Aboriginal people were supported by the trade unions and elected politicians opposed to the exploitation of the underground by foreign companies. Since the truck drivers' union refused to drive the convoy, some *scabs* were employed. When the convoy arrived it bore into the crowd who waited until the very last moment before moving aside, jeering. The police brought out their truncheons and a handful of demonstrators were arrested.

In Noonkanbah, men had painted their bodies and danced the Goanna Dreaming, the protector of the threatened site. The miners refused to work, and a new crew was to be parachuted in. All that was recounted to us in Fitzroy Crossing where the Aboriginal delegates for the fight committee had gathered. I learned that among the different tribes who came to dance and assist the people of Noonkanbah there was a delegation from Lajamanu. Despite the distance of 1,000 kilometers, traditional ritual exchanges had united the two communities for a long time. We decided to edge closer to Lajamanu in the hope of coming across some Warlpiri people.

---

41. Including songs from Bran Nue Dae, an Aboriginal musical known nationwide, written by Jimmy Chi, an Aboriginal artist from Broome (Western Australia), and played by a crowd of local Aboriginal musicians, singers, and dancers.

THE TRIAL

Kalkaringi, a Kurintji community. No need for a permit here, but going beyond was forbidden. We were 100 kilometers from Lajamanu. While I was filling up with gas, I heard:

"Nungarrayi! Nurgarrayi! There you are, coming back then? You're going to Lajamanu?"

I explained to the Warlpiri man who had recognized me that I had crossed the ocean to come back, but that the Council did not want my presence because of an article that displeased the missionaries. The man replied evasively, he did not know about it. I added I intended to wait here in case some women from Lajamanu came to visit their relatives.

"The Kajirri *business* has started," he warned. "Women are not allowed to leave Lajamanu for two weeks."

I had not forgotten those prohibitions, which during the previous year had given me the impression of being a prisoner. I managed to contact the Chairman of Lajamanu by radio-telephone.

"Has the council agreed I can come for a day to explain myself?"

"If I remember correctly, the Council hasn't changed its decision," the Chairman replied in a rather vague tone.

"But what about the telegram sent to the CLC giving notice of a meeting during which the Council would reconsider the question?"

"Can you recall what that telegram said?"

I no longer knew what to think, but nevertheless asked to speak to Betty Napanangka, the Kajirri assistant. The Chairman did not raise any objection and promised to call back before 5 p.m. There was no call. I had a strange feeling Betty had not been informed at the camp. A Warlpiri man took Michel aside and advised him to go and see the missionaries at Kalkaringi, as they would phone the others at Lajamanu. This couple, who had replaced the previous missionaries the year before, welcomed us warmly.

"We know you are honest and we don't have any grudge against you," they said. "The article is probably a pretext. It's something to do with money. We testified in your favor when the police were looking for you."

"Looking for me?"

"Yes. Something to do with the money collected to buy a truck for the women. Some youths wanted to use that money. The elders refused, and the rumor spread that there was no money at all in the account because you might have taken it away when you left. In reality, the account is intact. We said that, in any case, you don't have a signature to have access to it."

The sky was falling down on my head. Even if I had been cleared, the fact the women had not yet received a truck had certainly not ended the rumor. The missionaries said that if they did not manage to see their colleagues in Lajamanu before the next morning, we would have to go there without a permit. The Warlpiri man agreed. Though he advised us not to wait till the morning.

"If there's any problem, I will be there tonight."

My heart was beating hard when, in the night, we sped past the police station in Lajamanu and went directly to the camps. The women's camp had changed place. A tractor arrived, a beaming Japanangka climbed down, shook my hand and led me close to the new site. He was the younger brother of Peter Blacksmith, the Kajirri *boss*. He immediately disappeared, taking Michel with him to the men's camp. Many children encircled me in the darkness, dogs started to bark, and I caught sight of some painted women. At last Betty Hooker, the Kajirri acting *boss*, appeared. I called out her name, delighted. She looked distinctly annoyed. I took her hand. She turned her head away.

"Betty, if I've done something wrong, tell me. I came here only for that, to understand."

"You know what's the matter?"

She went away. Annie, Abe Jangala's spouse, the delegate we met at Ali Curung, pulled me by the hand.

"Come into the *business* camp. There are too many children here."

I followed her. The women crowded around. Some had an impassive look on their faces, others smiled at me, like Rosie Tasman Napurrurla, the woman in charge of the *kurdungurlu* managers in the Kajirri ceremony. Betty pointed her hand to the West.

"Do you remember over there?" she asked.

I thought of the day when we were all gathered in the undergrowth during a mourning. Then of the meeting of the new secret cult of Balgo when some Warlpiri women complained the missionaries treated them like dogs. But I did not know what Betty was getting at. Again she went away. Annie and Rosie urged her to speak with me, to listen to me. She returned briskly, in anger.

"You've rubbished Yapa *business*!"

The accusation was terrible. I defended myself.

"That's not true." I said. "I was happy with you and I like Yapa *business*. I wrote in my country that the *business* is a good Law."

Rosie turned to Betty:

"You see, Nungarrayi didn't do anything wrong."

Her daughters, two extremely beautiful Napangardi, mothers of toddlers, joined in:

"See, she likes Yapa."

I learned that Betty, not wanting the women to watch my film about the rituals I had sent her, had taken it to the mission. She frequented the Baptist church assiduously and had been offended that I had written that missionaries call their traditional rituals devil business. Nobody spoke about the devil anymore and I had been wrong to reawaken a matter considered to be smoothed out. As for the money in the account for the women's truck, it had not disappeared. It was no use. There again, it was my fault for I had made vain promises that had divided the community.

I talked of my letter in which I informed Betty about what I was told in Darwin by the officials of the Aboriginal trust fund which provided the trucks, namely, that the Lajamanu Council, having been given numerous vehicles that year, should have allotted one to the women. The letter had not been passed to Betty. She reflected at length before telling me in a softer tone:

"Undoubtedly someone doesn't want the women to have a truck."

I came to the conclusion that that *someone* had perhaps read my letter and did not want the women to know they could lay claim to one of the vehicles allocated to the Council. It was clear my presence was the source of many disturbances. The women started to sing and dance again.

"We'll talk about it again tomorrow, we have plenty of time."

Michel was brought back from the camp where the two Jangala from the meeting at Ali Curung had wanted to welcome him. We were shown a place to camp, right at the border of the women's ritual camp. A Jampijinpa, the husband of one of Rosie's daughters, told us what had happened since my last stay: an old Nakamarra woman was dead, which explained why the women's camp had been moved. There had been a big *business* during the rainy season. Some men had gone to fetch a boy in Noonkanbah so that he would be initiated with those from Lajamanu. Men and women had danced for three weeks, camping in the bush. Tonight, the Rain Dreaming was being celebrated. In two weeks some Kurintji people would come to Lajamanu, and a ritual convoy would go down to Yuendumu to celebrate Kajirri, perhaps with some Aranda (Arrernte) and Pitjantjatjara people. The man left, after taking Michel by the shoulder:

"Tomorrow morning, 9 o'clock, be at the Council."

We unrolled our blankets. Betty called me. She was carrying two logs in her hands, a sign of reconciliation. I showed her the wood stored on the flat back of our old Holden. Early morning I made the fire. The songs started again. The custodians of the Rain Dreaming danced to erect a sacred pole. Betty, seated on a jerry can, watched us from a distance.

Jimmy Burns arrived, the *postcard from Paris* Jangala. Many children clung to his tractor. He accepted some coffee. We talked about one of his cousins we had met in Western Australia. Moved, he evoked memories of the time when they both looked for work from station to station, offering to muster cattle. The cousin had showed us around the land claimed by his group for some years, Bamboo Springs, a river running through the sacred rocks of the Snake Dreaming. That place was as magic as Kamira, the site of Jimmy's Rain Dreaming, a wonderful natural well formed by a pile of rocks and rock shelters. Jimmy explained that he would like to set up a cattle station together with his cousin, with their bush pastures stretching between their respective lands.

Other men joined in and shook hands with us. We showered them with photos taken during the wait for the mining convoy for Noonkanbah.

"There is big trouble between Yapa and Kardiya," Jimmy commented with a disapproving look. "That's no good."

I had to come to terms with the idea that most Warlpiri people do not like conflicts between Aboriginal people and Whites. The elders avoided talking about the first half of the century when some clans were decimated by the settlers, and about the persecutions they had suffered in the cattle stations and reserves. If they complained about the abuse of power of such and such Europeans, they hesitated by contrast in confronting it openly. In 1978, a policeman, a member of a local association allied with the Ku Klux Klan, subjected Lajamanu's population to victimizations that were denounced in the press. A deputy intervened and the policeman was transferred, but the Warlpiri people refused to testify against him at his trial.

I noticed Betty going to fetch water with a plastic jerry can at one of the taps in the camp's waste ground. I caught up with her and showed her the photos. She was surprised to see Aboriginal women in the crowd. I asked her for news about the single Napangardi who slept next to me when I camped with the women. She had married and lived in a house. And Maggy the blind? Betty led me there.

Maggy occupied a *dog house*, a small kennel in a set of so-called houses reserved for pensioners. She was sitting against the wall in front of a fire. At her side was Nganjiljiya Napanang-ka, the *number one* singer. Both embraced and re-assured me. I must not worry. Everything would be alright. I left them for the Council. An old Jangala accosted me:

"You are with your Jangala this time? Bring him to me later."

I promised, startled. I knew that Aboriginal people often hide what they think and behave cordially with Whites just to live in peace. But here nothing forced all these people to show me any friendship. We took the road to the Council and there we saw the Toyota of the police coming toward us. Two White policemen whom I did not know stepped out.

"Do you have your permits to stay?"

"No, we've come precisely to arrange that."

"Well then, if you don't leave immediately, we'll have to arrest you."

"We would like to talk with the members of the Council."

"None of them want to see you."

I could not hold back my tears. Nobody dared to move in the camp. We were not even allowed to say goodbye. The policemen escorted our car as far as the Lajamanu exit. Abe Jangala was there with some men. He waved to us. Michel stopped the car and shouted through the window.

"They don't want us to stay!"

We got out of the car to greet these men. The two policemen put their hands to their belts as if they were ready to shoot. A shadow of terror flashed in the eyes of the Warlpiri men. Did they remember the old shootings? I articulated a few words between two sobs. Abe said in an unperturbed tone:

"It's all right."

The police car followed us for ten minutes along the track then did a U-turn. As we approached Kalkaringi, we passed a car full of men which stopped. The Warlpiri man who had encouraged us to go to Lajamanu without a permit climbed out. Hearing that the Council had sent two policemen to expel us, he shook his head.

"That's not right. The Council should have talked to you. There are perhaps some people who don't like you, but others do."

He wished us good luck, then added:

"See you soon! Do come to the sporting events at Yuendumu."

If they did not want me in Lajamanu, I had no intention of going to Yuendumu. In Kalkaringi, the missionaries advised us to sue and receive compensation based on the fact that coming to Australia we had a Lajamanu permit that had been withdrawn subsequent to new elections at the Council. I refused. To resort to law would be interpreted as an attack against the authority of the Aboriginal Councils. I had no intention of playing into the hands of some Whites.

On return to Alice Springs, we went to visit the Warlpiri people camped in houses on the outskirts of town. There I met two Japaljarri brothers who lived in Lajamanu the previous year. One managed a rock band whose singer was his wife. She pointed out that people had not appreciated my behavior on the day when the missionaries had made the Christian Warlpiri act out a scene from the Bible.

I had laughed upon seeing Herod, covered in the Warlpiri fashion of white cotton wool stuck to his body and face, threatening to kill the children. These youngsters had laughed too, unintentional actors of the show. But I was not a child, and even if there were tensions between the missionaries and non-Christians, one had to respect the beliefs of others.

"What do you know about our beliefs?" reproached Martin, a slightly drunk, young Japanangka.

I talked about the songs, dances and paintings which bind people to Dreaming trails and about the sacred sites which inhabit them. He objected that they were not only beliefs but the truth. Seeing I was not upset he quieted down.

"OK. I would like to write a book about my people which would be called *Forced by bullets*. You have to help me."

I promised I would help him to apply for a grant from the Aboriginal artistic department which financed steps of that kind. The next day, his uncle took me aside and explained I should not help him write a book about his people since he had refused to submit to the trials of initiation and therefore

143

the elders would not speak to him. Martin had fully grasped the situation. He hoped to obtain the status of anthropologist to gain the confidence of the elders. No use to look for him, the uncle added, he had been in a fight the day before and was nowhere to be seen.[42]

I was feeling more and more crushed by the pent-up violence in the feelings going through these people. The husband of the rock singer complained that recent visits of governmental officials had made some Warlpiri too smart, in other words that power had gone to their heads. In the end I realized it was the political situation that was making an intruder out of me. Lajamanu had just changed status, becoming the first Aboriginal settlement of the Northern Territory whose government campaigned for all Aboriginal communities to follow that example and to leave the protection of the federal legislation — which permits land claims and restitutions — for direct dependence on the State.

The leaders of Lajamanu, having already retrieved part of their traditional lands in trust, had accepted the new deal with the promise of numerous financial advantages. Only later would they gauge to what extent their so-called self-determination would be subjected to the instructions of the authorities of the Northern Territory. In that recent compromise, to play the journalist was tactless. I learned that my article in Le Monde had just been translated into English for the Guardian, a diplomatic weekly paper rather popular in some Australian circles.[43] It was quite normal for the Warlpiri people and the Whites involved in the strategies of local power to protect themselves from all external eyes which threatened to spy on them, pen in hand.

Having no disposition whatsoever for spying, I was devastated at the idea that my desire to make the situation of the Aboriginal people popular in France had been transformed into such a misunderstanding. I even decided to abandon anthropology. An Australian friend talked me out of it. During the

---

42. Two years later, French artist Michel Potage paid homage to Aboriginal struggles with a series of paintings displayed at the Galerie Donguy in Paris in an exhibition titled *Le Rire dans le désert* (Laughter in the desert). He also displayed a big book of sand he called *Forced by bullets* and dedicated to Martin Johnson: page markers were made of red ochered strings with bullets at their ends. In the 1990's Martin was to become the Chairman of Lajamanu.

43. See note 23.

following months, in Paris, I wrote the thesis for my Ph.D. on the relationship of time and space with the Australian Aboriginal people.[44]

One day two policemen from Interpol came to see my partner and I. In parka and jeans, those Starsky and Hutch characters made us sign a statement on our past activities in Australia. They had taken over an investigation on a misappropriation of funds in the CLC. By talking with us they came to the conclusion that it was probably a fabricated story aimed at preventing us from returning to Australia. I was overwhelmed, not wanting to believe that my article could have caused such a measure. In reality, the policemen had it all wrong. Later we heard that all Australian and foreign anthropologists working with the Aboriginal people from Central Australia had been interrogated. It was confirmed that the misappropriation of the funds had been accomplished by an Aboriginal secretary at the CLC whom nobody had wanted to denounce.

It took me quite some time to recover from that failed trip. A raw wound had destroyed something deep inside me. It had even ruined my relationship with Michel, which became a painful reminder of my failure.

---

44. Glowczewski, B. 1981-82 *Le Rêve et la terre : rapports au temps et à l'espace des Aborigènes australiens: les Walpiri à Lajamanu (Hooker creek, une communauté du désert central australien)*, 400 pages, Université Paris VII, Jussieu, thèse de 3e cycle (PhD). One chapter was published in English: Glowczewski, B. "Death, Women and 'Value Production': The circulation of Hair Strings among the Walpiri of the Central Australian Desert." *Ethnology* 22(3), 1983: 225-239. "Walpiri" used to be a way to spell "Warlpiri."

REUNION

"Having surrendered to a land outwardly desolate, you've wandered from laughter to tears, ecstasy to despair, highs to lows, love to annoyance. You've wandered, and like every wandering traveller, you've built for yourself a myth from moving to meeting, from signs/events to signs/memory. Like an animal circumscribing its survival territory, you've prowled a perimeter of several hundred kilometers around a familiar point in your dream, you've covered a mythical triangle whose center is Hooker Creek.

From north to south, Darwin to Alice Springs, south to west, Alice to Broome, you've woven with invisible threads the tiny fragments of trails relayed by glances, voices, smells and touchings. At the beginning without references, you've been traversed by a multitude of references which came to embody your own shattered body. But those references to the image of Western technology filtered into the traditions which at the same time go beyond and hollow our understanding, those references perhaps come as some contemporary metamorphoses to repeat the ancestral script of the animal/vegetable/mineral process of becoming of human beings, the process of becoming of ceaseless transformations whose land is the witness/trace. A land which is no more a surface than a volume, but a suspended space/time in which through a multitude of centers the

147

Aboriginal people still know how to penetrate discontinuous totalities."

I believed I was accepting the empty space left in me by the people of the end of the world when I wrote that text for the catalog of an exhibition of paintings that Michel dedicated to the Aboriginal people.[45] Writing, painting, ways of exorcising the journey that had pulled us apart. The exhibition was a pre-text to invite Shorty O'Neill, the ambassador of the Federation of Aboriginal Land Councils who lived temporarily in London. He told us that the dancers from the Mornington Island of Queensland were currently touring Europe. They had danced in Italy and were on their way through Paris to appear in Britain.

Visiting the Beaubourg esplanade, the group from the Lardil tribe decided to dance there. Within a few minutes a crowd had gathered at the strange sound of the *didgeridu*, the long wooden horn typical of the Aboriginal people from the Northern coast. For hours, retaining their town clothes, eight men and two women sang, danced and talked with the Parisians and tourists from all over the world. The other entertainers in the place passed hats around the audience and lay the money at their feet. The Lardil asked for a drink.

An employee from the Pompidou Centre sent a waiter over with beers on a tray. Other spectators took turns bringing them cans. At 11 that night when the police arrived to disperse the crowd, the ground was littered. The Lardil were enjoying themselves. Later, in the premises of the exhibition, they started to sing again before the tent that Michel had set up on a ton of sand dyed red, a tribute to the tent *embassy* the Aboriginal people erected in 1972 in front of the Parliament building in Canberra, hundreds of them camping on the lawn as a protest against their living conditions.[46] Delighted with that unexpected welcome, the Lardil invited me to come to visit them on Mornington Island.

Soon after, I heard the Warlpiri were participating in the next Autumn Festival in Paris and I was contacted by a journalist from *Autrement* who asked me to write a series of articles

45. Potage, Michel. *Le Rire dans le désert* (Laughter in the Desert). Paris: the Donguy Gallery, Autumn 1982.

46. http://indigenousrights.net.au/land_rights/aboriginal_embassy_1972/background.

on the Indigenous Australians for a special issue on Australia. Aboriginal people were decidedly fashionable. While I thought I would never see this people again, the opportunity was presented for me to try to make contact once more with the Warlpiri.

June 1983. I was travelling on the Australian roads, interviewing different people in charge of Aboriginal organizations. Arriving at Cairns in Queensland, I obtained a residence permit to spend a month on Mornington Island. The Island was still a quasi-virgin land for the wallabies. On one of the coasts the old mission was the only development, for it had become a community self-managed by the Lardil, some seven hundred inhabitants assisted by White officials. A lot of things here looked like Lajamanu, but it was different.

First, there was the sea. Women fished with hooks attached to the end of a thread spooling from a plastic wheel held in their hand. Men caught fish with a spear and captured dugongs, sea-cows, quasi-fantastic beasts which were at the origins of the universal myth of mermaids. The flesh of those herbivores, cooked in a pit dug in the ground and covered with leaves, proved delicious.

Everybody lived in bungalows whose windows were fitted with blinds. Ritual life occurred less than in Lajamanu for it had been forbidden at the beginning of the century by the missionaries. Regaining their freedom, the Lardil had however asked a tribe from Arnhem Land to initiate their youth into the rituals their elders had lost. Traditional culture was integrated into schooling, children were taken on picnics near the sacred sites in order to hear the stories of their Dreaming heroes.

Alcohol was authorized, but rationed. Every day between 5 and 6 beer cans were sold to the men and women who wanted this ration in the shed that acted as a party hall, with a limit of 6 per person. Nobody had the right to assign their ration to anyone else. Women, constantly bugged by their husbands or sons, either surrendered them or drank the beer themselves to prevent the men from getting drunk. A pleasant euphoria bathed the community every night.

Leaving that enchanting island, I promised not to publish anything without first sending the text to the Lardil Council to obtain their agreement on the contents. Three months later, with its consent, the research was published.[47] I pursued my research in Alice Springs. The project for the artificial lake, criticized three years before at the CLC meeting, was on the verge of becoming a reality. Some Aranda people were squatting the sacred site under threat of being flooded: Welatye-Terre *Two-Breasts*. The women were especially active for the Dreaming concerned was the Two-Women Dreaming, a mythical trail which crosses Australia, handed in relay from one tribe to another, from the South Coast right up to the Bathurst and Melville Islands of the Tiwi people in the North. According to the Aboriginal people, destroying the site meant risking drying up the milk of all the women, aboriginal or not, living in the area. The story made the front page and the project was finally abandoned.

At the CLC, Stanley, the Aboriginal field officer of mixed ancestry who had taken me to Lajamanu on my first stay had succeeded the Aranda (Arrernte) Chairman, Wenton Rubuntja. I also met, once again, the ambassador of the Federation of Land Councils who had come to Paris. He was returning from Roxby Downs in South Australia, the location of a uranium deposit where, with his cousins of the Kokatha tribe, he had camped for three weeks to demonstrate their opposition to the destruction of ten Dreaming sites. A few kilometers away, a gathering of White ecologists protested against the uranium exploitation. They would obtain only partial satisfaction. Australia is so rich in uranium that this vein would be preserved only for subsequent exploitation.

The atmosphere in Alice was slightly tense. There were different factions of Whites working with Aboriginal people and others who despised them *en bloc*. To be accepted by the former, one had to show that he/she was co-opted by Aboriginal people. I attempted a rehabilitation, my stomach tightened with anxiety and hope. Wishing to make another long fieldwork in Lajamanu, I asked for a week's residence permit to discuss it with the Warlpiri.

Four days passed and I obtained permission to visit them. I was taken to Yuendumu, the community of the Southern Warlpiri. Françoise Dussart, a French student, had just settled

---

47. Glowczewski, B. "Au pays du Dreamland et de la terre rouge: les Aborigènes." *Aventure Australie, Autrement.* hors série 7: 1984. 130-183.

there. When she came to see me in Paris before she was given an Australian grant, Françoise did not guess she would find herself with the Warlpiri. The latter found it funny, they were the only Aboriginal people *specialized* in French anthropologists.

In Yuendumu I saw a few Aboriginal people learning to use a computer in order to compile a Warlpiri encyclopedia directed by a linguist.[48] Françoise informed me that another linguist had been enlisted in Lajamanu to direct a Literacy Centre where school books in Warlpiri were created. Furthermore, the school had a new director who had gathered a team of young teachers immersed in Aboriginal culture. That evolution worried me a little.

Lajamanu. Nobody on the landing strip. My bag on my shoulder, I entered the deserted village. It was midday, siesta time. A White woman came out of the new building bearing the inscription, Literacy Centre. I approached her. She was the school principal. She told me she had heard about me but could not speak to me until I had seen the Council. Malaise: the paranoia of the Whites from Alice had followed me here.

Thus I waited in the empty building of the Council. At last the imposing Chairman arrived, a big smile on his face.

"We are going to see your country soon! Tell us how it is."

I spoke to him about France. The other members of the Council listened, amused. I explained the new research projects I would like to do with them, to gather the public versions of the stories relating to the fauna, flora and all the things that name the Dreamings, to understand the relationship between the ritual knowledge and the resource of dream visions.

The men told me the past was forgotten, but that I had to be careful what I wrote in the future. They reminded me of that damn *Le Monde* article (translated in *The Guardian*) wherein I had indicated the Warlpiri preferred camping to houses. That was not right, more and more wanted housing. Would they be able to obtain it following such remarks? I had to realize clearly that the stakes went beyond my nomadic utopia. The Council agreed I could visit the women to see if they agreed for me to return the next year to carry out further fieldwork.

---

48. Laughren, Mary. "Warlpiri Dictionary Project — Entries: Fauna Domain; Flora Domain; Body Parts; Verbs." Yuendumu: mimeo. See the *Kirrkirr* digital Encyclopedia, she continues to develop it with a team of linguists and Warlpiri people.

I set off for the camps. A group of women called me. I recognized Pampiriya, the wife of Jimmy, the Jangala-with-the-Paris-postcard. How was he? All of them went silent and lowered their heads. A chill went through me. I understood, he was dead.

A girl hung around us at a distance. I identified the face of the little girl straightaway from before as the one who was always looking to see if I had head lice. She was Marjorie Nungarrayi, my little *sister*, Nakakut's daughter. I called her. She came to a standstill with a very shy look about her. Pampiriya pushed me to follow her. Like a kid, Marjorie ran forward then back to check I was still following. Suddenly she shouted:

"Mum! Mum! Nungarrayi is here!"

Nakakut was seated on the ground. Her penetrating look made my heart sink. I melted with emotion. Next to her, Beryl, her inseparable sister and co-spouse, stared at me while squinting her eyes. They were lean and really very beautiful with their long black hair, low-cut T-shirts and straight skirts. We embraced. Tears rolled down Nakakut's cheeks.

"I was not here when you came. And I was ashamed they let you go. Have you seen the missionaries? You have to make friends with them again. They still have the film of our *business*. Now that you are here, we'll be able to watch it."

I went to the mission and talked at length with the couple of Baptist ministers. I acknowledged my past mistakes and recovered the film.

"Think carefully," Nakakut warned me. "Two women passed away since last time you've been here. Remember, look around who's missing. We cannot tell their names. They have become *kumanjayi*. When you've found out, erase them from the film. And then, only then, can we watch it."

It was then I discovered that the traditional taboo on the names of the dead also applied to photographic or filmed representations of the deceased. Still the same concern, not to cause grief to the mourners, nor to risk holding back on earth those who have to be dissolved in the time-space of the Dreaming. How to identify the two who passed away? There were so many women and some, absent today, could simply be on a journey. I was set on the track: one was a Nampijinpa, the other a Napurrurla.

Studying the images, I immediately guessed, as if not having seen those two women at the camp had created a hole. Lacking an editing table, I thought I could blacken the film. But one or the other appeared on almost one out every four shots. That idea made no sense. The women agreed that I should take the film back with me and show it the following year, once it was re-edited.

Meanwhile the *businesswomen* invited me to their camp. I heard that they had finally obtained not a truck but a car capable of carrying fifteen people. As none of them knew how to drive, a son had been appointed to take them around. They only benefitted from it for a few months. The Holden was borrowed by the men, who had an accident, fortunately without serious injuries. Betty Napanangka, who was the car *boss* showed me the wreck at the edge of the camp.

"That's the car, perhaps we can have it mended?"

That seemed rather unlikely. They were already talking about something else.

"You've helped us to get a car, now you help us to get a *museum* like the women of Yuendumu."

They wanted a building to store their sacred objects and asked me to talk about it with the Council and the *topmen* in Darwin or Canberra. I accepted. The tone was set for my next stay. I could come back to collect the *Yapa culture*, but on condition I serve as an intermediary for the women in the administrative processes. First, I had to record their explanations for the *museum* and take the cassette to the Council. A dozen *businesswomen* declared, in turn, they wanted the building in the middle of the camps next to a water tap.

The men of the Council listened to the tape and nodded.

"We'll see what we can do with the community budget for next year. But on your side, make inquiries about the possibilities of outside financing."

I was told that Maggy Napangardi the blind had lost her old husband and married a Jangala, a skin *son* and not a potential *spouse* of Jampijinpa skin, as she should have done. That type of marriage was called *warrura* (against the Law), and always provoked scandal and conflict. In her case, the Jampijinpa man had finally made up their mind. Maggy was an important *businesswoman* and a seductress who scared people because of her love magic.

With her new husband and the family of another Jangala, they had settled in Lullju, a Rain Dreaming site, some fifteen kilometers from Lajamanu. Her father Peter Blacksmith, *boss* of the Kajirri ceremony, had settled in Parnta, the region of the Insect Gall Dreaming where I had camped with the *businesswomen*. The two places had become Outstations. In recent times, a White man had been employed by the Council to manage the budget allocated by the State for the development and maintenance of those new bush camps. Each Outstation was supplied once a week with a stock of food paid for by a governmental subsidy and the personal income of its members. I climbed onto the tractor that supplied the food to pay a visit to Maggy the blind.

Lullju was a totally rudimentary camp, apart from its windmill. There were no prefab houses yet, or gardens which would blossom as a result. The blind woman told me how she had liked the glacé chestnuts I had sent her, for she had wanted to taste a food from a tree in my country. They had also appreciated burning the bits of coal which accompanied the confections. She told me coal should be provided in vast quantities in Lajamanu for it was becoming more and more difficult to find wood nearby.

I translated an article for her into pidgin that I had written in English about the hair strings.[49] The Council had asked me to inform the women about what I was writing. But I noticed the degree to which it was difficult to translate my scientific jargon however inspired by Warlpiri data. A strange paradox that many anthropologists experience. Maggy enjoyed herself.

"I should go to your country and explain to the people they make a mistake when they call the children of their father's brother *cousins* and not *brothers*. This time it's our men's turn to go to your country. Next time, you have to invite the women."

---

49. Glowczewski, B. "Death, Women and 'Value Production.'" *Ethnology* 22(3) 1983: 225-239.

THE WARLPIRI IN PARIS

September 1983. Twelve Warlpiri men arrived in Paris. For a week, sheltered from all witnesses, they worked at the Museum of Modern Art. Red sand had been delivered which covered the vast room of ARC. They created a ground painting on it with white kapok and red meanders which joined the two circles: the *pirntina* Python Dreaming linking the Jurntu *limestone* site to another sacred site. The night before the opening, a dinner had been organized at the museum for them and a group of journalists. I met them there. They introduced me to the organizers of the exhibition, announcing proudly that they already knew somebody in Paris. For my part, I had the impression I was living in a dream.

"We agreed to do that painting to make an alliance with the French people."

The journalists found that hard to understand. Most had not made any effort to read the catalog or the wall with its long declaration, each word carefully weighed by the elders to present the cultural context of that painting. They hesitated between taking those imperturbable stars as artists or as some last vestiges of the Stone Age disguised as modern men.

Some said Arboriginal as if that *r*, evocative of a population living in trees (*arbre*), had crept into the unconscious, replacing the long-gone preconception that the Indigenous people of Australia represented some kind of missing link between man and ape. The so-called savages were bewildered. They behaved like noblemen, inaccessible and ironic, yet benevolent toward those who plagued them with questions.

Three weeks in a row, in the evening, the Warlpiri danced at the Théâtre des Bouffes du Nord,[50] their faces and bodies covered with glued down and designs painted in red. Three of them remained seated in a circle to sing and keep the beat with their boomerangs. It only lasted a quarter of an hour, a sort of strange mime almost in slow-motion. The dancers were old and their dancing stomp, around the man who crawled on his knees before succumbing beneath the spears, dumbfounded most of the spectators. What was the meaning of this sacred dance?

The booklet said the danced scene had been revealed in a dream in the Sixties. The victim represented a keeper of the Jurntu site who, in the Thirties, had a fight with his brothers because, instead of waiting for them, in order to celebrate the mourning of one of their nephews, he had taken flight bearing the cut hair of the deceased for himself. Why was it sacred? Because it happened to be a thing of the past which had been integrated into the mythical patrimony and the memory of the Jurntu site associated with the Python Dreaming, as in the ground painting. The historical incident had become a myth by being transformed into a Dreaming, and retranslated into a dance, paintings, and songs.

Also disconcerting was the performance of the twenty men and women from Arnhem Land, all very young, with their faces painted. The *didgeridu* accompanied them. Each minute they stopped with an impressive silence, before restarting their hopping from one foot to the other, each section illustrating a different Dreaming. The fragility and agility of the bodies suggested animals and birds from another world.

Some evenings, a part of the audience took offence at the applause that others tried to inject between the sequences. The dancers from Arnhem Land expressed surprise. Clapping was the only sign, in our convention, of participation by the audience which, in their country, manifests itself with exclamations of encouragement and even laughter. They found it strange

---

50. Established in 1971 in Paris by famous English theater and film director Peter Brook, this old italian style theater became straight away an important European centre of contemporary creation.

156

that their gestures, due to their sacred nature, were met with the conventional silence of our churches.

Some journalists were charmed by the modesty of the dances which were proof of the "*primaryness*" of the Aboriginal people. But what would we say if Western culture was judged on an extract of a Bob Wilson production and a Mondrian painting? The foreigner who knew nothing else could say that those artists were only capable of painting squares, and wonder if they have ever thought of dancing in another way besides endlessly repeating the same movements. The response to the foreigner would be that there is a history behind all this — the history of art, painting, and civilization — which gives a richness to the apparent poverty.

The Aboriginal people had agreed to come to France to show precisely that they too have a history, a civilization, without which dances and paintings have no meaning. Each new generation needs years of initiation and apprenticeship to understand it. But the journalists were not invited to the Franco-Australian round table during which a man from Arnhem Land and the imposing Chairman of Lajamanu, Maurice Luther Jupurrurla, took turns explaining what they had come to present was a living sign of their culture.

Another misunderstanding. A professor insisted that anthropology was in the process of discovering the role of creation in traditional societies — and that the artists there had perhaps the same problems as ours.

"Creation doesn't have the same meaning for us as for you," replied the Warlpiri Chairman. If someone dreams a painting or a song that are not linked to his land, he has no right concerning this dream but has to give it up to the custodians of that relevant land, who will do with it what they judge is right."

The Warlpiri man specified that it was not sufficient to dream in order to enrich the heritage, the agreement of others was also needed. A dream vision was certified "real" only if it was linked to pictorial and narrative forms which were transmitted as such for hundreds of generations. While the man from the desert gave us a lesson in Warlpiri philosophy, the usual roles suddenly seemed to reverse. Claude Lévi-Strauss, invited to respond, said in great humility:

"The signs produced by those cultures are less to be interpreted than to be shared."

During their entire stay in Paris, the Warlpiri rightly sought to share our signs. They were impressed by the contrast between the ever-so-young Australian towns and Paris, which bore testimony to a distant past:

"Why did the Europeans leave all that to come to our country? To think that so many generations have seen the same golden angel on that square (Châtelet), it means something to be there."

Accustomed to wooden or corrugated iron houses, the constructions in stone caught their attention. I told them the story of the African woman who, arriving at a friend's flat under the eves of the roof, decided to build a room above it. She thought houses were built floor by floor at the will of each new tenant. The Warlpiri burst into laughter:

"We thought each street was a single house that was spreading!"

Housed on one of the floors of the university center, they found it strange to live above the heads of other people and chose to settle whenever they could on the terraces of cafes:

"It's like in our country, one takes time to watch people come and go. French people show their feelings much more than Australian Whites. But those Black people are different from us."

They thought it very amusing to observe the heated exchanges of drivers in traffic jams. Finding it strange that people could get excited over so little, they concluded that living like that, without space, would drive anyone crazy. I could not help but think that their first view of Paris in its way summed up people who live in cities, because before seeing up close the bread, or *baguettes*, they had thought that Parisians wandered around with a stick in their hands! They were very sensitive to the tensions prevalent between the organizers, French and Australian, bustling around them.

"They shake hands as if they were the best of friends, but to do their *business*, they become enemies. It's the other way around in our country, our *business* consists in making peace and erasing eventual conflicts."

Shocked by the homeless sleeping on the pavements and in the subway, they did not understand why the government could not give them houses. After a few explanations about our society, one young man from Arnhem Land remarked in a mischievous tone:

"When the day comes that it is like that in Australia, we will always have the bush to shelter and feed us."

Amazed that a 50 French francs note was worth less than 50 Australian dollars, the Warlpiri asked why the French did not use the dollars that would allow them to buy more. I tried to explain my limited rudiments of economy and the Warlpiri Chairman concluded:

"OK, the French are like us, they want self-management in their affairs."

At the end of the show, with their bodies covered with ochre, covered with a blanket and ready to leave in the car that would take them back to the center, I introduced my parents to them. They all wanted to shake their hands. And the Chairman said solemnly to my father in English:

"Don't worry about your daughter, we are taking good care of her in our country."

One Sunday we went for a hike through the woods at Fontainebleau. They were searching for animal traces in the sand and grieved at the sight of the "dead" trees. They found it hard to believe that fresh leaves grew back every year, for they did not consider the dry trees of their country which were covered with flowers after each rainy season to be "dead." Then a Warlpiri picked up an oak leaf:

"But it's the same as in Kurlungalinpa, a desert oak!"

Curiously, those men whom one would think as being closer to nature than us, preferred the parks at Versailles and Saint-Germain-en-Laye to the woods. They had noticed the similarity of the geometrical organization of the alleys and greenery of the uninhabited châteaus. These evoked the Warlpiri's own geometrical drawings of trails linking their sites:

"What is the special story of those designs on the ground?"

I explained to them that it was the style of old French formal gardens and that the labyrinths of hedges and bushes sometimes took up the traditions of the checkered stone plans of the crypts of some churches.

"OK, you don't want to answer us because it's a secret."

Visiting the Australian collection at the National Museum of Arts of Africa and Oceania, a dancer from Arnhem Land was very happy to recognize the animal paintings of the so-called *X-rays* style made on bark by his grandfather. They had been gathered in the 1950's by Karel Kupka, an artist of Czech origin, the first French researcher to do fieldwork with Aboriginal people.[51]

The Warlpiri men on the other hand discovered carved stones, collected in the Thirties and connected to the ritual cycles they shared with other desert tribes. They looked at each other, aghast. Those sacred objects should not be displayed. Following the example of a recent museographic movement, the curator proposed a restitution. Later, after a long discussion, the Warlpiri decided it made no sense. Having been exhibited, the stones were no longer sacred. Besides, if the hereditary custodians of those objects retrieved them, they would find themselves accused in the name of their fathers of having let them go. The ritual responsibility had enough complex political implications without it being poisoned by painful memories. They ended up declaring with solemnity:

"We have the same sacred objects that we still use today. The French can keep the ones they have in exchange for the way they have welcomed us."

The day before their departure, the thirty-two Aboriginal men and women were invited to the Australian Embassy for the opening of an exhibition of paintings on canvas from Papunya, a community from the desert where a few Warlpiri live with some Pintupi and Luritja people. The Warlpiri men immediately recognized in the dotted signs that covered the canvases the designs representing the trails of the Kangaroo Dreaming and the Emu Dreaming which, by crossing their territory, unite them to their neighboring tribes.

Deeply moved to once again see those images, they stepped aside from the crowd of visitors. An unbearable sadness went through their deep-set eyes. For them, some designs were too

51. Kupka, Karel. *Peintres aborigènes d'Australie.* Paris: Publication de la Société des Océanistes (Musée de l'Homme), 1972.

160

secret and should not be given to the public in that way. They themselves did not yet paint on canvas with acrylics. That movement, started a few years before at the urging of a White man who had provided the Aboriginal people from Papunya with the materials, was, however, beginning to spread. In Yuendumu, the elders had just painted their ancestral Dreamings on all the doors of the school.[52]

In the middle of the general frenzy, a Warlpiri man sat on the floor, lowered his head beneath his cowboy hat, and said with sadness:

"They talk, and talk, just like birds."

I discovered later that it was through a certain bird that the ancestors of the Goanna clans learned to speak. But from the mouth of the Warlpiri man that remark was not a compliment.

---

52. Myers, Fred. *Painting Culture: The making of an Aboriginal High Art*. Duke University Press, 2002; *Warlukurlangu Artists, Kuruwarri: Yuendumu Doors*. Canberra: Australian Institute of Aboriginal Studies, 1987; Ed. P. Sutton. *Dreamings: the Art of Aboriginal Australia*. New York: The Asia Society Galleries in association with Braziller Publications, 1988.

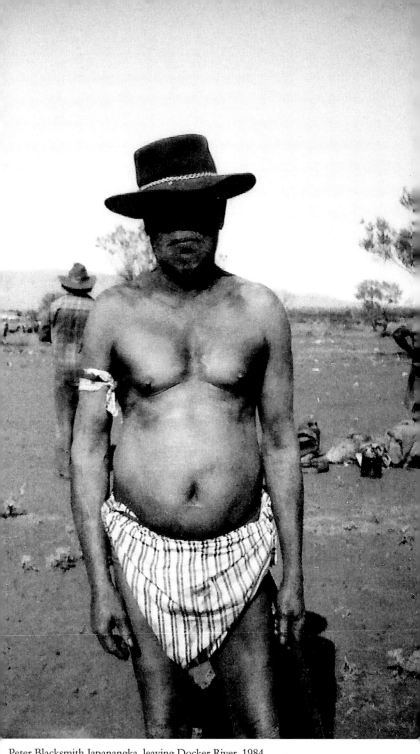

Peter Blacksmith Japanangka, leaving Docker River, 1984.

PART FOUR

(1984)

Paddy Patrick Jangala making a video to protect this sacred site at The Granites from mining.

Lajamanu women walk around the sacred site Yarturluyarturlu for the video.

Nakakut Gibson Nakamarra laughs with other women after the Yarkinpirri dancers throw sparkles of fire during the Initiation ceremony, 1984.

Nakakut Gibson Nakamarra leads a *yawulyu* ritual for the *yawakiyi* Black Plum and *janganpa* Possum Dreamings, Lajamanu, 1984.

166

Kungariya Napangardi (front) and Kajingarra Napangardi dance the journey of the *pilja* Goanna Dreaming holding *yukurrukurru* boards painted, like their bodies, with the *pilja* trail passing through Mount Theo, Lajamanu, 1984.

Hunting at Kurlungalinpa: Marjorie Gibson Nungarrayi, Maudie Nakamarra, Molly Nangala, Beryl Nakamarra and Tony Gibson Japaljarri.

Lajamanu girls painted with their Dreamings for the end of the school term, 1984: back row (right to left); Monica Napangardi Blacksmith (*karnta* Insect gall), Dulcie Napaljarri Herbert and Vanessa Nungarrayi Hector (*yarnjilpiri* Stars), Lillian Napanangka Johnson (*kana* Digging stick), Selina Nangala Robertson and Vanessa Nangala/Napurrurla Nelson (*ngapa* Water), front row (left to right): Melinda Napurrurla Simon and Sophia Nakamarra Donnelly (*ngurlu* Seed), Patricia Nakamarra Patterson (*puurda* Yam) and Valerie Nangala/Napurrurla Nelson (*ngapa* rainclouds).

Lily Hargraves Nungarrayi and two Napaljarri dance the *ngatijirri* Budgerigar Dreaming when the ancestral birds fed themselves during their travel, Lajamanu, 1984.

Lajamanu women dance around two ritual *kuturu* as *kurdungurlu* managers of the *kana* Digging Stick Dreaming.

Women of Napanangka and Napangardi skins painted as *kirda* bosses with the *kana yawulyu* dance to get the gifts of blankets deposited by their relatives for the reopening of their Dreaming after a two years period of mourning.

A HOUSE FOR WOMEN

March 1984. Three weeks after settling in the mission flat in Lajamanu, I had to vacate the place for a pilot appointed by the Baptist authorities. No question of camping when more and more Warlpiri were living in houses. I spotted an abandoned prefab. The Council agreed to reconnect the water and electricity in exchange for rent.

Originally it was a five-room house with a kitchen and bathroom. But after the departure of the last tenants — two White builders, who had seriously damaged the place before being thrown out as a result of their alcohol abuse — all the partition walls were pulled down and the children enjoyed themselves in what had become a large shed. Eventually, the space only interested a herd of roaming goats that took shelter there from the sun.

I was rather satisfied. With its knocked down partitions, part of the windows blocked with corrugated metal and the floor covered in linoleum tiles, my new home looked more like a trendy loft in Paris! The women thought it would make an ideal *jilimi*. I was not asked who might settle in that new women's camp. The future occupants came by themselves to help me clean the house and tidy the garden.

"You cannot live here by yourself. If you didn't have a house, you would have camped with us," said Pampiriya Margaret

Nungarrayi, my *sister,* widow of the *postcard from Paris* Jangala, Jimmy Burns.

She was joined by four women whom she had camped with for two years with a dozen children: two Nungarrayi grand-mothers; a Napangardi widow, my *mother-in-law*; and a di-vorced Nakamarra, my *mother*. Our furniture was reduced to the strict minimum, mattresses and blankets. The women hid their sacred objects in a stone container at the entrance of the house. I squatted the kitchenette in order to place my typewrit-er and papers there. The children didn't touch them. After a while Pampiriya's younger daughter stored her school drawings in the oven that didn't work. On the walls, painted with gaudy colors, we stuck more and more drawings, postcards, and pho-tos.

Before long our house became a turntable with incessant comings and goings, everybody sharing their joys as well as their most intimate dramas. Sometimes young newly-wed women would take refuge there, fleeing a marital conflict. I learned never to be alone and to always be available to the de-mands of others. It was not easy but, slowly, a way of life was established, which made an ideal solution from that open door co-habitation.

At daybreak a fire was lit in the yard to heat a large billy can of tea. Men of all ages, married or not, stopped for a chat or breakfast. During the day women came through one after an-other to use the bathroom or the old washing machine. Many visitors liked to spend hours in the shade of our enclosure. Some showed up for the sole purpose of telling me their ances-tral stories.

Nakakut had agreed to help me decipher the recorded tapes of myths and songs. Day after day that work weaved a deep friendship between us. The most inexpressible things for her, as for me, seemed to cross the cultural barrier that separated us. Nakakut used to come almost every morning. At midday, like a hurricane, her children and their friends and cousins arrived from school. We improvised a meal that I cooked in a big heat-ing dish. After their departure, we resumed working until the shop opened and Nakakut rejoined her family. At closing time, around 5 p.m., the women of the house placed a padlock on the door to prevent dogs and children from rummaging in the food stock. We eventually went into the women's ceremonial place for some *yawulyu* rituals.

We returned at nightfall, assailed by children who needed to be fed. Sometimes there was no food for the pot and the kids left for other camps. Frequently, a son or a brother accompanied by their children, came in search of food. In exchange they often brought from the hunt a kangaroo, an emu, a wild turkey or a *killer,* a bullock turned wild after the Warlpiri had stopped raising cattle on the reserve. Those much appreciated meats were grilled or cooked in a pit dug beneath the hearth.

Late in the evening, while I was writing in my diary or typing the transcriptions of the day, the women stayed up outside near the fire or played cards indoors. For lack of money they gambled with their clothes. When all the lights were out, amid the whispers, laughter and sleeping sighs, I gradually felt that I was growing attached to this strange family life.

When there was nothing left to eat, no more washing powder, no more wood, no more brooms, no more money and the children were running wild, I had the feeling that my companions became little girls whose grandma I would have been. If I undertook quieting the children or cleaning the floor covered in litter, they repeated, half-amused, half-disheartened, "*wiyarpa*," a Warlpiri expression of self-pity or pity for others. Yet the day after I was the one who became an impotent little girl when they baked me a bread or brought me a goanna, adding with gentle irony that I could not make bread or hunt.

The contrast between such a solicitude and periods of abandon was part of the Warlpiri art of living. Nobody was ever held responsible. The collectivity easily absorbed the crisis of apathy, anger, and even delirium of any of its members. By contrast, everyone had to in turn face up to the requirement of taking care of others. Such was the functioning of the gift.

One never said "thank you" or "please," but "give me" and one took. The person who refused to give would quickly be discredited, the only acceptable excuse would be to have nothing left. Then, one would lend, knowing perfectly well that the car would come back broken, for it would be used for a pub crawl, or that the tape recorder would not come back for it would carry on circulating from house to house until it was worn out.

At the beginning I was irritated when one of my companions gave all her allowance to a relative who wanted to place a big stake at cards. But one day when all the blankets of the house disappeared, given here and there, like the other women I threw up my arms and laughed. Not caring any more about eating with my fingers, from a tin can instead of a plate, I waited for the kids to proudly brandish bowls and forks collected by others. That circulation of material goods and the detachment of private property finally appeared to me as the way Warlpiri people maintained a certain social cohesion and tribal identity.

An angry man approached the house. Pampiriya seized me by the arm and told me to do what he said. He ordered me to open the door. Why did he want to go in when we were all outside?

"I have the right to take the girl promised to me," the man shouted.

I was told that during our absence, Roselyn, one of Pampiriya's daughters, aged thirteen, had taken refuge in our house. Did I have to let that furious man take away the young girl? Her mother had told me to obey. I agreed to open the door on the condition that I talked with her first. I knew Whites should not interfere in Aboriginal affairs but, by living constantly with those women and children who called me "mum," I didn't quite know what my position was.

"If you don't come out, the two of you, in ten minutes, I break the door open. I'm in the right," the threatening suitor warned.

I went in, accompanied by Nakakut's daughter, Marjorie, who knew that type of situation all too well. She too had just resisted the fiancé who had come to claim her, but she had to submit to familial consensus. I blocked the door behind us with a latch. The vast room was empty. Nobody in the bathroom either. Marjorie pointed with her finger to the wall where there was a hole that opened into a tiny room in which women stored their reserves of flour and cooking fat. Through that hole, only dogs and kids could enter. Women had access to the room from outside, by a door whose key they kept.

I drew closer to the hole. It was impossible to discern anything in the darkness, but I heard a jerky breathing. I called softly to the girl. There was a long silence, minutes, then:

"I have a knife. If he comes closer, I will kill him like he killed my father."

She burst into tears, sobbing. What to say? Her father had been killed in a car crash following a collective drinking session at the Rabbit Flat gas station. No witness had really been able to describe what had happened, nor to identify who was driving. Roselyn's father was said to have been knocked over following a brawl. Was she accusing all the accomplices of the drinking session of being responsible for his death?

"He's a murderer, a murderer…" her gasping voice repeated, tirelessly.

I talked to her about her father, who loved her, and was respected by everyone. She finally came close to the partition. I pushed my hand inside to draw her toward me and hold her in my arms. She was trembling, shaken by spasms which made her huddled little body stiff and tense.

"Nobody will make me leave this niche. I'll stay in here like a dog. I'm not destined to that man. I'm promised to another."

I decided to call her mother to clarify that promise business. I half-opened the door and Pampiriya came in, metamorphosed. The woman, who earlier seemed to be resigned to fate, had disappeared.

"My daughter is still too young to get married," she said in a voice both tender and fierce.

I stated that, on those terms, I was ready to take on responsibility not to allow Roselyn to leave. Pampiriya went out. I closed the door again. Marjorie discreetly raised the piece of material used as a curtain and announced joyfully:

"The Japangardi just left!"

The young promised came out of hiding. I asked if she was hungry. She immediately opened a tin of corned beef, another of beetroot and ate without a word. I showed her some sheets of school exercises the children had deposited on my table. Grabbing a sheet with the drawing of a fish, Roselyn settled down on the floor and did some coloring, as if she had forgotten everything else. It was not easy to imagine that the same girl held a knife to defend herself just a few short minutes before. Her seven year-old younger sister arrived.

"Do you know how Roselyn escaped the Japangardi?" she said, a note of pride in her voice. " She climbed to the top of the tree in the garden to jump onto the roof. Then she ran to the other side of the house to go down the drainpipe and slid inside between the bars of the small window in the toilet!"

The acrobat looked mischievously at the younger and both burst out laughing. They crawled into the little dark room to play. The drama seemed completely finished. I went out to talk with the mother and the other women gathered outside. They all confirmed that Roselyn was really promised to the suitor and she would have to follow him sooner or later. Did he "kill" her father? Roselyn had said "*kill*," an English term which, for the Aboriginal people, has the same ambiguity as the Warlpiri word meaning either "kill" or "hit."

"Don't believe what my daughter says," Pampiriya replied, angrily. "There has already been a *payback*."

For the Aboriginal people, the English expression *payback* means *settling of scores*, either by ritual presents, or a death sentence. Traditionally, a person who did not die of old age was avenged by a punitive expedition or some witchcraft aimed at the guilty one. That scapegoat was determined by divination on the corpse. The Warlpiri remembered the case of some of their contemporaries who, having offended the Law, had been *sung to death* or *pointed at*, even sometimes killed. The justice of the Whites turned a blind eye on such incidents settled by traditional Law.

I returned to the house followed by Pampiriya:

"Don't make up stories!" she shouted at her daughter. "Or there will be big trouble because of you!"

Roselyn glared at her mother with hatred, then smacked her. Pampiriya smacked her back and left without a word. I had never seen a mother strike her child. That gesture meant she considered her an adult. One thing was clear, despite all the rumors, the death of the Jangala was considered as *settled* by the Warlpiri. Had there been reprisals that should not be divulged?

Or perhaps could the Warlpiri Law not be exercised any longer? It was out of the question to make an enquiry, I had to submit to the unfathomable in Warlpiri society.

The *businesswomen* had gathered together in the vast building inaugurated the previous year to receive shows of itinerant performers. The open air cinema had disappeared that same year with the emergence of videos. That was the reason I transferred to video the new editing I had made of my film of their rituals. They had enormous fun recognizing themselves on screen after five years.

All of a sudden, terrible laments of mourning tore through the room. I stopped the projector immediately. It had been confirmed that no other woman had passed away among the women I had filmed. The scene that had caused the cries showed boys in the last phase of initiation. I was told that one had recently been killed in a car crash. Some spectators wanted to destroy the film, in the same way that they tore up photos of the deceased. Others dissuaded them and told me to keep it.

"When we won't be here any more, our children or grandchildren will appreciate watching that film. Perhaps then, there won't be any more *business*."

The Warlpiri were beginning to fear the disappearance of their traditional ritual life. The girls regularly refused to follow the men, sometimes 30 years older than them, to whom they had been ritually promised. The young men did not wait any longer for the end of their initiation at around thirty to settle with a girl their age, or an older widow. And the elders, the last witnesses of bush life, hesitated passing on to the young the ancestral secrets or even the dramatic episodes of their first contact with Whites.

The conflict of generations openly broke out when the teachers organized a video projection of *Women of the Sun*, a television series setting four Aboriginal heroines who, in different eras, rebelled against the bad treatment inflicted on their people by the settlers. The program had been applauded all over Australia, but in Lajamanu it scandalized some Whites, and right away many Warlpiri joined them under the pretext that past quarrels should not be reawakened. The youth, extremely affected by the film, urged the elders to tell them about the past on which they had chosen to remain silent.

Consequently, the Warlpiri started to reconsider their pedagogy of the last thirty years. As the children now learned to read and write in Warlpiri in the context of a bilingual program, the elders agreed for their life stories and some episodes of the Dreaming to be written down in schoolbooks. They knew something would be lost that way, for there was not one unique version, but as many versions as contexts which should be lived to acquire a true meaning. Nevertheless, faced with that dilemma, month after month different women, and some men too, would come and tell me their Dreaming trails so that I could record them in their language and transcribe them into English and my own language.

POSSUM AND THE MEN

In the shade of their leafy shelter, some *businesswomen*, seated one against the other, were painting each others' chests while singing. Suddenly my neighbor stood up and signaled for me to follow her. We did not go very far, just a few steps away, to where a beautiful Nangala in a red skirt and printed T-shirt stood. Two other singers joined us. Nangala turned to look in the direction of her husband's camp. A malaise overtook my companions. Something serious was about to be said. In what way could it concern me?

I did not know this Nangala very well. She had participated in the female rituals for a short time only. Married to an ex-police tracker much older than her, they had no children. The couple camped with the family of an old man wearing glasses, well respected for his ritual knowledge. It was the old wise man she talked about.

"Jungarrayi said the *yawulyu* the women painted and danced yesterday is not right."

She said it with the voice of a little girl caught red-handed, for she had also participated in the *yawulyu* ritual of the previous day. She added that the men were annoyed and trouble lay ahead. Turning to me she motioned with her lips toward the notepad I held in my hand.

"You must remove the drawings you did yesterday of the body paintings, do not show them to anyone. Same for the photos, forget them for now."

Nangala left. My companions had not asked any questions. Soon after the whole group of *businesswomen* were informed and stopped singing and painting. The situation was serious for the men never became involved with rituals restricted to the women.

"If the men are dissatisfied, we can expect reprisals," one remarked. "Perhaps they will forbid us to make our planned journey to The Granites?"

Anxiety. Several women started to talk at the same time. The old ones watched the agitation in silence.

"In what way was our *yawulyu* not right? We danced the Possum Dreaming for The Granites."

"We were only getting ready for that journey on which the men asked us to go with them."

"That's true, it been agreed that women will show a *yawulyu* to the Kardiya of the mining company so the topmen understand they shouldn't touch the rocks of The Granites."

Annie Nungarrayi promptly stood up, palms turned toward the sky as a sign of anger.

"It's all very nice to celebrate The Granites land. But I have never in my whole life seen those paintings and that dance! Nor have I ever heard the songs that accompanied them! This is not a true *yawulyu*!"

General silence. The debate was closed. Eventually I obtained an explanation. If the songs, paintings and Possum dance were *unknown*, it was because it was perhaps a secret knowledge. The day after, the elders who had gathered specified their accusations. The celebration of the Possum Dreaming was restricted to men. Women are supposed to have another ritual responsibility linked to the sacred site of The Granites.

Nakakut immediately summoned me to the women's bough shade with my tape recorder. She wanted to record a tape of ancestral songs to show the men that women had not forgotten their ritual responsibility. Eldest daughter of the most important keeper of The Granites, she was clearly concerned by that challenge.

For hours, Nakakut directed a group of singers, rediscovering hundreds of verses which marked step by step, site by site, right up to The Granites, the long epic of the *janganpa* Possum ancestor. I learned then that that Possum had gone to fetch the *yawakiyi* Black Plum people to fight against its own Possum people. If the men celebrated Possum, women had to celebrate the Black Plum people: a symbolic allocation between the genders to celebrate the same Dreaming trail.

The tape circulated among the elders. The old bespectacled Jungarrayi was moved as he listened. He smiled, his eyes closed, his face lit up at certain words sung. He was reliving the journey of the ancestral heroes. His two spouses and the other women who surrounded him pinched their thighs as a sign of complicity. It was dark now. The children stopped playing to come and listen to the old man.

"Possum is my first name for I'm born from a spirit-child of that Dreaming. He entered my mother when she passed near The Granites rocks. I carry in me the Possum Images I received from the father of my mother. He travelled with the Black Plum people. Without them, he wouldn't have been able to confront his own people."

The knowledge that Nakakut had acquired from the elders of her clan was thus confirmed, and she gained prestige with everybody. The elder women pointed out that the young woman deserved their teachings for she had known how to wait for the right time to show what she had remembered from her learning years. Nakakut was asked to stage the *yawulyu* ritual corresponding to those songs.

"For the body paintings of the Black Plum Dreaming," she explained to me, "besides red ochre and white clay, one has to use black from charcoal. If there's a lot of black that means the design corresponds to the end of the story, once the Plum people have melted into a vast black soup which has washed over the earth."

Nakakut specified that, like all women from her clan, she was born with the mark of her Dreaming. At each season when the plums grew, when the sun was burning, the outside edge of their lips blackened. As for the men of the Possum clan, they were born with a curved sole, like that of a marsupial's foot. As she painted a little arc inside a circle on a woman's shoulder I asked her what it represented.

"It's the print of the Possum, the father of my clan's Dreaming as well as the Jupurrurla and Jakamarra skin's clans. In the dance I learned there's only one woman who carries that design embodying Possum, the other dancers are painted with the Black Plum design."

The body paintings executed during the *incorrect* ritual were composed of many arc-prints. That is what had displeased the men when, upon their return, had seen their wives still painted. They considered those sign-prints to be restricted to men.

A few days later, thirty or so women, a dozen men and as many children, set off for The Granites. The women crammed on top of blankets and mattresses, among cans of flour and sugar, in a truck named: Possum. It originated from the first compensation awarded to the Warlpiri a few months before by the mining company that had been authorized by them to look for gold in the old Granite mine.

I was invited to make the journey on the flat back of the Toyota of my *brother*, the old bespectacled Jungarrayi. All the possessions of the family camp were piled up. I sat on them with four women and three children. At the time of departure, between our interlocking legs, two dogs found some room to nestle themselves in.

In front of us, 300 kilometers of rugged tracks. If everything went smoothly, we would need two days to travel across the Tanami desert furrowed by the running waters of the recent rainy season. The earth shone with a fluorescent green, speckled with tiny yellow, red, purple and white dots, shoots sprung up from the showers and flowers bloomed on the bushes. We were in April, in a month all of this will be dried up in the sun and melted into the ochres of the earth.

The nights of that season started getting cold. We camped on the edge of the track. Fires were lit and, as usual, single women settled down together apart from the families. Until late into the night, the campers told each other either funny or chilling stories. Words flew across the space, from one end of the camp to the other.

A young custodian of The Granites, Victor Jupurrurla, recalled the opposition that occurred there when, seeing White prospectors for the first time, the elders asked them to leave their lands. The foreigners did not understand. Later, when spears faced guns, the place became cursed.[53] For years, the Warlpiri had not returned there. Chased from their other waterholes by the arrival of cattle breeder settlers, they had become reconciled with the gold mine and some had agreed to work there for basic rations of tea, flour and tobacco.

"Now, we've got our land back," Victor continued. "If Kardiya want to start digging again, they have to pay us. With that money, we'll be able to set up wells and houses near The Granites so we can live there again. We'll organize our own school to train our children in our own ways, children who will be proud of where they come from. We can be our own bosses with the mining royalties."

Eyes lost in the stars, I tried to imagine the future of those authentic aristocrats, perhaps the last on earth. Our postmodern society was in the process of transforming them into a people of artists. I told myself that provided the mining company respects their wishes, does not touch the sacred rocks, plans its wells at the places the Warlpiri choose, and supplies them with an advantageous contract if it finds gold, then…. It was almost like a prayer addressed to the God of my childhood, or perhaps to the Dreaming spirits who protected the Australian land. Why could those who said they belong to the land as much as it belongs to them not live on it as *rentiers*?

The day broke. The magic of the light. The earth stretched as if the horizon pulled it in all directions. Small fires crackled here and there. Standing up, wrapped in their blankets, women and men warmed their hands or backs at the fire. Children off exploring the environment came back announcing they had found water. It was stagnated between the pebbles of a dry sand bed. I helped the women to fill billy cans that they placed on the fire for tea. When the water boiled it was mixed with cold. The

53. Baume, F.F. *Tragedy Track — The Story of The Granites*. Sydney: Johnson, 1933.

tea circulated from hand to hand, drunk straight from the billy can, tepid and very sweet, as the Warlpiri liked it.

Blankets were already rolled in the canvasses used as ground sheets and thrown loosely into the vehicles. A few handfuls of sand to extinguish the fires and off we went. Before us, an infinite plain. The bushes had given way to tall bright yellow grass which undulated in the wind like a wheat field. Called spinifex or porcupine grass, it cut like a blade and contained an inflammable resin that was once used as paste to hold the sharp tips on the spears and the cutting stones on the wooden axes and spear throwers.

We left the track to drive at full speed through the grass, flattening termite mounds of red earth. The car leapt in bounds, the women bounced, laughing, their eyes fixed on an invisible spot. As if at a tennis match, heads turned, anticipating the zigzags of the vehicle.

"Kangaroo," a child whispered in my ear.

We had to keep quiet. The vehicle stopped, a gun poked from a window. A shot was fired. Missed! We resumed our crazy race. Another stop, another shot, then two, three. The vehicle started again, more slowly this time. The women pointed at a trace of blood in the grass. The kangaroo was wounded and the vehicle caught up with it. It stood still for a few moments and looked at us as if it wanted to know the face of its hunters. The men seated at the front did not shoot.

The kangaroo bounced back on one leg, helping himself with his long tail. The driver got down from the vehicle. He picked up a stone and threw it. The beast toppled over. Its head injured, eyes open, it thrashed around in its blood. Shouting gleefully, the children finished it off with stones and turned the carcass on its back. It was a female. From its pouch they withdrew a miniature kangaroo, hairless and pink. The baby was alive. Delighted, the children passed it from hand to hand. In a day or two, even if it was fed, it would die for it had been weaned too early. In the meantime it became the journey's mascot.

The hide wedged between the cans and blankets, we sat on it. We needed to keep moving and take full advantage of the morning freshness — all somewhat relative. My skin was already burned and the puffs of wind were getting hotter.

At midday, huge eucalyptus trees lined the horizon. We entered the undergrowth of a Budgerigar Dreaming site. They were there, the small bright green birds, fluttering around silently from branch to branch. We climbed down from our vehicles.

"*Ngatijirri*, the Budgerigar people came here to initiate their boys and they have lost their feathers," the old Jungarrayi explained, indicating a vast swamp. "They were so numerous that they formed a giant nest with their feathers which, at the time of their disappearance beneath the earth, became that swamp called Kartarda. It's always supplied from the rain draining into a secret cave that keeps enough water for the whole year. Budgerigar is my father's Dreaming flesh."

The moment had arrived to prepare the kangaroo. A man eviscerated it through a small hole that he reclosed with a small stick. Women took turns to dig a deep pit on the edge of which they lit a huge fire. Flung into the tall flames, the carcass was turned several times until all the hair was singed. Then, the tail and front legs were cut off with an axe and the rest of the carcass thrown into the pit and covered with embers. On the pile the cut parts were laid out, sprinkled with burning cinders.

After an hour, the tail and legs were cooked. Everyone took turns to bite into the meal. It was an hour before the rest of the meat was taken out of the pit and sliced onto leaves spread out on the ground. Children gave away big chunks to groups napping in the shade of the trees. A single large kangaroo was sufficient to feed thirty people.

Pieces of meat in hand, we set off along the tracks again. The truck in which the women travelled did not have any more oil and we made a detour to ask for some at a cattle station. The reception was rather cold. Through the barbed wire of his property, the stockbreeder told us he did not have any oil for sale. We made a U-turn and the truck plunged through the brambles instead of going back to the track. Our Toyota followed. I was about to have a most wonderful lesson in bush survival.

Before us, the wreck of a crashed car. The truck piled into it in and tipped it on its side. Then the driver jumped from his cab and, armed with an old tin, retrieved the oil from the motor, using it to refill the crank-case of the truck. The abandoned car seemed to have already been used for other emergency repairs. The land carried on supplying the people as a free shop!

Two hours later we arrived at Rabbit Flat, the gas station of the South, owned by a long-bearded White man and his French wife. The Warlpiri had given to their children (twins who had been born there) local names linked to the Two-Dingo Dreaming whose ancestral trail went through that spot. But the attempt at integration failed. The pump attendant and his wife lived in the heart of the Warlpiri territory, only caring about one thing, to make their alcohol business profitable, serving it day and night through an aperture cut in a thick iron fence that went right up to the ceiling, isolating them from their customers. It was said they had settled there for shelter in case of a nuclear war.

Our vehicles filled, we continued on our journey. The track became as wide as a motorway, having recently been cleared by the workers of the mining company. Soon the caravans and corrugated iron shelters of the geologist's camp appeared. A meeting had been planned with them for the following day. That night we slept twenty kilometers away from the sacred rocks of The Granites, at the seasonal camp of Victor Jupurrurla, where a stock of jerry cans filled with water were supposed to be found.

We arrived beneath a huge tree, divided and spreading in all directions with its knotty branches.

"That tree is an Image of Possum, which has passed here after having rallied the Plum people," Nakakut whispered to me. "The Plums made a detour while it took this short cut to watch its people settle at the foot of the sacred rocks."

All the vehicles were unloaded. Some women uprooted tufts of prickly grasses using crowbars in order to spread their blankets on the ground. Others lit fires and heated billy cans. The children enjoyed themselves playing in the thickets. Noticing the jerry cans were empty, the men announced they would go back to Rabbit Flat to refill them. The women looked at each other with a knowing look and let them depart.

Returning in the middle of the night, the men shouted loudly and lustily: "Where's my wife?" All the women hid beneath their blankets, giggling like girls at boarding school. The men lurched around, knocking over billy cans, stepping on sleeping dogs. Some risked lifting up the blankets. Not a good idea. A wave of abuse forced them to lose their balance.

"Don't come any closer," shouted the women, "it's the camp of your mother-in-law!"

Faced with the taboo of the mother-in-law, the men's only option was to retreat. They settled beneath the Possum tree and sang. My neighbor pinched my thigh as a sign of connivance. They were *yilpinji*, love magic songs. The Possum Dreaming was particularly effective for seducing women. The women laughed, hearing the name of so-and-so in the middle of the verses. Reinvigorated by their songs, an audacious one rose and went in search of the one he lusted after. A new stage of the game took place. Without any discretion, among the screams of the other women, the *chosen one* left her bivouac to come and take refuge beside me. It was Pampiriya Nungarrayi. The seducer approached, laughing.

"Come here, I want you!"

He bent down over our heads.

"Here she is. And it's very good! I want them both, all the Nungarrayi for me. I'm a Jangala!"

The whole camp burst out laughing. I had to play the game.

"*Yantarra!* (Go away)," I shouted in Warlpiri. "You have a wife to make your tea. She's a Napanangka, not a Nungarrayi. You're not a Jangala but a Jupurrurla!"

A fresh burst of general laughter. The man in reality had two skin names for his parents had *wrongly* married. He was Jupurrurla by his father and Jangala by his mother. But, having married a Napanangka, as Jupurrurla are supposed to do, he could only flirt with women of that skin name, and not with Nungarrayi.

Pampiriya ran away, doubled over with laughter. The skirt-chaser followed her. She grabbed hold of a stick and stood in front of him:

"Go and lie down now, Toby. We want to sleep!"

He capitulated and rejoined the group of other men who welcomed him as a hero. The songs of seduction resumed, only to die down quickly in a series of snores. Suddenly, Toby emitted a painful cry: the name of his young wife left behind in Lajamanu. He cried and called her softly, declaring his love for her.

THE REVELATION

The geologists from the mining company did not come to the appointment near the sacred rocks of The Granites. Nevertheless the *businesswomen* danced to pay tribute to the Possum and Black Plum heroes who killed each other at that site. At the foot of the chain, where strange piled red blocks materialized the petrified bodies of the fighters, they planted two sacred poles and re-enacted that drama of the Dream Time. At nightfall, after having lit a gigantic bush fire, men and women took turns singing the long journey of their ancestral heroes.

Early the next morning, I drove the women onto a vast plain that had shrubs covered with smooth pale green balls, bush tomatoes, *ngayaki*. They systematically stripped it as in a grape harvest, filling up their cans. Upon our return to the camp, seated in the shade of the bushes, they opened each *ngayaki* with a wooden spoon and scraped out the insides to dispose of the little black seeds and its bitter juice. Prepared like that, those Indigenous tomatoes are very sweet, juicy and crisp like apples. Those not eaten straightaway were strung on long sticks to be conserved in the same manner as dried dates.

Each year, for two months, that plain supplied tons of bush tomatoes, without the necessity of treating the soil. Other resources exist in the desert. The places are known to the animals who have their seasonal routes, the same routes that the Aboriginal people used to follow to feed themselves. Do those nutritious trails echo the Dreaming trails? Have the bush to-matoes a Dreaming that traverses the plain? "No," the women replied. Their Dreaming sites are found elsewhere. On the other hand, at The Granites, the site of the Possum Dreaming, many possums lived before. When the Whites imported rabbits, their breeding supplanted the small marsupials, which have now dis-appeared from that area.

And the Black Plums? No elder remembered having ever seen any around The Granites, although there were some in an-other site of the Black Plum trail. The coincidences between the places of a Dreaming and the animal or plant of the same name did perhaps refer to the ancestral migrations of the men and women who identify themselves with that Dreaming.

At the beginning of the afternoon a young Jangala, Paddy Patrick, father of two, arrived with a video camera borrowed from the school at Lajamanu. He proposed to the campers the idea of making a documentary for the mining company so that they would understand why they had to leave the sacred rocks intact. The project enraptured everyone. While waiting for the shooting to begin at 4 p.m., the women decided to record some songs. It would serve as musical backing for the live commen-tary that Victor Jupurrurla would make, since he was the one who had started negotiations with the mining company.

A Napurrurla began a song. It was the *unknown* verses of the now famous ritual that had annoyed the men before the jour-ney. Other women joined in. They signaled me to record while the singers started to paint their bodies. The time for the video shoot approached. Jangala fixed the camera on a tripod.

The cameraman signalled to the crowd to take a course along the sacred rocks. Barefoot, wearing skirts and with their chests painted, there were around twenty who walked in a line among the yellow grass. Jangala shouted to the women to de-cide which one would scale the rocks. It was a Napangardi with huge breasts, the widow living in our house, who was unani-mously chosen. While she was being filmed, Victor, his finger raised, explained that behind that rock was the most secret part of the site, restricted to men.

Then she pointed at three waterholes in the rock: the tracks left by the heroines of the Possum Dreaming who camped on that spot. That is why, Victor pointed out, that side of the hill is called *jilimi* and is restricted to women. Recording was finished for the day. Victor's first wife, showing me the three sacred holes, two round and one elongated like a spindle, added mischievously that it looked like the hidden part of women.

The morning after, recording recommenced.

"That place is another sacred site for the women," Victor explained into the microphone. "A Possum woman stood there with her baby. She saw Possum the renegade leaving to fetch allies to fight his people. But she didn't forewarn her brothers."

The women came closer to the North side of the chain of rocks and disappeared behind a narrow passage that harbored a spring. They took the opportunity to quench their thirst. It was very hot. The cameraman followed them as far as the East side of the chain where a second spring was located and ordered them to head toward another pile of granite blocks. Shouts of disapproval from the women. It was a secret site restricted to men.

The women hesitated. In the end, Rosie Napurrurla volunteered herself and led the way, on the condition she could carry a sacred dish, which would protect her from the secret Images of the Possum Dreaming. Victor explained into the microphone that, in that spot now forbidden to women, the Possum heroines did something very secret.

At the heart of the rock chain an unexpected oasis was hidden, a sort of natural arena whose steps encircle a big pool of transparent water. The day before the women had washed there. Now, they had to dance there. Forgetting they were being recorded, they danced with all their hearts to saturate themselves with the forces of that sacred place.

Two evenings later, I was invited to the camp of the old Jungarrayi to watch the video. His elder son, the father of four children, set up the video on top of his car and unrolled one hundred meters of cable across the camps to the electrical outlet of the shower building. The spectators sat on the ground or on top of cars. As soon as the first images appeared, the women in the audience shrieked with laughter. The colors of the small screen

191

were fluorescent. The landscape vibrated under the zigzagging screen. At each flash of the red of rocks or yellow of grass, an approving breath went through the audience. Captured that way, that Dreaming site suggested another world in which the light source would not come from the sun but rather from the earth itself, walked on by the crowd as if by elves. For forty minutes, even the dogs seemed to succumb to the spell.

The following day, after the video had made the rounds of the camps, the elders decided that Victor's commentary was incomplete and had to be redone. They did not say anything about the body paintings and songs of the film, those of the famous female ritual which had scandalized them previously.

"Everything is OK now," the women told me. "We've given them a *kunari*."

Kunari, a ritual payment of flour, sugar, tea, material, blankets or sometimes even money, goods that replace food or, in the past, hair strings. I was told that upon returning from The Granites, the women had negotiated with the elders to make them accept that the so-called *wrong* Possum ritual was in fact a revelation dreamed by an important *businesswoman,* Rosie Tasman Napurrurla. The acknowledgement of every ritual innovation generally supposes discussions and the eventual retribution of the custodians concerned through the place to which it relates. By accepting payment, the elders had given their consent that the revealed ritual was integrated into the patrimony of ancestral celebrations.

"I have dreamed about Jinma (a site of the Black Plum and Possum Dreaming)," said Rosie, the initiator of the ritual, a small woman with a taciturn face. "I've spent my childhood in that area because of The Granites where my parents used to acquire their supplies of tea and tobacco from the miners. In my Dreaming, I was sitting on my own, and I heard the sound of the clapping sticks men play at the Jardiwanpa fire ceremony. I dreamed of the Emu people and I heard a new song for Janganpa. They were travelling toward Yarturluyarturlu. There, I saw the Possum women singing and painting themselves. The Possum Dreaming gave me the new songs, paintings and dances."

To my great joy, Rosie agreed to relate her dream in detail for me.

"First, I followed my *wampana* Wallaby fathers who were travelling with the Emu people. I saw the Emu paint themselves with circles, their eggs. They took me up to two rockholes near Kulpulunu, place of the Water Dreaming. They sat there in the shade. Then I followed them to Warpinypa, the place of the *kalajirdi* Grass Dreaming where the Wallabies, Emus and *kurlukuku* Doves met the fire ceremony. This is where my *kurruwalpa* (spirit-child) of the Wallaby Dreaming came into my mother to be born as me."

Rosie stopped talking and gazed in the direction of her native land.

"In my dream, I saw a baby lying on a wooden dish," she added. "I saw her rolling on the side, then crawling. Then she was bigger and grabbed a stick to get up. But she fell. My mother and my two grandmothers took her hunting. She cried and screamed: "Mummy! Mummy!" then, "Daddy's coming, *yati yati*, I'm happy!" She was able to articulate, despite her young age. She was given some meat, but she carried on screaming: "Mummy, milk!" Then, I saw her growing, making her first steps. What I saw was my *kurruwalpa* (myself as the) Wallaby spirit-child. I was travelling with my Wallaby brothers, to The Granites and Papinya. My spirit-child followed the track I was going to follow during my life: every dry season, my people used to meet other groups in Papinya. My spirit was adult, now, going back and forth between The Granites and Jinma. I saw all the Dreaming of the region: the *wampana* Wallabies, Emus and *kalajirdi* Grass. I followed them to Jarralparri and Jawalarra, two *wampana* places, my spirit-child said: "Mummy, Daddy, let's stop here." So they sat, the three of them, at Jinma, and I woke up. I dreamed the *Kurumindi lakurrlakur Yarturluyarturlu lakurrlakur* song. "In Kurumindi they were sitting in a group, in Yarturluyarturlu (The Granites)," that is the Black Plums who went underground there and the Possums. I dreamed the *Jilimi lakurrlakurr Yarturluyarturlu lakurlakwrr* song. "On the big flat *jilimi* stone, at the women's camp, were seated the Possum heroines. I saw them painting themselves with the new designs which show the prints of the possum. And they sang *Yarturluyarturlu yirrarninya Wajungunpalu lakurrpa*. They sang their *Wajungu* Possum name. They sang *Jalparla lakurrlakurr...*,

193

jalparla, the other name of the *jilimi,* and *Jilimi karlarkarlar wa-jungu pawulu karlarkarlar,* for they were seated in a line (*karlarkarlar*)."

Rosie explained to me that, after having dreamed those songs and paintings, she had taught them to some of her Napurrurla sisters and Nakamarra aunts and nieces. They had danced this new ritual in the bush for the first time over the 1983 Christmas holidays, but had to wait more than a year for a propitious opportunity, the journey to The Granites, to allow them to make the ritual public.

"The ancestral women I saw in my dream had unknown faces. They left The Granites, dancing, heading toward Kurumindi, the last of the Eastern rocks where Possum men stood. I heard the Jakamarra Possum singing his ancestral journey to the East when he went to fetch the plums as fresh supply. I followed him on the way back to The Granites where the butterfly ate the flower of the plumtree and the leaves from which grew new Plums after the old ones disappeared underground. In the new *yawulyu,* we dance the Butterfly eating the flower and the leaves. In the old *yawulyu,* we dance as if we held a flower in our hands while the singers sing about the petals flying during the trouble. For this story ask Nakakut Nakamarra who is the custodian by way of her father."

One morning, Nakakut arrived at my house asserting I could put the *Kuruwarri* in my book, the Image-story of her clan, but also that her testimony would be used first for the negotiations with the mining company. It would be the guarantee of her rights and the rights of all those linked to The Granites. She asked me to turn on the tape recorder and, with a singing voice, began to recount in Warlpiri a strange story woven with poetry and prodigies.

"Possum ran from Piyayi, heading toward Yiwalpiri. He ran toward the East while the sun rose. He went to the Alyawarri and Wankangurru tribes, looking for allies to fight in the West, against the Pintupi tribe, his own people. In Yiwalpiri, Possum, of Jakamarra skin, he found the big Black Plum people, some Jakamarra and some Jupurrurla, and the little Green Plum people, some Jangala and some Jampijinpa. Possum solicited both peoples. In great numbers, men and women agreed to follow him to fight at his side. They went as far as Mijitinya-nu where they camped. The little Green Plums asked the big Black Plums: Who are you? They replied: We are a very ripe food, a fruit good to eat. Poor little Green Plums, not being ripe enough to be eaten, they had to abandon the journey!"

Nakakut burst out laughing and told me that before I too was like the Green Plums but now I was ripe like the Black Plums, and that was why she had decided to give me the name that designates those in the songs: Nganjiljiya. I was very taken. She carried on with her story.

"Possum had rallied a small group of Possum Jakamarra and Jupurrurla in Jangankurlangu, in Warlpiri country. When he rejoined them, the Black Plum people started off again. A bird with a black beak, *yarrindakurdaku*, as small as a shrike and of Jampijinpa skin, followed them. Because it has followed the Black Plum Dreaming those birds have a black beak today. Moving away from Mijitinyanu, the Black Plum people turned to look at the Green Plum people it had left behind. They had disappeared underground, forming a big waterhole in the rock. Saddened to have lost their little companions, the Black Plums cried. In that place called Jinma, a waterhole was born from their tears.

"The Black Plums set off again behind the Possums. And now from the South another people arrived, the one of the Black Sap Leaves, *parrawuju*, some Jungarrayi, and some Japal-jarri. That Dreaming, which came from Ngarnka, decided to pursue the Black Plum. Stopping at Warntapari, the Plums rip-ened even more and formed a sort of black soup. Guided by the Possums, the black tide of the Plums moved forward. Be-hind, the Black Sap Leaves approached to attack. The bird took flight and watched the advance of enemies. Coming to a halt at Pirnki, Possums and Plums built shelters with branches to sleep under. Not far away, in Parrapardupardu, the Black Sap Leaves people settled for the night too. Early in the morning, Possum and Plums resumed their journey to Mulyukariji. Spying on the Plums, the Black Sap Leaves said to themselves: We are going to take a short cut and divide them in two. And they went, the men and the women of the enemy people, in their turn forming a black tide. They cut the black tide of the Plums in two, attacked and then disappeared underground to return to their country. The Black Plum people had succumbed to the attack. There remained only a few survivors who went underground to try to return to the East, to the country they had left. Exhausted, the Plums soon came out and began to boil. They tried to revive themselves but each time fell again. Dripping, like a torrent roused by black foam, they pierced the rocks, forming the Lirrinjarra waterhole. In a last attempt, the Plums boiled again in a multitude of bubbles, then went down underground for ever.

"From the boiling liquid a butterfly *pintapinta*, a white flower *yintilyapilyapi* and some leaves *wikirri* sprung. Possum took the flower and the leaves and set off again with the Possums of the East whom he had rallied to his cause. The butterfly followed the flower, its food, and the bird with a black beak flew at their side. On the way, the flower having wilted, the leaves gave seeds from which another Plum people grew. Arriving at the Mirnangi waterhole, Possum gathered the new Plums and his Possum companions to show them how to enter the territory of his people whom he wanted to attack. You are going to split into two groups, each will take a different path and we will meet once more at the Yunturru waterhole, he said. Possum left alone on reconnaissance by the shortest route. Stopping near a huge gum tree, ever since called Janganpa, he noted, not without annoyance, that his own Possum people were gathered not far away from there in great numbers. When his allies arrived at the gathering point, Possum explained to them: It's here we are going to fight my people. I wanted to attack later in Piyayi (in Pintupi country), but they have come here (in Warlpiri country).

"There was a big battle, opposing the Western Possums (Pintupi) with the Eastern Possums and the Plums (Warlpiri) guided by Possum, the Pintupi renegade. All of them killed each other and perished in battle. Their bodies became the granite boulders piled one on top of another at Yarturluyarturlu (The Granites). Abandoning their petrified bodies, Possums and Plums entered the earth and formed the sacred cave Mukuri. Most of the Plums, however, went underground further East, in the direction of their country, marked by another granite pile called Kurumindi and by a few isolated boulders, located on the same trajectory. As for the bird with a black beak, it became the messenger of the killings for other Dreaming people."

Having finished her story, Nakakut insisted that it was very important to write down all the other Dreamings associated with The Granites for they gave land rights to their depositories. First, the Two Serpents *warna-jarra*, a man and a woman from Jarluwanya, in the West, who stopped close to the ruins of the old goldmine where a big acacia, called Warriji, stood all alone. They witnessed the fight and carried on their way to the East, as far as Parulyu, where they hid in a spring and swallowed the two heroines of the Acacia Dreaming *watiyawarnu* who had come to draw water. There was also the Flying Serpent Dreaming *lingka* which created the spring on the South side of the granite pile. Some say the Possum women fell in love with the Flying Serpent and that, unable to console themselves after having seen him disappear, they refilled the hole he had left while disappearing with their tears.

At last, even before the formation of The Granites, two heroes from the Two-Men Dreaming, who came from Patilirri, in the East, strode for a long while across that land they dug in many places. In this way they discovered the wild carrots, *jatipiji*. By uprooting them, twice they made water rise that became the spring on the North side and the big pool around which the battle took place. A secret hill is also linked to the Two-Men Dreaming.

"When I was little," Nakakut recalled, "my mother always made me go the long way round to fetch water on the other side of that hill. And all the women repeated to the children not to go there for it was dangerous. There were *kuuku* (night spirits that steal children). We didn't go there because we were very scared. We knew that somewhere there was also two sacred places belonging to the women, but we were far from guessing they were located exactly there where we children played. Such was the secret. It was only when I returned to The Granites that I recognized the two spots we celebrate with our songs, paintings and dances: *jilimi*, the big stony platform where the Possum women camped, and the flat rock where one of them, carrying a baby, unexpectedly caught the renegade Possum on his search for allies."

Nakakut specified that part of the Possum Dreaming did not belong to her father's group but to the members of the Pintupi and Kukatja tribes, custodians of the West site, Piyayi, who lived in Balgo. She inherited from her father the land corresponding to the segment of the story between The Granites and Mulyukariji, the big waterhole in the rock in which the Black Plum ancestors changed into a torrent.

"This is the place I was conceived," she said slowly. "A spirit-child of that Dreaming entered my mother. It was living there, left by the Plums, and became flesh through me. I received its name, Nakakut, before my birth for my mother knew in dream I would come into being from that spirit. It's my secret name but you can put it in your book. I've always heard the elders saying they had been initiated to the Plum and Possum Dreaming by the father of my father."

"He was the *boss* of his clan and had a ritual authority over other clans," Nakakut continued proudly. "My father, who had taken over, transmitted to me, the eldest of seven sisters from different mothers, the responsibility of organizing the women's *business* for our Dreaming. Our only younger brother, although heir to the rights of the land between Mulyukariji and The Granites, is still too young to participate in the men's *business*. So other clans have taken over after my father's death. Those men and women, from other countries, acquired a claim on The Granites since they were born in the area at the time when their parents worked at the old goldmine."

Nakakut explained that in the past, it was not sufficient to be born on a land to own the land rights and ritual responsibility. But, as that region represented now a source of mining income, the Warlpiri tried to stand together and not to privilege some clans to the detriment of others. Fate of the place: since the mythical battle of The Granites, the Possum Dreaming rightly advised the men not to follow that murderous example and to maintain peace.

"It's not easy, White people set us against each other and money provokes a lot of conflicts between us," Nakakut remarked. "Those who talk loud and eagerly know how to be heard by Whites and gain advantages. It's not like in the past, when all of us had to submit to the Law dictated by our Dreamings. The elders have more and more trouble earning respect for those ancestral principles which should govern our rights. However, it's still thanks to that Law that we live as human beings, and not as wandering dogs."

THE VOICE OF THE NIGHTS

Nakakut returned from Yuendumu, where she had attended a meeting of the Central Land Council, gathering all the representatives of the groups who had rights on The Granites land. Being the only woman invited, she told me of her shame to have had to speak in front of so many men.

"In the plane that was taking me to the meeting, I was sick. But it was not only the flight. The night before, I had a dream. I was seated with Yakiriya and some ancestral women under a bough shade. We were getting ready for a ceremony and a crowd of Whites were taking pictures of us! My mother-in-law accosted me, very angrily saying she didn't want the Whites to take photos of us. I answered back: Don't worry! They are going to give us a truck!"

"And didn't you want to ask for a truck at the meeting?" I observed, bursting out laughing.

"That's true!" Nakakut confessed, having a laugh too.

She added that, if she had dreamed about having her picture taken, it was undoubtedly because of the photo she had asked her daughter to take, a photo of herself, her sister Beryl, me and Yakiriya, when the latter had given me a wooden egg, a sacred object of the Emu Dreaming.

"But my dream carried on. I heard two new songs, one for the Emu Dreaming and the other for the Rain Dreaming of my mother-in-law. The two trails follow each other in parallel from

North to South of the Warlpiri territory. Emu guided me. More accurately, it's the egg that has sung for me. Not the male egg that you own but its little sister, the female egg that Yakiriya has kept. I'm the one who made them for her, on the occasion of an old ceremony. The poor little egg has been separated from its brother, that's why it sang for me."

Nakakut talked at length about a long journey which, in her sleep, she had undertaken with other women, Yakiriya and Betty among them, on the ancestral trail of the Emu and the cloudmen of the Rain people. While they danced that last Dreaming, a sandstorm had awoken her in the middle of the night. She had remembered with sadness the old deceased relatives who had taught her the Rain Dreaming in her childhood. Falling back to sleep, she had resumed with a few companions that journey on the ancestral tracks. Dancing all night they were hurled from a swamp with black stones called *Black Clouds* to a site with several rockholes. They *tasted* the water from all the holes with their feet and did the same with the sea on the coast of Darwin where the brother and sister of the Emu Dreaming disappeared. Then a giant wave took them back to the swamp, the final site of the Rain Dreaming, and Nakakut had woken up.

"You know," I recounted, taking my turn, "while camping with the family of the old Jungarrayi on the way back from The Granites, I had a funny dream. I was floating with them in a kind of boat on an immense black lake. The water rose and a gigantic silhouette appeared, bigger than a mountain, very thin, with the face of an unknown Black woman. She stretched out her hand toward us, palm up, with a terribly sad look on her face. We placed a handful of earth in the hollow of her hand, that earth was in fact really our boat. The giant smiled as she disappeared beneath the water that became earth."

"You dreamed about water because the Nangala spouses of the old Jungarrayi came from the Rain Dreaming," Nakakut told me. "The gift of earth to water is a sign of a good meeting between the land of Jungarrayi and the Rain Images of the Nangala. That should be the same between you, Nungarrayi, and the Jangala who will marry you."

"The Nangala noticed that that dream had perhaps been given by *Wapirra*, the Christian Father," I said, "but that, above all, it came from the land as a sign that it welcomed me."

"It is possible that White people receive their dreams from the one they call the Word," Nakakut said. "But it is *Mungamunga* or *Yiniwurru* who gives their dreams to the women of the desert. For the men, it's different."

I was extremely excited. With the story of the oneiric revelation of Rosie for The Granites, and now with Nakakut's dream, I could at last tackle the subject which haunted me since the beginning.

"What happens when someone dreams?" I asked point-blank.

"Well, *pirlirrpa*, Kardiya would say the *spirit* or the *soul*, leaves the body and travels. If someone wakes up the sleeper too abruptly, one risks preventing *pirlirrpa* from regaining its place, loins for the men and uterus for the women. And then the person falls ill."

Nakakut explained that without a *soul* every Warlpiri becomes weaker, cannot act anymore, or concentrate. Similar to a robot whose batteries are no longer capable of being recharged, he wastes away and can die, unless in the course of another sleep the soul finds its way back to the body. Sometimes, it lodges itself in the foot instead of the belly. In that case, a ritual cure helps to direct the soul toward its vital center.

"And what becomes of *pirlirrpa* when one dies?"

Nakakut hesitated a little before answering. After a long discussion, I discovered the destiny of that individual *soul* varies according to the age of the deceased. For a child, *pirlirrpa* seems to mingle with the *kurruwalpa*, the spirit-child which, returning to the site where it had entered its mother, waits to be reincarnated into another child-to-be-born. For the youth and adults who perish through illness or a wound, the soul is condemned to wander in the shape of a dead ghost, *manparrpa*. It has to find the way of the trail of its Dreaming clan to rejoin the Dreaming time-space both subterranean and interstellar.

Sometimes the lost soul of the deceased becomes a *kurdaija*, a sort of vampire who attacks the living isolated in the bush, rendering them unconscious to drain their blood and steal their own *pirlirrpa*. The victims wake up without remembering what has happened to them, but from that day forward they are no more than a semblance of life and die soon after.

Finally, the soul of old people who die of old age are carried directly onto the way of the Dreaming time-space. It leaves the body at the moment of agony. The relatives make the dying person repeat, site by site, the steps of their Dreaming trail. And through that last journey, which makes them relive their life, their soul enters the earth at the place where the clan's dead join to find itself carried away into the sky, beyond the Milky Way. It is said that one can see the milky stain of Magellan's Little Cloud drawing slightly nearer to the Big Cloud, a sign that the two galaxies are drawing the soul into another dimension.

"But what is the relationship between that soul, *pirlirrpa,* and *Mungamunga* or *Yiniwurru?*" I asked Nakakut.

According to the anthropological literature I had read, *Yiniwurru* was a word used by women for spirit-children,[54] while *Mungamunga*, a term originating from the Northern and Eastern tribes, designated the ancestral heroines who had sown the spirit-children.[55]

"*Mungamunga* and *Yiniwurru* are the same thing," Nakakut told me. "It's like a womb, our common mother who guides the women's soul *pirlirrpa* in their sleep. She inhabits other caves and dark holes. But in dreams, she speaks to us with the body and face of who we know."

And so I learned that *Mungamunga-Yiniwurru* is a truly cosmological system restricted to women, designating the principle generating dream images. The mythical elements which appear in the dreams — landscape, animals, plants, phenomenona, ancestral heroes, spirit-children, songs — seem to be a manifestation of that *Voice of the Nights*. Feminine, for it is called *Mother*, the dreaming womb was nevertheless moved by a masculine force, *mangaya*. Phallic symbol? Rather, sexuality is transcended here in a cosmic embrace.

---

54. N. Munn. *Warlpiri Iconography.* Ithaca: Cornell University Press, 1973.
55. D. Bell. *Daughters of the Dreaming.* Melbourne & North Sydney: McPhee, Gribble Publishers & George Allen & Unwin Australia Pty Ltd., 1983; Berndt, C.H. *Women's Changing Ceremonies in Northern Australia. L'Homme* 1, 1950; Spencer, Sir B. & Gillen, F.J. *The Northern tribes of Central Australia.* London: Macmillan & Co., 1904.

Sung in the most secret feminine rituals, the *mangaya* force is the exclusive power of the desert women who often designate by that name their sacred poles. One of the rituals that aimed at activating it consisted in the *businesswomen* smearing their pubic hair with yellow ochre and depilating them by burning the hair. The depilation was carried out in the greatest secrecy during different ritual contexts: by the widows at the beginning of a mourning; by the mothers-in-law during ceremonies of conflict resolution, called *of the fire*; finally by the custodians of the Kajirri cycle just before the boys are released from their initiation seclusion.

I could not help comparing that pubic depilation with our aesthetic *ritual* of depilating our legs. Warlpiri women have virtually no hair on their limbs, which the men value as a sign of their femininity. However, men do carry out pubic depilation[56] and, in some South-Eastern tribes, the entire body was depilated during the masculine initiation. They were submitted to that ordeal prior to the marriage, using beeswax. Curiously, Warlpiri women associate the ritual with the Honey Dreaming, but they do not use wax. What was the symbolic function of the masculine or feminine depilation? To differentiate humans from animals? To remember the hairless body of the newborn babies? To control fecundity? Or to make sexual difference ambivalent?

Considering that *mangaya*, the power of the Voice of the Nights is the women's secret, I asked Nakakut if the men have another power.

"They have *maralypi*." Nakakut murmured.

During several stories narrated by women, each time they pronounced the word *maralypi*, it was always whispered and in connection with the secret site, inaccessible to women, where the souls *pirlirrpa* of the dead of a clan merge with the Dreaming time-space. Of all the sites of a Dreaming trail that place is the most sacred and most dangerous precisely because *maralypi* is there, that mysterious power which condenses all the *Kurruwari* Images of a clan. Because of that link with the dead, *maralypi* also designates a funeral ceremony which consists in *opening* a Dreaming and a site whose celebration had been

56. Peterson, N. "Buluwandi: A Central Australian Ceremony for the Resolution of Conflict." *Australian Aboriginal Anthropology*, Ed. R. Berndt. Nedlands: University of Western Australia Press, 1970.

made taboo by the disappearance of an important ritual custodian.

Nakakut told me she could not explain to me if *maralypi* operated in the men's dreams. The men simply said that their soul was guided in their sleep by a spirit-child that they incarnated. Like the women they too saw the spirit-child of a future child announcing its birth.

In reality it is often in dreams that the spirit-children signal their forthcoming birth. The stories of annunciations of birth are absolutely fabulous. I had quickly succumbed to their magic which showed the extreme poetry with which the Warlpiri handle their desires. The spirit-children often penetrated a future mother through the ingestion of a fruit or an animal which had placed itself in her path to seduce her. They were *ngampurpa*, desirable. For that reason, they could light fires, provoke conflicts and urge men to fight. That is exactly what happened in the *conception* of one of Nakakut's sons. I was also told masculine ceremonies attracted them and at that time they *caught* mothers and fathers. For the Warlpiri it was thus the children who, before being born, chose their parents.

STORIES OF SPIRIT-CHILDREN

At Mounts Yarunkanyi, one of the sites of the Initiated Man Dreaming, there are two rockholes, a big one and a small one. Between the two water flows underground. Called Yupajarrayi, they are the trace of the pits the Two-Cannibals dug to cook their victims. Having eaten, they threw the bones around them. Skulls, femurs, and ribs arc found there today in the form of little rock crystals. One of my Nungarrayi *sisters*, a small woman with sparkling eyes, told me that before having her children she had come upon that Dreaming place by chance while hunting on her own.

"Seeing the two dry rockholes, I told myself: That must be the spot where the Two-Cannibals cooked men. Suddenly I fell. To regain my senses I covered myself with wet earth. But I felt nauseous and threw up over and over again, it didn't end. That bad place had made me ill. I went back to the cattle station feeling awful. The Kardiya gave me medicines that didn't help at all. Neither they nor I knew I had been struck by a spirit-child. I had a pain in my chest, and my two legs were swollen for the child was a cannibal."

Nungarrayi had to be taken to Alice Springs. She was scared at the thought of having an amputation. That is when she felt her child-to-be inside her for the first time. At the hospital, Nungarrayi saw him in her dream coming toward her, several spears in his hand, the same spears the Two-Cannibals had made to attack humans. On his head he carried human flesh. He put down the spears and human flesh in his shaded shelter. Then he hid in Nungarrayi's belly.

"It was true, my elder son had followed me with his spirit of death. He had struck me when I looked at the rockholes at Yarunkanyi. Perhaps he came out of the hearth in which he'd been cooked by the Two-Cannibals. Eaten by them, his spirit became cannibal. He followed me to give me this dream. When my son was born, I didn't have any milk to feed him for his spirit was dry from being cooked."

Nungarrayi told me that those two Dreaming heroes killed men at the Raparrapanu rockhole. At Larrilpi they sharpened their spears and looked for other victims. Not finding any, they went to Pirpirpakarnu, the site of the Lizard Dreaming, *liwirringki*. There they killed adults and children in great numbers. Later they went to Yinilpi where they ate an old man covered with pustules. That made them so sick they had to crawl on all fours and ended up disappearing underground.

"Those two *loathsomes* got the fate they deserved! My son is from Yupajarrayi, their country. The daughter of Ngaripalang's older sister also comes from there. She bears the name of that site: Yupa. Write it down in your book, for that's the truth."

Nungarrayi had five children, all custodians of the Rain Dreaming, a totem inherited from their father, a rain-maker almost two meters tall. But each one of them possessed a different conception Dreaming. The first son from the Two-Cannibals Dreaming at Yarunkanyi was born on the Initiated Man trail of his mother and not on his father's.

"My second son, Walpajukurrpa," Nungarrayi continued, "was sitting on a tree and he flew away in the shape of a red and white cockatoo *ngarnkamarda*. The bird settled in the spinifex grass before going back to the tree. A flock of cockatoos was going from one tree to the next. I tell you the story of my son, as my husband saw it in his sleep."

Nungarrayi explained that, in her husband's dream, the cockatoo spirit-child of her second son was the image of his father, with the same face and body. Huge, he flew away, leaving behind a flock of innumerable little cockatoos. He hid in a hollow trunk and began to pick at the bark with his beak. He was hollowing the wood to go deeper into the warmth. One could hear him talk like cockatoos when they peck at wood.

"Those birds are very strong and dangerous, they make a terrible racket. The cockatoo which hollowed his hole was the spirit-child of my son. He went back to his tree. And the other birds flew off in their turn. Together, they settled near the water, at Pikilyi. It's a place for the Digging-Stick Dreaming and the Red and White Cockatoo Dreaming, near Mirrawari, a Rain Dreaming place, my husband's. Later, the spirit of my son will return forever to the trunk he'd hollowed."

Nungarrayi told me she was camping with her husband when the spirit approached their shelter, the one of the father he had chosen. Seeing his father and mother, he said to himself: "Here are the parents whom I shall enter! And he gave that dream to his father. When the husband woke up, he said to Nungarrayi: I saw a cockatoo changing into a child! A child has come to us from that bird which lives in this country, I dreamed about it!"

"And it's true, my son entered me. Soon after, I had nausea. I couldn't eat anything for the spirit moved the child inside me. The child made me sick. Later I gave birth at Pikilyi, where White people had set up a cattle station. The lady from the station took care of my baby. But he caught a chill. He almost died, my poor child! The chill struck him when he was too small! It was because of the cattle. The bullocks brought those new diseases. Fortunately, the lady gave the baby several injections to help him regain his strength and he got better. He is big and strong now, like his Cockatoo spirit!"

Nungarrayi's first daughter came from the *yurampi* Honey Ant Dreaming, the Dreaming of the Yuendumu settlement where she was born.

"I was carrying my son at the time, still young, on my shoulder. While digging the ground, I found some honey ants in great numbers. I filled my billy can. On the way back to the camp, I suffered a sudden terrible headache and I said: What is it that I've caught? Perhaps it's not ants I'm carrying. It was my daughter who caused those disturbances. She said: Hey, mummy! Why have you been seeking those honey ants? It's me who looks after those ants, me, Malkirri! Now I'm coming back with that name you have buried!"

The spirit-children could be embodied in the newborn babies with the memory of the deceased bearing the same name which had inhabited them previously. If the identification of the Dreaming and the conception place did not provide any sign for such an ancestral name, in the past the child was given the Warlpiri name of a long-deceased relative, often a brother of the father's father, for the boy, and a sister of the mother's mother, for the girl. That naming happened during the weaning. Today many youngsters only bear an English name acquired at birth.

"That's true, we buried the old Malkirri, my mother-in-law. And her spirit-child took refuge in that honey ant's hole. It returned to its Dreaming place. I saw the body of my future daughter covered with round black spots — ants. Then she told me: Yes, I look after the ants! Other men and women came to hunt nearby and they found nothing. But you, mummy, you came to me. That's how the baby who made me sick talked: Me, the spirit of your mother-in-law, I went to your husband, my son, so that he'd become my father. I came to you, my new parents!"

Nungarrayi explained that the spirit of her daughter having entered her, she could not bear eating meat. So the taboo, which forbad pregnant women from eating certain game on the pretext that it would place the child or the mother's life in danger, became here a physical repulsion. The child was born at the camp, like her brothers. But the nurse took her away to wash her and put a diaper on her before bringing her back to the young mother.

"When he saw the baby coming and me breast feeding her, my son said: Mum! Throw away that filthy baby, it's no good to give her your milk! I replied: The poor baby, she's your little sister! My son cried: No! No! Throw her away! That's my milk she's drinking! He was jealous, my son, for I was still breast feeding him. So the nurse took the baby away to feed her instead of me."

The boy must have been around two, an age when the little Warlpiri can already master speech very well. Traditionally, Aboriginal women rarely weaned their children before they reached four. I asked Nungarrayi why her daughter was called *warungka*, a word for mad or deaf-mute. I learned that when she was a teenager, she camped with a friend, a girl who had an illicit affair. That transgression made her momentarily mad, and ever since, she has had to take pills regularly. Each time she forgot to take them, she became paralyzed and slept.

"My poor little one," Nungarrayi concluded sadly, "she was married at fifteen but her husband agreed to let her go for she didn't want to stay with him. Since, my daughter lives with us. She's a good girl, she's twenty now, but she's not interested in boys."

Soon after her daughter's birth, Nungarrayi's husband was employed again by the boss of the cattle station, and the whole family left the Yuendumu Reserve. One day as they were going hunting, Nungarrayi carrying her daughter on her shoulders and the two sons walking in front, they saw a kangaroo.

"My husband fired, hitting the kangaroo in the hip. It fell. It was not an animal he killed but his daughter. He didn't know it. There, under the tree, was that little girl and he had shot her in the hip, making the bones split. Our son Walpajukurrpa picked up the animal. His father and he made a fire to cook the meat. They cooked my daughter! The sun was at its highest and we ate, leaving nothing!"

Back at the camp, Nungarrayi could not swallow anything and during her sleep she had a dream.

"When I woke up, I told my husband: It's not a kangaroo you killed! It's a little girl, you shot the hip of the child whose mother I am! I saw her coming toward me, like that, holding her hip and limping. She told me: I entered your belly! Mummy, I entered you because Daddy was shooting me. I felt her inside me. That's why I couldn't eat or drink."

Nungarrayi specified that her second daughter was born with a bone at her hip that stuck out because of her husband's shot.

"I said to myself: Oh! That bone is bad, perhaps she will not be able to walk! And I asked myself if I would keep her. I said to my husband: That child is not well, she is handicapped! He replied: The poor girl, keep her! But I was not convinced: No, look, the bone is deformed and sticks out! In the past, if it was like that, we didn't keep handicapped children. My husband insisted: Keep her, it's because of the Kangaroo I killed. I kept that child who has the Kangaroo Dreaming *marlu*. I took her to the reserve, where the nurse asked me: What's that bone sticking out of her hip? I explained that came from her Dreaming. When my daughter grew up, the bone went back into the body by itself, and she was able to walk. My husband said: You see, our child is healthy and you wanted to get rid of her!"

The birth marks on the body and every other sign, dreamed or not, helping to identify the ancestral links of a Warlpiri, were traditionally at stake in territorial strategies. The interference of mothers and relatives in the interpretation of those signs counterbalanced the tendency to patriclanic monolithism. Sometimes the situation implicated a tribal consensus. That way a whole generation of children born in Lajamanu have Wallaby for conception Dreaming, a totem whose trail crosses the community and which gives them a legitimacy of residence over that land which used to belong to the Kurintji.

Nungarrayi finally told me the story of her youngest. At the foot of a big plum tree located near the Yuendumu settlement, in a suitcase containing female ritual objects, was his spirit-child.

"He was holding in his hand a light like a firebrand. My brother-in-law saw him and informed his wife: A child came from the men's ground. He climbed to the top of my shelter! He was not alone, another spirit-child accompanied him, his female companion. They took refuge in our camp. My sister replied: My poor child, you've seen two children, right? He explained to her: They came during the day and made me sleep in order to show themselves in my sleep!"

It was an opportunity for me to learn that it was not uncommon for someone other than the mother or father to receive the sign of a future birth. Here, it was the brother-in-law, Warntapari, so-called, for he had been *conceived* in a place of that name, crossed by his Rain Dreaming and the Black Plum Dreaming.

"He had said it right, the old man. My husband and I shared his camp, and it was in me that the spirit-child entered to become the little Pana! As for the girl accompanying him, she entered one of my Napurrurla cousins."

Nungarrayi explained that the two spirit-children came from the Goanna Dreaming *pilja*.

"That's what happened. My cousin was caught by the little spirit-girl while camping with her group on the land of the Goanna Dreaming at Yinapalku. She put on a ritual headband without knowing her daughter was hidden there and went to Yuendumu. My son, in order to follow his little companion, hid in the spear-thrower.

"On arrival in Yuendumu, they settled in the suitcase containing the sacred objects of the Goanna Dreaming. And they hung about in the camps. We could see something like two blue jumping lights around the plum tree where our ceremonial ground was. All the women saw those lights. We thought they were the signs of bad spirits. No, they were only two spirit-children who wanted to be born together."

The identification of a Dreaming and the land of origin of Nungarrayi's last child had been the object of a genuine investigation in the fabulous world of the spirits. The deduction of the Dreaming and the place of a child's conception often provoked the ingeniousness of his relatives, a mix of poetry and politics.

Traditionally, if the place seen in dream was not indexed in the ancestral cartography, one had to find signs helping to link it to an existing Dreaming. That place could be integrated in a totemic trail found nearby and given a toponym that would constitute a new verse integrated in the cycle of songs celebrating that totem-Dreaming. As in the case of the verses transmitted for generations, the new verse became the secret name of the child.

In the past, it has also been the case that when a child was born into an expanding clan, his place of conception was located in a *No Man's Land* and he or she was characterized by a Dreaming-totem without a clan trail. That allowed the grown-up child to start up his own clan and elaborate a corresponding trail from his conception dream. Generation after generation, rights were adapted to the needs of men's survival, always guaranteed by the Dreamings.

Kajingarra Napangardi painted *kana* Digging Stick leads the *kirda* bosses of that Dream Lorna Fencer Napurrurla (on the right) acts as *kurdungurlu* manager, Lajamanu, 1984.

PART FIVE

(1984)

THE BLACK DOG

September 1984. The end of the cold season was approaching but the nights were still chilly, and the wind blowing up as if a storm were coming. Janjiya, an old Nakamarra custodian of the Curlew Dreaming fell very ill. Neither the massages of the women, nor the medicines of the health clinic had managed to relieve her. She proclaimed she was going to die. The Voice of the Nights had predicted it to her by revealing the Black Dog in her sleep, the one every Warlpiri dreads to see.

When he comes close to you in a dream, licks his lips in a smooth manner and scratches your shoulder in a sensual way, it is the sign of approaching death, probably yours. Nakamarra was prepared to die and nobody tried to force her to eat, take her medicines or protect herself from the cold. Not any longer.

Was she condemned beyond hope? I proposed to my companions to take care of her in our house. At first there was a slight reticence. They probably feared the patient dying in our place. Eventually they agreed, in that way giving a sign there was still some hope. Nakamarra let herself be carried from the camp, where she slept under the stars, into the house where we made a place for her between the mattresses of the other tenants. Washed and dressed with clean clothes, she agreed to eat a little and take her medicines.

Her hips were swollen from dehydration and the pain prevented her from standing up. I massaged her several times a day.

217

Each evening, after hours of immobility and silence, her eyes closed or open, she was seized by verbal delirium and spasms that shook her violently. They continued into her sleep with murmurs and screams, the words always incomprehensible.

After a few days, she asked me to lay her down beneath the shade of a tree in our enclosure. I went back to the house to do some typing when suddenly a vicious barking broke out. Through the open door, I caught sight of a female dog rummaging in the stone container where the women placed their bottles of oil for painting and other bric-à-brac. I approached and found in the bottom of the container a second dog rolled in a ball, shaking and barking too. The intruder withdrew a few steps before coming back immediately to lean across the container. This little game was repeated several times.

I pushed aside the undesirable dog and looked in carefully at the other one. A slimy substance was coming out of her, that she was licking steadily, revealing a tiny black thing, so small, fragile and unreal that I felt my throat knot with a strange emotion. I could not hold back my tears, I was completely moved, as if I sympathized with an irrational pain. Was it not simply an animal having a premature delivery? I went out on the veranda.

"The dog has had a pup!" I said to my patient. "But it's real tiny."

Nakamarra, as if she already knew the birth had just happened, remarked in a grave tone:

"It is black, isn't it?"

I nodded, the pup was as black as its mother was grey. Again, I felt totally shattered. A gruesome shiver went through me. The word *black* became the abyss of an endless night. The day after Nakamarra had completely recovered. I confessed that when the pup was born I had cried.

She looked straight into my eyes with her strange smile which reminded me each time of the *babayaga* of Slavic tales of my childhood.

"The Black Dog of my dream has gone. You've fixed me."

For a few seconds my mind reeled. There was a relationship between the image of her dream and the dog's delivery, as if the dreaming obsession of Nakamarra had been made flesh to exorcize her disease. And me, a witness from both sides of the story, had I become the involuntary catalyst?

Two nights later, when Nakamarra had returned to her camp, my companions had a fit of giggles. Between chuckles, I heard:

"Kajirri has eaten her pup!"

Irony of the spells. Our dog, which bore the name of the Kajirri initiation ceremony, had swallowed the thing she had given birth to, exactly like the Kajirri heroines are reputed to *swallow their sons*, the novices, in order to engulf them for the duration of their initiation in the subterranean depths and Dreaming time-space. Simple coincidence or the destiny of her name?

In any case, it seemed that the words *Kajirri* and *Black Dog* had played a role of transference which had allowed the recovery. The pup had come to materialize the Black Dog of the Dreaming and to suppress another possible development of that image — the death of Nakamarra. The fact that the dog bore the name of mythical heroines considered as initiators, that is to say *rites of passage mediums,* had allowed the place of a possible transference to be made out of her momentarily.

That her pup was premature confirmed that it had another destiny than that of living. As for my own intervention in that *cure*, it was induced when I invited the patient into the house, then attended the birth. When the dog re-ingested her pup, the coincidence with the attribute of the *ogresses* of the Kajirri heroines became a pretext to laugh, for the dog seemed to perform a role without her knowledge.

Of course, the pup digested by its mother did not prevent the Black Dog from returning to haunt Nakamarra or anybody else in their sleep. But it was not a question of a reversible process like the eternal return. Rather, similar to a feedback in an infinite spiral, the passages from dreaming to awakening were numerous and constituted, from the Warlpiri point of view, the condition itself of the development of things and their transformation.

To be born, in Warlpiri, is said *palkajarri*, to become flesh. What becomes flesh in a human being is a spirit-child, that is to say a virtuality of life crystallized in the verse of a song sown by the

Images produced by a Dreaming name. In that sense, the human development materializes words, images and a rhythm at the same time. And everything reproduced outside the human is equally a manifestation of images and sung words coming from the Dreaming time-space.

The Warlpiri philosophy does not set images in opposition to the substance or essence of things. The two are indissociable. If every hero or heroine is *Kuruwarri*, Images that unroll in the stories and register as visible traces in the sites, he/she is also *Kuyu*, Flesh which gives form and substance to all that bears his/her name: the clans, animals, plants, phenomenona, etc.

A Warlpiri man or woman talks about their Dreaming, their totemic name, as well as their Flesh which they share with their mythical ancestors, the members of their clan and the things that act as totems: the goannas, yams, rain, stars or digging-sticks. Without Dreamings, that is without original names, all things that exist would not be. The words are in a sense a guarantee of the fact that the real is already in the image: the Kangaroos can only exist because, while saying the word "kangaroo," one perceives corresponding images that allow the numerous forms and substances which give meaning to that word to be recognized. But, on the other hand, without movement which animates the images, the names could not materialize.

The Warlpiri do not conflate dream and reality, but build their relationship upon a discrimination other than our opposition between imaginary and real. The cosmology is explained as a movement to and fro between *kankarlu*, the *above* which refers to the present and all that constitutes the celestial and terrestrial environment, and *kanunju*, the *below* which refers to the past, the underground, the interstellar space and all that can occur. In certain circumstances, the *above* is identified with women, and the *below* with men. Finally, one is sometimes synonymous with public and the other with secret. One could also translate the *above* as the manifest and the actual, the *below* being the latent and the virtual. In other words, beneath all apparent things hide secret principles. What men virtualize, for example, reproduction, women actualize by giving birth.

Ritual life consists in reaching the world of the *below* by way of the fabrication of forms from the *above*, songs, paintings, dances and coded gestures, which in this way acquire a sacred and secret attribute. In that process, the role of men and women differ. Women transform *below* into *above* by giving birth to embodied spirit-children as well as by propagating the forces of the Dreamings in their rituals. In reverse, men transform *above* into *below*, by making the boys *die* and *be born again* through initiation and by going into the sacred caves forbidden to women. As for the dreaming experience, it is, for both sexes, a journey into a dimension situated at the crossing of the *below* and the *above*.

Whether it be in sleep or while awake, the Warlpiri distinguish *true* from *false*, *lying,* or *mad.* Falsification and lie are a deceitful use of language, while madness is a disorientation, a lack of reference marks which beacon the paths of speech. That is the reason why the term *warungka* (mad) also designates babies, the very old, those who lose their way in the bush and deaf-mutes. It is the absence of recognition of words and places which makes the vision and hearing incomprehensible while awake or in sleep. The discourse becomes *senseless* in the proper and figurative sense.

It is amusing to note that in the XVth Century, the French *rêver* (to dream) was *desver*, a word derived from the Latin *esver*, which meant *wandering* and gave the word *endever*, to go mad. In our tradition, the dream was thus also linked to spatial and mental disorientation.

Twenty years before the story of the Black Dog, Nakamarra, who had just arrived in the old reserve, following a long delirium, received the revelation of a ritual for women and another for men. Everything had started with that bough shade where the suitcase in which she kept her sacred objects was to be found. One day, upon her return from the mission where she worked as a cook, she was told that her sacred objects had burned. Flames had mysteriously sprung up from her shelter and, although her companions from the camp had tried to smother the fire with branches, it only extinguished after consuming her suitcase. Straightaway, Nakamarra thought: It's a spirit of the Fire Dreaming which has thrown a spark in my suitcase. Why though?

221

"A terrible sadness took hold of me and I lay down," Namamarra told me. "That night, in a dream, I saw two Nangala coming toward me, each carrying a sacred board *yukurrukurru*. They shook them while dancing and put them down before me when they sat. Then a crowd of women of the Dreaming arrived and danced, I didn't know their faces. On the other hand I recognized in the two Nangala, two of my *daughters-in-law*. When they danced, I saw myself looking at them. And I felt ill each time I caught sight of the boards they were carrying in their hands. Those boards were painted with designs I didn't recognize. Seeing them in dream really weakened me."

Waking in the morning, Nakamarra was so exhausted, she had to go to the health clinic. The nurse, panic-stricken by her strange state, wanted to send her to the hospital in Darwin.

"But I knew I wasn't really ill. It was only the dream which hit me too hard. The spirit of my dead mother and all those women of the Dreaming had taken hold of the forces of my spirit, making me act mad. Remaining in the health clinic for the night, I had the same dream again. The day after, some women came to visit me, among them my two *daughters-in-law*. As soon as I saw them, I pointed to them with my finger and shouted: You two! I can still see you dancing! I was delirious."

Nakamarra stayed at the health clinic for one month, one month of delirium. Night after night, she dreamed of the same thing, otherwise she dreamed of new things which related to her first dream. Meanwhile, two of the men elders received similar dreams. Nakamarra recovered her health. She asked the women to come together with the men. They all came to the camp where her shelter, with her sacred objects, had burned. It was the Mosquito camp which borders Lajamanu on the West side.

"I said to the women: I'm going to give a new *yawulyu* to the Nangala and Nampijinpa, custodians of the Fire Dreaming. And to the men, I announced I was going to give them a new *purlapa* for the Jangala and Jampijinpa, custodians of the sacred site Jurntu. They listened to me."

Nakamarra taught the women and men a new way to paint their bodies, and to sing and dance in celebration of the Fire Dreaming of Jurntu.

"If I had seen in my dream my two *daughters-in-law*, it was because their deceased fathers, two Jampijinpa, wanted to use me to teach us how to celebrate the Fire Dreaming in a new way. It's one of them, Munkurturru, who had set fire to my belongings. The spirit of my dead mother told me."

The two deceased Jampijinpa were the custodians of the Rain Dreaming in Lungkardajarra. In her dreams, Nakamarra saw them in the company of a third Jampijinpa, Werrilwerrilpa, custodian of the Fire Dreaming in Jurntu, who was killed by his brothers because of a transgression when she was small.

"I saw the spirits *manparrpa* of the three Jampijinpa lighting a big fire in Kartarda (a site of the Budgerigar Dreaming). The three men carried on their way, flying toward the North to arrive at Lajamanu. I heard the music of clapping boomerangs and I came closer to the place where the sound seemed to be coming from. It was the big hollow trunk of the Mosquito camp. I said to myself: Well! They are singing a *purlapa*! Then, all the men of Lajamanu appeared and sat down near the ceremonial shelter. The three spirits came out of the tree trunk. They wore a head dress, *kutari*, very big with a tuft of emu feathers on the top. The Fire and Python Dreamings *pirntina* shone in red on their bodies covered with white down. At the same time, I saw big white clouds coming, carrying rain. A fourth spirit accompanied them on their journey but he didn't stop, carrying on his flight, far away, toward the North, as far as the sea. He dove into the ocean and re-appeared, forming huge splashes. Seeing the sky, he said to himself: I've gone too far. He turned back to land here, in Lajamanu, on the landing strip. He brought back a spear that he brandished to dance at the meeting with his three newly found companions. Then the Munkurturru spirit exclaimed: Look! *Kamangirpa*!"

Nakamarra explained to me that Kamangirpa, which designates that type of spear, is also the name of that fourth spirit of death. In her dream, she followed the four spirits to Palwa, a sacred site of the Wallaby Dreaming *wampana* that women usually cannot approach. But it was there the dreamer saw them showing the men of Lajamanu the *purlapa* dance, which mimes the murder of Werrilwerrilpa and her arrival at Kamangirpa, the man with the spear.

"You saw that dance in your country when our men came to present it to your people," Nakamarra reminded me. "Would you believe it, the Voice of the Nights took us beyond the sea, further than the Kamangirpa spirit which had plunged into it! The men are proud of the *purlapa* I gave to them and, each time they dance it, they have to *pay* me the *kunari*. But, when they accepted the *purlapa* and danced it for the first time, it was me who had to *pay* them the *kunari*: dampers (flatbreads) and tea. The women to whom I had given the *yawulyu*, the Nangala and Nampijinpa, helped me to pay the *kirda* custodians and *kurdungurlu* managers of the Fire Dreaming."

After that ritual gift, the *kirda* men made *yukurrukurru,* two sacred boards, for Nakamarra so that she could paint the designs she had seen in her dreams on them. Except for the digging-sticks and the fighting sticks which are used as sacred poles, it was always the men who carved wooden objects.

It was twenty years before Nakamarra received a new revelation, this time for her own Dreaming, *wirntiki* Curlew. That happened when she camped with her niece in Yiningarra, her Dreaming place she had not visited for a very long time. The niece dreamed about the *kunarnturu* Bean Dreaming whose people followed the smoke of the beans they cooked on their way until they disappeared underground, whence came out the Curlew Dreaming. Nakamarra dreamed about the Curlew, the bird-man who saved his people from a gigantic bush fire coming from Jurntu. She saw the Kajirri heroines burning their pubic hair before leading the boys underground for the initiation. She saw women dancing and painting themselves in a new way while singing new songs. Nobody contested her vision. Nakamarra had already proved she was a dreamer chosen by the ancestors.

THE SHIELD CEREMONY

Three twelve year-old Jungarrayi had illicitly entered the shop's store to steal fizzy drinks. The Chief of Police threatened to call in a magistrate who dealt with young offenders. The elders, refusing any interference by the Kardiya in what they considered to be their own business, decided to show the aspiring delinquents their traditional authority. Although still a bit young, the three offenders were captured and submitted to all the trials of the Kurdiji *Shield* initiation.

I was extremely happy to witness that ceremony again. Five years earlier, I had had a bit of trouble following its different stages. Disorientated by the nocturnal moves of the participants, I had been swept up by the magic of a mysterious spectacle. After all, the Warlpiri sometimes call their rituals, *manyu*, a term meaning play and pleasure.

For the first ritual evening, a field was cleared on the East border of Paddy Japaljarri's camp, as two of the boys were his twin sons. Their father's sisters Napaljarri and their *mothers* Nakamarra, that is to say besides their actual mothers, their co-spouses and real and clan sisters, painted their chests with the *liwirringki* Lizard Dreaming, associated with circumcision. In each cycle of the Shield ceremony, the *mothers* and the father's sisters of the novices have a crucial role to play. In fact, it is only after playing that role in several initiations that women become *businesswomen.*

225

The painted women danced, immediately followed by the men who struck the ground with the shield which gives its name to the ceremony. On their bodies, covered with white down, were traced the red designs representing the wild fruit *markirdi*, associated with the Initiated Man Dreaming. Whatever the clan Dreaming of the novice, the Shield initiation always refers to that Dreaming of the tree-man children of the stars who inaugurated it.

On the East and West of the ceremonial ground, two shelters made from branches represented the ancestral shelter that fell from the sky and changed into the long hill at Kulungalinpa. At nightfall the men sat down to sing, their eyes turned toward the East, staring at the stars whose trajectory indicated the various stages of the night. Behind them, women and children settled, taking turns to dance. Behind their backs, hidden by the Western shelter, the three novices sat cross-legged, heads bowed, in the company of some Jangala brothers-in-law, their ritual tutors. Every half hour, they were made to stand and look up, arms folded behind their necks, and follow the course of Mars chasing the Pleiades across the sky.

Just before day break, at the appearance of the Morning Star, the tutors made the novices pass among the women, as they had to rejoin the men. It was a very solemn moment, contrasting with the merry atmosphere of the night. The *mothers* massaged the boys and gave them each a firebrand, that had passed from hand to hand during their dances, in order for the boys to light the first fire of the day, in this way marking the beginning of their retreat into the bush that would last for one week.

In the past, novices were taken on foot on an initiation journey lasting several months. They used to visit different local groups without being able to see any woman, receiving from all their potential fathers-in-law ropes made out of hair, intended for their fathers and mother's brothers as an offer of alliance. Today such journeys usually occur from one community to another by car.

The *mothers* and father's sisters had organized a special camp during the day where they painted themselves and danced their respective Dreamings to give strength to the future initiated. Three times a day they prepared and cooked food for the recluses and their tutors who came to fetch it and tea. At the end of the week, a hundred women brought their blankets and big billy cans of tea into that camp so that a truck could take them away to a new ceremonial ground.

At sunset half of the painted women, followed by others and numerous children, passed under the barbed wire that lined the landing strip, crossed it and sat down at the edge of the scrub. For half an hour everyone waited, in strained silence. Finally the expected howling occurred, emitted by an elder. We hurried past the prickly bushes to arrive at the old landing strip furrowed by several seasons of rain. The men's silhouettes appeared, merging into the shadowy light of the sky the sun had left behind.

The *mothers* and aunts moved toward the novices whose shoulders they tapped with the sacred boards they had painted during the day. Then they disappeared behind the new shelter made from branches located on the West of the ground. The other women and children sat in front, rejoined by the novices' *fathers* and mother's brothers who sang, facing the rest of the men settled in the East, against the other shelter. All of a sudden they rose and the *mothers* and aunts came out of their hiding places to join them. We followed to sit there, our gaze turned toward the East.

A hand forced me to bow my head. The men sang a very guttural chant. I heard footsteps, hoppings, cries set to the rhythm of breathing — the men were dancing. It was forbidden for women to look. A fresh signal, it was finished. We went back to sit against the Western shelter. There the *mothers* and aunts, covered with the ritual headband *minyeri* — a hair string smeared with red ochre — danced, accompanying their moves with little cries: "Pou! Pou!" Like the Digging-Stick heroines who received such a headband from Goanna, they hopped, their legs slightly parted, palms open to the sky as if weighing a necklace in their hands, from time to time flinging a hand behind their ear as if pushing aside very long hair.

The men called for all the little boys to come near the Eastern shelter where they were decorated with two vertical white lines on their chest and a horizontal one on their nose. As a joke the men asked the boys if they had a sister to offer in marriage. The little ones, holding a stick on their neck, were ordered to make a turn around the dancing women, who pretended to be scared, laughing, and encouraging the boys.

Night had fallen. Women and children set off again to sit in the East, this time their backs against the shelter and their eyes turned toward the West. In front, the seated men sang. A huge fire was lit, around which a line of dancers appeared, stomping from one foot to the other, their knees high, beating the air with their hands as if juggling. Decorated with white dots on their chests, a special design representing the stars, together they bent down over the fire and lifted it with their hands, producing a shower of sparks that made the women scream with laughter and scatter.

Three women each seized a novice whom they placed on their shoulders and took flight toward the East, followed by the other woman and children. In that way they re-enacted the kidnapping of the little hero of the Initiated Man Dreaming, who was carried away through the air on the back of the seductress of the Rain Dreaming. For years, furious that she had taken him away from his seclusion, he refused her advances, until eventually he ended up succumbing to her charms and they had a little girl.

After a short walk, the three novices were set down and laid their backs against the chests of the three *mothers* who were stretched out side by side. Some women lifted the novices' heads to make them drink fizzy drinks and eat bread with corned beef. After that modernization of the ritual meal they massaged the boys as they sung. They reminded them of the secure comfort of their world and placed them on their guard against man's world, repeating the ritual formula:

"Do not follow your brother's path, go your own way." Meaning, do not covet the women promised to others.

The Nungarrayi *sisters* of the novices began to dance, and I was pushed into doing the same, for the twins were my *brothers*. In the past, at the final moment of the boys' circumcision, the real sisters underwent, on the side, a ritual scarification, marking their solidarity with the circumcised. Most of the women over thirty bore the trace of that now abandoned practice, scars in the form of a line or arc between the breasts, or on the belly if the woman was pregnant at the time, or breastfeeding a child.

A disturbing silence followed until a signal indicated that we could approach the ground. Two Jungarrayi came to recover their little skin *brothers*. A further wait and the *mothers* moved toward the novices to lay them down, their backs against the stomachs of three of their *brothers-in-law* lying down one against the other on the ground.

Eight in the evening. Scattered here and there, fires were lit and blankets spread for the *break*. Some men sat a few meters away from the women and commenced a cycle of songs relating the story of the transgression of an ancestral hero who slept with his mother-in-law. The women responded by cracking dirty jokes at the singers. The other men disappeared behind the Western shelter to perform secret dances.

Two hours later they came back very happy, pretending to burn the blankets of the women who were also laughing. The women rolled up blankets to clear a space for dancing just behind the men already seated, ready to sing. Turning their backs on the assembly, the three novices and their tutors settled near the Eastern shelter. Past midnight, the tutors erected three spears, on which they suspended piles of material, presents destined to their mothers-in-law, the mothers of the novices. At once they made the mothers rise and, passing through the assembly, go and sit against the other shelter.

The singers, retracing stage by stage the trail of *ngarrka*, the Initiated Man Dreaming, recalling *ngapa* and *kana*, the Rain and the Digging-Stick Dreamings he met. Each time a song referred to the Digging-Stick heroines, the female dancers took hold of a tall branch reaching their waist and mimicked the dancing-walking of the ancestral women who planted their sticks to grow acacias and sow spirit-children. At other moments, they passed around the three firebrands with which the novices had lit their seclusion's hearth the previous week.

All of a sudden, three old women rose brandishing sacred boards. The men sang the Kangaroo Dreaming *marlu*. What that Dreaming gave to the men cannot be revealed, say the Warlpiri and their Western neighbors, all of them associating it with the initiation. Any reference to circumcision is so secret that the word that designates it is never publicly used. If women have rituals for numerous Wallabies Dreamings, they have none for the big Kangaroo. To celebrate the corresponding trail, they paint and dance the Lizard *liwirringki*.

However, in the Shield ceremony, the women's sacred boards are exceptionally painted with a design of the Kangaroo Dreaming. The dance with those boards announces the crucial moment of the night: the novices' real mothers each hand down a firebrand to the respective mothers of those they have chosen as future mothers-in-law for their sons. It is with that ritual of the firebrand that the assembly discovers the decision of alliance, the promise of marriage passed between the women of the matrilineage of a new initiated and that of his future spouse who is often not yet born. It has to be emphasized that the prohibition forbidding a boy (or any man) to ever associate with his promised mother-in-law (or any woman in that skin category) prevents risk of incest, the risk being that he could become the father of the girl he will have to marry.

The men, for their part, chose for the boy a circumciser who, in that way, also becomes a potential father-in-law. Traditionally, although they secretly take counsel together, the choice of men and that of women does not necessarily coincide. If the chosen circumciser and mother-in-law were not married or promised to each other, and so were not predisposed to have a daughter together, the circumcised could claim the daughter of one or the other, even the two of them. This on the condition he fulfilled his duties of assistance toward his circumciser and his mother-in-law, promised during the years preceding the wedding. Sometimes promises were renegotiated, especially if a promised mother-in-law did not give birth to a daughter.

Around six in the morning the songs and dances stopped. The novices, smeared with red ochre from head to toe and covered with tufts of white down, passed among the women. The *mothers* stretched out their arms to pluck off tufts and place them in their hair. Then we ran to sit against the Eastern shelter. Two young Jungarrayi bent down, threw dust in the air and, running, one toward the North, the other toward the South, accomplished a big semi-circle before meeting behind the shelter. Then the women covered their heads with blankets.

I heard footsteps and a repetitive song whose words did not sound like the Warlpiri tongue. The men laughed and the song came to an end. Silence. The same ritornelle started again, accompanied by a sound of shaken leaves right behind our backs, as if something was moving in the branches of the shelter. In reality, the men were hiding the ritual objects they had used for the secret dance. Among the novices' father's sisters, those having already taken part in several Shield ceremonies do not have to lower their heads, they are authorized to see the designs painted or carved on objects: shields, big mother of pearl shells or poles. As for me, I would not have a chance to see them.

Seven rather old male dancers, painted with circles on their torso, now moved one behind the other, stamping the ground very hard with each foot. The first and last had a tuft of emu feathers fixed at the bottom of their backs. When they sat around the fire, the women carried the novices on their shoulders again, followed only by the *mothers*, the aunts, the sisters, as well as a Napanangka, *maternal grandmother* of the novices and a Napurrurla *maternal grandmother* of their future spouses. I was invited to attend the very moving ritual about to take place. We went much further than the previous day, taking shelter in the scrub.

Before I had noticed, some women uprooted bushes to clear a small space where the novices were stretched out upon the three *mothers*. The novices were fed with tea and a damper, then smeared with red ochre. They looked exhausted. The ritual headbands taken from the heads of their mothers were placed on their heads. All the *mothers* sat behind those lying down and rocked the boys to the rhythm of a monotonous song. In front the aunts made waves on the boards painted with the Kangaroo design, then pressed them firmly on the backs of the novices, imprinting the sacred Image. When the boys lifted their heads again, they were ready to cry. One clutched a toy truck in his hand.

Having dug a round pit, the women lit a fire that they covered with eucalyptus leaves, emitting a very strong menthol smell and a thick smoke. The *mothers* set the three boys upright in the pit and made a tight circle around them. The other women pressed around, singing. The Napurrurla and the Napanangka took hold of the heads of the boys and pressed firmly on them. The group, screened by the smoke, had become a sort of spiral about which one did not know if it was going in or coming out of the earth. A reminder of the traditional smoking practiced on a newborn and its mother just after birth. I was overwhelmed by that simulacrum of the passage from one world to the other.

Leaving the pit, each woman *dipped* her foot in to absorb the power of the Dreaming that supposedly arose from it. The boys were seated again on their *mothers,* between their backs and the bellies of their *mothers* the long hair rope *makarra* (matrix) used in healing rituals and to link sacred *witi* poles was stretched, then shaken. The boys withdrew. On each side of the three *mothers* the others stretched out, all gripping the three poles arranged in a line end to end. The aunts pulled them up to set the women on their feet again, miming in that way the Milky Way associated with the Initiated Man Dreaming.

The boys received the three firebrands, a sign of their future alliance, and threw them on a little hearth made for that purpose. Then we left. Two men were waiting for us halfway. The sisters accompanied them to take the novices back to the ground and returned. The *mothers* went in turn to collect the materials and hair ropes from the three spears. They spread those gifts on the ground and, two by two, a Japaljarri *father* and a Jakamarra *mother's brother* of the novices helped themselves. The *mothers* took away what was left in buckets and we returned to Lajamanu as fast as we could.

Seven in the evening. After a long day of waiting, we set off once more for the ceremonial ground. In the afternoon, the *mothers* had shared their materials with the father's sisters and replaced their body paintings of the Black Plum Dreaming with those of the Yam Dreaming. The aunts and sisters had only erased their paintings of the Lizard Dreaming. All the women carried leafy branches that they dragged on the landing strip and into the scrub to cleanse the ground, as done during mourning.

When they arrived on the ground, the *mothers* struck the novices with other branches they had cut on the way. They started hopping about like kangaroos. I went to sit with the women and children near the Western shelter, then followed them toward the Eastern one that sheltered some decorated men carrying thin poles several meters high. In front of us, other men began to sing and, in the front line, the novices, their backs covered with horizontal lines, small circles and crosses, were ordered to place their fingers in their ears.

In the South and North of the ground were two huge piles of wood. When the first one caught fire, dancers looking like tree-men arrived. Fastened to each foot, moving up their bodies and over their shoulders to the height of a man, was a thin pole lined with leaves that rustled with each of their movements. The novices were ordered to listen and watch carefully.

Those *witi* poles were fastened to the feet with *ngalyipi* vines, two totemic names which often designate the Initiated Man Dreaming in remembrance of the branches which grew magically on the ankles of that ancestral people. To celebrate Kurlungalinpa where that happened, women often paint the *pole* and *vine* designs.

Only the Jangala *brothers-in-law* and the Japanangka *fathers of mothers-in-law* danced this time. The first ones bore on their torsos and backs designs traced in black in the shape of an escutcheon or "S", representing the flashes of lightning from the Rain Dreaming. The seconds were decorated on their chests with circles representing the Insect Gall Dreaming, and on their back with a strange shape called by the women *mamu*, spirit.

Individually, or in twos, the dancers stood squarely before the novices and, as if shivering, shook their shoulders and knees. The effect was rather erotic and the women, still seated, did not hold back from showing their excitement, stretching out their arms toward the dancers. Sometimes one singer or another stopped to ask such or such dancer to start again, while other men controlled the swaying of the tall poles with sticks .

Suddenly, except for some initiated, the women had to lower their heads again and I was asked to switch off my tape recorder. I just caught sight of a new light. The North fire had just been lit. For a quarter of an hour, the footsteps and other non-identified sounds seemed terrifying to me.

When I was allowed to lift my head once more, I saw three new dancers who, one after another, fell to the ground upon their backs. The thin poles they had on their feet covered the three novices, who, in the meantime, had been laid down against the other men. The novices' aunts cried. They were about to be circumcised, and the women had to leave quickly. I followed. It was out of the question for a woman to attend that final ritual of the Shield initiation.

SHAMANS

My head was full of rituals and myths that I was turning over and over in my mind for days on end looking for numerous associations and the principle of organization which would bind them together. For nearly seven months I had not left Lajamanu, except with the Warlpiri for trips into the bush or an epic journey to Katherine. Men and women had gone there to march in the street and dance for it was the National Aboriginal Day commemorating the death in 1876 of Trucanini, the last of the Tasmanian women the first settlers had met, who had become a symbol for the call to establish a national celebration of Aboriginal history.

One morning I woke up paralyzed by a pain in my kidneys. Impossible to stand up. The illness forced me into a welcome respite. One of the teachers lent me a book, *Gödel, Escher and Bach* by Hofstadter. What pleasure to rediscover Escher's drawings that had made me ponder so many times about optical illusions during my adolescence. On the other hand, I found it difficult to follow the comparison with Gödel's information paradoxes and Bach's fugues. But the hilarious dialogues the author placed in the mouth of Achilles and the Tortoise, characters inspired by *Alice in Wonderland*, kept me on track. The question that seemed to drive the book was that of self-reference. For example, in Escher's drawings, where the hand draws a hand that draws it, how can a system generate itself?

Again, I was sent back to my Warlpiri material, where most of the Dreaming narratives are self-referential. The mythical heroes and all that exists stem from their respective names, themselves stemming from the Dreamings of those names. No origin or finality. No Dreaming generator of all the others. Each ancestral or eternal being generates itself. Moreover, through the kinship relationships that link them to the other Dreamings, each can be seen as the generator of others. Hofstadter says that Bach died writing a fugue composed of notes corresponding to the letters of his name. Perhaps, like the Warlpiri, we all incarnate a verse of a song which unfolds our destiny toward the Dreaming which has generated that verse.

I had been lying in bed for three days and Pampiriya decided it was time to call in a *ngangkari*, a traditional healer. He arrived, accompanied by his two wives, "to reassure me," they stated. He leaned over me. I could not work out if he was smiling or grimacing behind his gray beard. His very thick lips were curiously flabby. He ordered me to turn on my stomach. I felt my T-shirt pulled up, my skirt down, then strange touchings around my kidney that came to a halt at the precise point of my pain. The healer said something quickly to the women.

"Don't worry! He's going to do *something* to you and after he will spit on that," they warned me, showing me a metal plate.

I was slightly worried, but thought: He's just going to do the number of the Amazonian shaman who spits a stone or a bone, making you believe that that just came from the sick person and thus been rid of their illness. I felt an unpleasant pricking on my back and I was told to look.

On the plate lay a little pool of blood in which floated a kind of kidney tinged with blood, all of it a rather brownish color. This time, no doubt, the man smiled at me, his teeth shining and his lips smeared, with what, according to him, he had just spat out. A vampire faced me and I did not find that very funny! I felt nauseous and could not help it, even thinking it could very well not have been my sucked blood, but what he already had in his mouth before his arrival.

I was dying to check the state of my back. Impossible, the operation was not finished. The healer started again. A new pricking. I identified the bristles of his beard rubbing against my back. He spat again: no kidney, only a little pool, very red, like fresh blood.

"All the bad blood has gone," Pampiriya commented. "You see, your blood has a good color now."

Third operation, on the left side this time. There too, the blood spat was very red and liquid. In the logic of the analogy between my illness and the blood there was nothing surprising, the pain came more from the right side. I was ordered to get up. That seemed beyond my strength. The women became impatient and urged me to try. Woefully, I got on all fours and pushed on my hands with an unbearable effort to lift myself onto my knees. Miracle! The pain had disappeared. The old man looked at me with a mixture of irony, tenderness, and assurance.

For the first time I trusted him. I twisted my body to see the state of my kidneys: on my skin, a big bluish mark on the right and a smaller one on the left. Had he really sucked my blood or were those traces only like the love bites one received during school-day flirtations? With that sudden memory, I was on the point of bursting into laughter. Not being sure the shaman would appreciate the comparison between his practice and that of teenage crushes, I expressed my content with a smile. Everything was alright, I was entitled to the diagnosis.

"I was told you had carried very heavy bags," my healer said in Warlpiri. "It's normal you had a pain after. But something else was needed for the pain to persist like that. A *stone* has hit you."

The word "stone," *pamarpa*, designates pebbles and rocks as well as the mountains. But here it concerned foreign bodies which crystallized in humans attacked by spirits or witchcraft. The shaman would have rid me of my "stone" by spitting the bloody kidney. I learned other diseases can take the shape of a bone or a real stone that every *ngangkari* has the power to extract with that same suction technique.

I could not help thinking the blood really came from my body. Most certainly I would have had more difficulty believing if the healer had spat a real stone or bone. The fact was that deprived of periods for months without any reason, I associated the kidney with a materialization of the blood which refused to discharge! Hysteria? Psychosomatics obliged: a few days after I had paid the flat rate of 40 dollars for my *cure*, I finally had my period!

Pampiriya told me that on the path I had taken when carrying the heavy bags was a zone that concentrated all the hitting *stones* of Lajamanu. Most Warlpiri avoided going that way: a place where, by coincidence, White people lived. For the Warlpiri, the association between an organic disease and a place is not unusual. For example, it is said that non-respect for sacred sites provokes pains defined by the corresponding Dreaming. Where the Digging-Sticks heroines have gone underground, women risk no longer having their periods. And where the Invincible hero discharged pus from a wound in his testicles, men risk infections.

In a word, every disease has its origin in a Dreaming and every Dreaming has its benevolent and malevolent sides. The first anthropologists who thought that the totems represented what men need to survive, did not understand why some tribes have totems like Fever, Cold, etc. That antimony disappears if one considers totemism as an attempt to regulate everything that exists. As there are some sites of power for the Yams and rituals associated to ensure the reproduction of those tubercles, there are also sites for illnesses and witchcraft practices to direct them onto enemies. Thus, men make every effort to control the circulation of totemic forces localized in places.

Soon after my illness, a Japaljarri in his forties, very lean and jolly, came to tell me about his own experience as a shaman.

"When I was little, one of my brothers-in-law heard a strange sound coming from my stomach, and exclaimed: Hey, listen, boy, to your father, there, speaking in your tummy! He explained that it was the voice of Jungarrayi the Invincible, *wawulja*, my skin father and the Dreaming father of the first *ngangkari*, the Two-Wind brothers."

It was a curious story, that one about the father of the Shamans. He married all his daughters, forcing them to kill their male offspring. But, secretly, they brought up the two sons of their lover, the Wind. And those two decided to kill their Invincible *father* by way of a stranger who died as well. But Invincible came back to life and, followed by his daughter-wives, wandered with wounded testicles. He finally went underground and from that sprung a huge Rainbow Snake which swallowed the women before hurling them into the sky where they became the Pleiades, chased for eternity by their jealous father-spouse. As for the Wind brothers, they went far away to the West, changing into tornadoes to sweep away the women they seduced on their path.

"Some men moved closer," Japaljarri continued, "and all noticed that there were small waves which undulated like a snake on my arm. That was the second sign: I had the *ngangkari* power inside me. When I was driving the cattle in Western Australia I was always asked to heal people. I was assisted by two little spirits with children's faces, the Wind brothers: one roots out diseases and the other sees through the body."

"The Kardiya doctor needs machines to see inside the patient's body. The Yapa doctor goes directly through the skin to find the disease." Nakakut told me that later when we talked about shamanic power.

According to old ethnographic narratives most Australian shamans pride themselves on possessing a kind of X-ray vision. There is also an *X-ray* art, the paintings on bark from Arnhem Land which represent animal or human figures with their skeletons and organs seen transparently through their external wrapping.[57]

That internal vision does not only refer to the perceptible inside of the body, the Shaman also sees *kanunju*, the *below* of the patient, his intimate identity with the Dreaming.[58] The figurative paintings on bark testify to that with the characters sometimes entirely hachured, the images of their mythical cartography. It is also the case for the apparently abstract

---

57. B. Glowczewski. *Rêves en colère. Avec les Aborigènes australiens.* Plon: Terre Humaine, 2004.
58. See p.140.

paintings of the desert which trace the signs of trails and sites of the Dreaming on the ground or the body.

The terms by which the Warlpiri designate the *medicine men* or shamans, *ngangkari* or *mapanpa*, signify their power of vision and extraction. That power is supposed to materialize itself through the *stones* — quartz that inhabits the body of their healer. It is the shaman's quartz which allow him to see through the patient.[59] And sometimes he spits one or two of his own quartz to catch and extract the disease. The *stones* are thus double-edged weapons: agents of disease or healing. Some shamans who practice sorcery can also use their *stones* to make their victim ill.

The sorcerers are called *kurdaija* from the name given to the death spirits who, for not having found their way, become vampires who suck the blood and soul of their victims. Curiously, it is precisely through the technique of *vampires* that the shamans heal. *Kurdaija*, a term taken from the Aranda (Arrernte) tribe, is also the name given to the shoes plaited with hair strings and emu feathers which allowed sorcerers or members of a punitive expedition to walk without leaving footprints, even to become invisible. Independent of all witchcraft practice, shamans were said to have the power to move about without leaving traces.

But witchcraft is not the shaman's prerogative. Traditionally, everyone could cast spells by following precise practices. Killing at distance by *singing* or *pointing a bone* is supposed to penetrate the victim and tear them inside, or make them ill, blind or unable to walk by manipulating a drawing or an object, etc.

"It's *Mungamunga* (the Voice of the Nights) which throws *stones*," Japaljarri had stated.

Up until then I had never heard anyone say that this oneiric matrix could be maleficent. On the contrary, several times I was told stories of children lost in the bush who were guided by the Voice of the Nights to find their way back. Some went on to become shamans just after getting lost.

"You do know that men don't talk about *Mungamunga*," Nakakut explained when she was transcribing my conversation with the Japaljarri. "He said that because you are a woman. You can leave it in your book, for it's somewhat true. As *Mungamunga*

59. Meggitt, M. "Djanpa among the Walbiri." *Anthropos* 50: 375-403, 1955.

can make us ill by showing us too many things in a dream, in the same way the stones hit us when we are weak in our head."

Does that mean that like the dreamer who succeeds in making out of his visions a ritual for others, the patient can transform his *stones* into a healing power? The answer was not clear, shamanism being a secret business. It seemed the shaman's quartz both *hit* him during an illness and was injected into his body by other shamans through an initiation. Numerous descriptions that I have read in old books concerning other tribes than the Warlpiri have remained incomprehensible to me. The body would be emptied of its organs to be replaced by new ones, the joints turned around before being put back into place, etc.

Strange people of the desert. In the past men and women knew the medicinal plants and poisons to throw into waterholes to send wild animals to sleep. Some could treat the teeth, using a small worm as a drill, filling the hole with a special amalgam.[60] They all munched the *pitchuri*, the wild tobacco which, mixed with ashes from a certain bark, takes the appetite away and allows one to stay awake. However, they did not resort to the magic mushrooms found in Australia. The landscape and the rituals were enough to make them lift off.

It is said that once all elders were more or less shamans. They not only had the power to see the *underneath* of things but also to feel in precise parts of their bodies when a particular relative was in danger, ill or on the point of returning from a journey. Today, a few sometimes interpret an itching in that way.

During my stay in 1984, a group of eight Pintupi arrived in a southern community. The adults had spent thirty years alone in the desert where their children were born. They returned to their tribe to marry off their daughters and also after the death of the patriarch who had made the choice not to allow his family to be made sedentary during the systematic *putting into the reserve* of the Pintupi in the Sixties.

The Pintupi, the southwestern neighbors of the Warlpiri, had been so traumatized at the time that some had let themselves die. The others persisted in returning to their land to set up the first Outstations. When they saw the return of that group who had remained faithful to the life of hunter-gatherers, they

---

60. Barrett, M.J. "Walbiri Customs and Beliefs Concerning Teeth." *Mankind* 3: 56-59, 1964.

decided to protect them by forbidding journalists and research workers to come and pester them. The Pintupi, however, asked an American anthropologist, who worked with them for years, to come and meet the group.[61] The press did not fail to grab hold of those "last nomads" and news spread throughout the world. The excitement was no less strong with the Aboriginal people of Central Australia themselves who attributed to those *returning people* (revenants) all the powers about which they felt nostalgic. They said that, like the shamans, those women and men could have travelled awake in the past of human beings, the past of the Ancestral Dreamings, and anticipate what will happen. They could simultaneously find themselves in two different places, materialize there and bring back an object. How was it so surprising, in such conditions, that the Dreamings generate themselves?

61. Myers, Fred. *Pintupi Country, Pintupi Self: Sentiment, Place, and Politics among Western Desert Aborigines*. Washington D.C.: Smithsonian Institution Press, 1986.

A RITUAL CONVOY

For two weeks, settled in the bush one kilometer from Laja-manu, I slept in a huge space cleared to serve as a camp and ceremonial ground for around sixty women. The well-known Kajirri ceremony, celebrating the sisters, the sowers of insect galls, had begun. And, as in each of those Warlpiri rituals, I re-discovered the pleasure of living in a kind of daily theater.

Women danced from daybreak, starting again at midday, and took shelter under a big leafy shed to take a nap and paint themselves before dancing again at the end of the afternoon. During the night, while the children slept, they sat in a circle and sang around the two sacred poles that they pulled up, re-painted and replanted each morning.

At midday, they laid down a pile of carefully folded blan-kets, a ritual present for the men who camped further away, sheltered from the eyes of the women and children. During the day cars went to and fro to supply both camps with food. Some married men came to fetch their spouses once they had finished their own ritual activities. The women pretended to ignore their presence or their calls if they had not finished their own *business*.

One evening a man, fed up with waiting for his wife, bran-dished a firebrand and threw himself upon the circle of danc-ers. Immediately they scattered, but not before pulling out the sacred poles. Contact with the Dreaming must be broken once violence erupts. The poles which usually serve as combat sticks exclude conflicts when they are planted for rituals.

The camp remained in suspense, waiting. Day after day rumor spread that we were going to leave the following day for a very long journey. The aim was to go to Docker River, 1,500 kilometers south, and give the Kajirri ceremony to the Pitjantjatjara tribe who had been asking for it for eight years. The previous year, some men had gone there to negotiate the conditions of such a ritual transmission. It was agreed that Warlpiri men and women would bring their teenagers to be initiated at the same time as the young Pitjantjatjara novices. The Warlpiri added that they wanted to be accompanied by a delegation of Kurintji, for it was from that Northern tribe that they had themselves received the ceremony some hundred years before.

The Kurintji agreed to be part of the journey. Months passed before the Warlpiri decided to go. In reality, the women were worried to go to a stranger's country. They were scared of the Pitjantjatjara because of their Red Ochre *Business*, a very *hard* ritual which requires the initiated to have their hair smeared with red ochre for months, with the added prohibition of washing, combing or cutting it ... on pain of death. The children of the initiated are systematically bound by the Law of that *business* which also punishes by death those who get drunk. The women feared that by going to Docker River the Warlpiri would be *caught* by the Red Ochre and that those who drank would be threatened with death. The men had invited me to join the journey to reassure the women. There would be no Red Ochre.

The Warlpiri had decided to set up their Kajirri camp on the day the Council received the telegram from Docker River announcing that six novices had been placed in seclusion and the Pitjantjatjara were waiting now for the arrival of the people from Lajamanu. The elders of Lajamanu did not dare chase after the young men who had fled when they wanted to place them in seclusion. Was the tradition subsiding? The women explained that they did not want their sons to make such a dangerous journey and, anyway, the Kurintji had undertaken the ceremony on their land in Kalkaringi with four of their own novices.

A new telegram from Docker River informed the Council that the Pitjantjatjara were growing impatient as some representatives from Ayers Rock and Papunya had already arrived and were waiting for the planned ceremony. The Warlpiri sent a delegation to Kalkaringi. The Kurintji, short on vehicles, decided their women would not be part of the journey, that only six elders would accompany their four novices. One hour after that decision, the order to prepare was given.

The women danced for the last time to pull out the sacred poles that they hid among the blankets, mattresses and cans of flour, tea, sugar and other tins piled up in the cattle truck. We were about thirty seated on that pile two meters high. Only two blind old men accompanied their spouses. Two other men rode in the cab to take turns driving. A little girl, the only child on the truck, joined them. One of the old men let out a ritual howling while waving his hand before his mouth. Women answered back with youyous and we left. It was almost nightfall.

Several hours later, a Toyota 4x4 was waiting for us by the side of the road. Six men got out, they were the ritual managers of the ceremony in charge of the liaison between the different vehicles of the convoy. They explained the women should not see the truck of the men with the novices, as well as another car that transported the male secret objects. Our truck was to be used as a shield to block all cars crossing in the opposite direction. If they contained Aboriginal men or women non-initiated to Kajirri, they would have to turn back or hide in the bush to allow the novices and secret objects to pass.

The two cars we passed obeyed willingly. Later, I was shown a spot where, a few years earlier, two men were found dead who had transgressed that rule of avoidance common to all tribes of the Centre and West. While we were driving in the night, an extremely violent storm took us by surprise. All around the sky was streaked with lightning flashes of incredible shapes. I was uplifted by that natural show, but my companions did not seem reassured. For them it was the Rain Dreaming which spoke in thunder.

The rain stopped. We halted to sleep, after the women had planted their sacred poles and danced. They started dancing again just before daybreak to pull them out. In the afternoon, while the truck drove at top speed, they took off their T-shirts and smeared their chests, arms, faces and hair with red ochre. We arrived in Yuendumu. Our truck stopped at the edge of the camps. The men left for the ground of the *businessmen.*

An hour later the *businesswomen* from Yuendumu arrived carrying two large billy cans of tea and dampers that they set down in order to dance toward us. Without a word, my companions danced to meet them. The two groups mixed together as they hopped about, then stopped to exchange news of their families.

Then tears burst out, that heart-rending cry which seems to come from a single throat to modulate itself while reverberating from mouth to mouth. In groups of two or three, the women knelt down and embraced, a mourning ritual for a woman from Yuendumu that had passed away a few days earlier. The sky became black, the storm roared anew. Everyone scattered to take refuge in the houses or little corrugated iron sheds. I went to Françoise's, the Nangala, my French *sister-in-law*, who was doing her field work in Yuendumu.[62] Our pleasure came from sharing our experiences in our language, rediscovered after so many months.

The morning after, the women of Yuendumu laid down material at the feet of the sacred poles erected by the Lajamanu women. They brandished two other poles that, in an impressive exercise of gymnastics, they threw among them. The women of Lajamanu danced as well. Then, in the blink of an eye, the truck was loaded once again. We left, preceded by a Toyota with six women from Yuendumu, driven by Françoise.

I was told a boy from Yuendumu had joined the Kurintji novices in the men's truck, while an important ritual custodian, a woman from Yuendumu had not come, along with one of the old companions of our household who had remained in Lajamanu. The former recently had an illicit love affair, while the second had settled down with a man against the better judgment of her relatives. The Law of Kajirri assumes that men punish such offenders during their celebration, but the women

62. Dussart, F. "Rêves à l'acrylique." *Australie noire, Autrement.* hors-série no. 37: 104-111, 1989; Also see Dussart, F. *The Politics of Ritual in an Aboriginal Settlement: Kinship, Gender and the Currency of Knowledge.* Washington D.C.: The Smithsonian Institution Press, 2000.

agreed to avoid that humiliation, the punishment of missing a journey in which their ritual authority would have been reinforced, was enough.

We arrived in the middle of the night in Alice Springs. The convoy was not supposed to stop there, but we had been driving with four flat tires for several kilometers. Hammering the asphalt with that infernal racket, we passed through the town to camp by the side of the road near the airport. Since nobody had enough money to buy new spare wheels, the ritual managers sent an emergency telegram to Lajamanu the following day. I went shopping with Françoise for the women were not allowed into town.

It became a day of waiting. By evening we still had no reply. The women erected their sacred poles again. Some men reproached them for having awoken the *jurtiya* Adder Dreaming, the cause of all their problems. Thus they painted themselves while singing and dancing all night long for the snake to go back underground and leave us in peace.

The second day, after the women had cooked a large amount of dampers for the novices and their custodians, good news arrived. The Council would pay for the repair of the spare wheels. The convoy set off again at the end of the afternoon. In front of us lay 450 kilometers of tarred road and 250 kilometers of dirt tracks.

We passed alongside the monolith of Ayers Rock and the gigantic Mount Olga rocks, two tourist symbols of the Aboriginal sacred sites. The silence was almost oppressive in the truck. The women's eyes rolled as if they reflected something invisible happening around us. Before we left, Nakakut's husband, Tony, had warned us that on the other side of the big red rock Uluru, which the White men called Ayers Rock, one sees some sort of little vapor trails coming from the ground on the horizon.

"When one gets closer, one can see spots of burned ground. But there are no traces of a fire just burned out," he added. "No, there are other burns, much older, which come from the Dreaming. In that country the ground burns with an internal fire, a very dangerous force which sleeps in the depths. One can also smell a very pungent smell which hampers breathing."

I did not see or smell the vapors, but I was extremely impressed by those rocks. The heat then became unbearable. We stopped near a water tank where all the women washed themselves. Once clean, they smeared their bodies afresh with red ochre and painted their chests with Kajirri designs, particularly yellow marks, prints of the Dreaming Dingos which chased after the two ancestral sisters. It had now been a week since we had left Lajamanu. We were only one hour away from our destination, Docker River.

We arrived in a narrow valley embedded between old eroded mountains where some shelters, made out of woven branches in the old style, in the shape of arcs and open at both ends, were scattered around. In the shade of a hedge made of branches planted vertically in a double line 20 meters long, the Pitjantjatjara women were seated, some with their chests painted. A slight apprehension went through the Warlpiri women. The minute they climbed down from the truck, they parted into four lines and, holding their sacred boards, danced toward the four poles erected near the hedge. The strangers rose and danced to meet them. The two groups interlaced, coiling in a spiral between the poles, then went to sit down a dozen meters apart.

Millennial diplomatic art: one dances before one talks. A woman from Yuendumu knowing the Pitjantjatjara language stood up to present the *businesswomen* of Docker River, Ayers Rock and Papunya, the four lines of Warlpiri dancers, by their skin names. Each line gathered together the women from the two skin names in the relationship *father's sister* and *niece*: on the one hand, some Napanangka-Napangardi and Nungarrayi-Napaljarri, the *kirda* bosses of the Kajirri ceremony, on the other some Napurrurla-Nakamarra and Nangala-Nampijinpa, the *kurdungurlu* managers.

I was told that most of the women from Docker River did not have a skin name and one of the reasons why the Pitjantjatjara asked for the Kajirri ceremony was precisely to be able to adopt that classificatory system. Why? Because this mode of organization of ritual roles and territorial rituals was becoming, it seemed, more and more popular. Several tribes had already adopted it during the previous decades. It represented a kind of dominant Aboriginal ideology, making both intertribal relations and interactions with White people easier.

The Pitjantjatjara women now walked in file to shake hands with the Warlpiri women. They offered them a large billy can of tea and dampers. Before eating, the Warlpiri women laid down at the feet of the ritual poles a pile of new material in honor of their hostesses. Late into the night, the two groups met again to sing and dance. The atmosphere was slightly tense, each group watching the other, trying to gauge their differences and similarities. One could hear the songs of the men in the distance.

In the morning, the Warlpiri women danced again to retrieve second-hand clothes and blankets that the Pitjantjatjara women had laid down in their turn at the feet of the sacred poles. Some showed a few women from Docker River how to paint the designs of the Kajirri Dreaming on the boards and sacred poles. Next to the four Pitjantjatjara poles they erected the two poles they had brought from Lajamanu and bound them with the sacred rope made of hair strings, *makarra*, the *matrix*.

At midday, our hostesses brought cardboard boxes filled with corned beef and fizzy drinks they had bought at the Docker River shop. They explained they were painted the day before with the Yam Dreaming and the Acacia Seeds Dreaming. The similarity I had noticed between the designs of their body paintings and those from Lajamanu were thus confirmed. But those designs could as well have belonged to different Dreamings for a similar drawing characterizes two Dreamings, while each Dreaming has several designs corresponding to different places.

My companions and I were told the last dry riverbed we had crossed before arriving at Docker River belonged to the Budgerigar Dreaming, another trail shared with the Warlpiri.

"If our Budgerigar Dreaming has come as far as here, we might have land in this country!" remarked a cunning Napaljarri with pride.

Warlpiri ethnocentrism. Lajamanu's women know very well that some of the trails of the Warlpiri Dreaming have been taken over by neighboring tribes, sole legal custodians of the sites of those Dreamings located on their territory. But the Warlpiri like to think they can appropriate foreign lands in the name of the extension of a common trail. It was probably in this way the rather fluid shifting of tribal borders used to occur in the past.

With every generation, local groups had to renegotiate their lands. Some intertribal marriages or other ritual arrangements, sometimes giving way to open conflict, could also modify the limits of a tribal territory. One has to understand that it was not a question of cutting up lands into little parcels, but rather of an open network whose sites alone marked the passage from one tribe to another. That way the mythical trails are like television series marked on the ground, with different tribes in possession of different episodes.[63] During certain intertribal gatherings, each group interpreted the episodes in its possession with a ritual for the other groups.

Following that custom, during the night, some Pitjantjatjara women danced their episodes of the Initiated Man Dreaming associated, like for the Warlpiri, with the stars. A wave of emotion swept through the Warlpiri women: the dancers were doing the same sacred gestures as them. It did not matter any longer that the songs accompanying the gestures were in a different language, those strangers proved to be the daughters and custodians of the same Dreaming.

The next morning, the men announced that the novice from Yuendumu, the four Kurintji from Kalkaringi and the six young Pitjantjatjara were to be brought out of seclusion. There was surprise in the women's camp. They had expected to stay in Docker River for at least one week, if not two. In reality some admitted they were relieved, they had begun to feel homesick.

Warlpiri and Pitjantjatjara gathered for the arrival of the eleven boys. They appeared in the distance, accompanied by an elder armed with a long spear. Two women were sent to meet them. They deployed in a big circle and danced at a running pace, brandishing spears. For a moment I was transported into another time. Their naked bodies and the contemplation of the scene were reminiscent of the photographs of tribes last century, which had made me dream even before I came to Australia.

The novices rejoined the men who covered them with multi-colored material. As I saw in Lajamanu five years before, each boy was presented to a group of women defined as his skin

63. Hamilton, A. "Dual Social Systems: Technology, Labor and Women's Secret Rites in the Eastern Desert of Australia." *Oceania* 5 (1): 4-19, 1980.

mothers. The Pitjantjatjara novices had each received a skin name, and in that way, their mothers, sisters and co-spouses were automatically classified by the *mother* skin name of one or the other boy. As soon as the *mothers* had removed the material and given some food and drink to the young initiated, the trucks were loaded again. We were leaving Docker River.

It was explained to me that, contrary to what had been announced, the whole of the Kajirri rituals had not been passed on to the Pitjantjatjara. It was not a breech in the relationships but a sign of the balance of power. The Warlpiri had said to the Pitjantjatjara that they would give them the rest of the ceremony if they came to Lajamanu the following year. Perhaps a way to avoid the Pitjantjatjara forcing them to be initiated into their famous Red Ochre *business*. Every ritual transfer should in principle be followed by a contra-transfer in order to re-establish the balance between the solicitors and the petitioned. For Aboriginal people from Central Australia, the *strongest* is always the one who can give while making the other desire what he has to give. In that game, the Warlpiri had become masters. The Pitjantjatjara had been soliciting them for eight years already.

If ritual life is *business* for Aboriginal people, it is more as a political activity than an economical one. To exchange rituals, sacred objects or mythical stories is not to exchange goods as we understand it. Rather it is a matter of exchanging signs which simultaneously guarantees the partners' identity, their ancestrality, and their inscription in the country.

By *carrying* the Kajirri ceremony to the Pitjantjatjara, the Warlpiri had extended the trail of the Kajirri heroines as far as Docker River. On the way back I heard the women explaining that this Dreaming in fact *always* led the two ancestral sisters to the Pitjantjatjara. Confirmation of the fact that anything new that occurs is already virtually within the Dreaming. It was now up to the Pitjantjatjara to inscribe the trail of the Kajirri Dreaming on their territory by once again *finding* new episodes for the mythical heroines, as the Warlpiri had done a hundred years before.

Thanks to that ritual journey, I had just attended the mystery of the Aboriginal actualization of a myth into the landscape. The Dreamings were traced by peoples' shifting and rituals. It was not a question of re-enacting a so-called mythical golden age, but of articulating a collective experience and an intertribal meeting in the terms that constituted such and such Dreaming, *Jukurrpa*, as an ancestral referent. In a word, the people were free to trace their paths of Dreaming, but that freedom was directed by the Law of the Dreaming itself, *Kuruwarri*, which presupposes that the people continually build new alliances.

Warlpiri men resting after bringing young initiates for Kajirri ritual in Docker River, 19

Lajamanu men during a Wulaign Outsation meeting, 1988.

PART SIX

(1988)

CHANGES

July 1988. After a long walk in the bush in search of wild honey, I was resting beneath the shade of a tree with Nakakut, her sister Beryl and their husband Tony, recalling memories of four years earlier.

"You remember when we came back from the Pitjapitja of Docker River?" Nakakut asked me mischievously.

"Oh yes, I couldn't stand it any longer."

Crammed in a truck with the women, we had travelled the 1,500 kilometers that separated us from Lajamanu, not only in an unbearable heat but also in an atmosphere of total paranoia. The Warlpiri dreaded crossing paths with foreign novices who were supposed to come up from Southern Australia. According to custom, if the women ever had the misfortune to see them, they risked the death penalty. Every hundred kilometers we hid on the edge of the road and, instead of following that tarred road to Alice Springs, we bumped along the railway track.

"You know, a man was killed on the way," Nakakut declared.

Really? Or was it rather the legendary version of that truly epic journey? Seeing my skepticism, Beryl burst out laughing.

"It's true! But sometimes, we feel scared for nothing. Last year, at the Yuendumu sports, some men saw some Pitjantjatjara all red. They thought it was the Red Ochre *business* arriving, and all the Yuendumu's campers fled into the bush, leaving everything behind. Even the kids had to stay with their teacher.

We didn't dare return to Yuendumu for two days! And the policemen of Katherine were mobilized to escort us to Lajamanu. In fact, it was a false alarm! The Pitjantjatjara were simply covered in dust."

I asked Nakakut and Beryl if the Pitjantjatjara had come as planned to Lajamanu to be completely initiated to the Kajirri ceremony.

"Oh no!" Beryl replied, scared. "Those people are too dangerous! Anyway, Peter Japanangka is too old to run Kajirri now and we don't yet know who's going to take over."

I was told that the Kajirri ceremony had not been celebrated since 1984. It had become taboo just after the return from Docker River, for the old legal custodian of the ceremony had died. On the other hand, there had been other celebrations and distant journeys. For example, to Borroloola, to meet the Anula and Warrumungu people. The women of Lajamanu have danced a *yawulyu* ritual there and, in return, some men and women from Borroloola had come to camp and dance for a week in Lajamanu. Ever since, some Warlpiri families speaking Warrumungu planned to go and live there for awhile.

"The men of Lajamanu really fancied Borroloola's women!" Beryl said with a laugh. "It's not the same with the Pitjantjatjara women who scared them."

More recently, there was also the journey to Western Australia, to Balgo, for the fire ceremony Jardiwanpa, connected to the Dreamings of Wampana Wallaby and Yarripiri Giant Snake. The Warlpiri have ritual exchanges with the Kukatja Walmajarri, Ngardi and other Western tribes since time immemorial. But they had to interrupt the ceremonial cycle, usually spread over several months, because of the death of its first ritual *boss*, a Jakamarra, step-father of Victor the *millionaire*.

I was informed the fire ceremony would resume when the time came to lift the speech taboo the widows of the Jakamarra had submitted to. Since his death, they had settled in Yuendumu. The end of the mourning was planned for 1989, but the meeting over the royalties of The Granites gold mine and the planning of new explorations had precipitated certain events. Considering the Jardiwanpa ceremony was traditionally carried out to settle conflicts, the Warlpiri had decided to perform it as an attempt to pacify the disputes that caused opposition concerning the royalties. Always that ingenious marriage between modern and traditional life. But would they succeed?

I could not help but notice an irreversible loss, the disappearance of most of the elders over seventy. With them disappeared the last adult witnesses of ancestral life in the bush, those who, never having used iron, knew how to hew stones. The youth did not know and the elders had much trouble rediscovering the effectiveness of the technique that consisted in heating the gum of the spinifex grass to fix the hewn stones on spears or wooden throwers. Sometimes the handles of iron axes were mended with an amalgam of gum, but not without being reinforced with wire and nails. Our machetes did not resist cutting wood in the bush.

I asked the old custodian of Kajirri, Peter Japanangka, if he could show an old quarry to my friend Bertrand, who was interested in stones. We travelled 200 kilometers with his wife, little girl, and baby to stop by the edge of the road in a zone full of pebbles but without trace of stone to be cut. Noticing that Bertrand was not fooled, Peter admitted he did not want to take us to a quarry. The Warlpiri preferred that White people did not see those places and, anyway, our car would not have been able to drive along the tracks that led to them.

I did not hide my annoyance at this lack of trust. Peter made us stop elsewhere, in an old camp teeming with chips of quartz from earlier hewing. He spoke with nostalgia about the time when the bush was full of people camping, when all the plains and hills surrounding us were animated with real life. He explained to Bertrand that if he stayed a bit longer, or came back, he could then see a real quarry. I asked him if there was a Dreaming for the hewn stones.

"Yes, of course," replied Peter, slightly sad, "but I can't tell you, Nungarrayi, the story is only for men. South of Rabbit Flat, there is a place with a big mass of stone knives stuck in the ground. They come from *Jukurrpa*. We used them before. But I can't show this place to young people today. They might kill each other with the knives if they go there after drinking in Rabbit Flat."

A terrible dilemma: to respect both the distribution of knowledge between men and women, and to ensure the young initiated will not betray the secret. Peter said to Bertrand that he would send a stone knife to him in France. We did not ask for that, we just wanted to watch and talk about it on the spot. That was much more difficult than it seemed. I suddenly realized my luck at having seen and heard all the things women and men had shown and told me during my previous stays.

Afterwards, Peter took us near a sacred waterhole in the rocks, a splendid site but already spoiled by the passage of cattle that came there to drink. The emotion of the old man rediscovering this place of his youth rebounded on us. A bird started singing and Peter spoke to it. For ten minutes an astounding dialogue took place between the man of the desert and the wagtail which responded. He called it my *mother* and paid tribute to its Dreaming.

The Wagtail Dreaming, *jintirrjintirrpa*, is the story of a woman-bird who kept an adult son in her womb and lived far away from men with her cousin Quail, *puntaru*, mother of two girls. The elder sister discovered in a dream the existence of the hidden son. One day when Wagtail had allowed him out so that he could hunt a kangaroo, the two sisters left in search of the young man and convinced him to marry them. Wagtail, furious, killed her cousin Quail, for she held her responsible for the loss of her son, and attacked the two sisters, who let themselves be beaten. The son, unable to bear the loss of his spouses, killed his mother. Then the three of them returned to their relations, whom they asked to judge them for those two killings. They were beaten according to custom before being integrated into the tribe.

Nakakut told me that story years ago, by drawing it progressively on the sand, the way her mother had taught her when she was a child. First she traced two small arcs and a dot indicating the two women-birds seated near the fire. Then she moved her fingers as if they were the heroines' walking feet, leaving prints on the ground. Some fascinated kids surrounded us, their eyes fixed on the sand *screen*. Sequence after sequence, the scenes of the story were superimposed at speed, Nakakut wiping them one by one with a sweep of her palm to make a fade out as in animation.

In the past it was the way the children learned to narrate the public episodes of the Dreamings, but also any daily anecdote, such as a hunt or a dream they had. Today it is much more rare for adults practice that form of direct *writing*. Teachers have taken over the technique to illustrate some school books. But on paper, the signs are fixed, as in acrylic paintings where, for the non-initiated, they no longer have meaning.

What would become of youth like Martin who, wanting to write a book on his people, could not do it for he had refused to submit to the initiation of the elders? Today, having stopped drinking, he was the father of four little girls and earned a good living from his paintings. Would he be able to plan a ceremony when he reached the age of forty?

In 1983 the women asked me to help them obtain a building to store their sacred objects. Unable to get anything from the budget of the municipal development or from the funds of state assistance, they had cobbled together to buy a corrugated iron garage that we had erected at the end of my stay in 1984. Four years later, I found the garage abandoned. I was reassured a delegation of *businesswomen* had to travel fairly soon to Darwin to discuss the construction of a *real* women's center in Lajamanu. Would they dance in there or would they only do paintings to be sold?

Four days earlier, the little girls from a school group were painted with their Dreamings on their chests and danced in front of the concert hall. Having gone to cut wood with Pampiriya and two other women, I had returned too late. I was reproached for my absence by the dance leaders who admitted that, contrary to the past, almost nobody had come to watch and encourage the girls. During my previous stays, the women noticed with satisfaction that my interest in the *business* changed the attitude of some children who, under the influence of school or mission, were *ashamed* of the traditional activities. Thus by not coming this time, I had failed in my role.

However, my companions did not seem worried about missing that event, finding it more important to chop wood. They were delighted to walk in the bush in search of trees which could provide adequate pieces to carve out carriers. Beneath a scorching sun, forgetting hunger, thirst and weariness, they exerted themselves with evident pleasure. One tore, without a moment's hesitation, her brand new dress in order to mend an axe, and carried on working with all her strength on a rebellious trunk. Upon their return, and without any feelings of regret, they shared the pieces of wood already roughly prepared for the carving of water or baby carriers. By making others benefit from their effort, they followed the old, constitutional rule of the networks of alliance.

Many Warlpiri from Lajamanu complained that the relationships of solidarity and obligation were not really like before. Marjorie, Nakakut's daughter, already a mother of two little girls, regularly took shelter in her parent's camp to escape her husband's beatings. However, he returned continually to fetch her without any respect for his in-laws who, according to custom, he should have helped in various ways. Before, in such a situation, the mother's brothers of Marjorie would have seen that her husband did not beat her, and Nakakut and Tony, unsatisfied with their son-in-law, could have had the marriage annulled.

Roselyn, Pampiriya's daughter, escaped the man to whom she was promised by marrying an Aboriginal policeman from Katherine with whom she had a son. The boy understood English better than Warlpiri, and, when Pampiriya visited her daughter in town, she no longer respected the traditional taboo which forbade women to approach their sons-in-law and talk to them. Was it the beginning of the end of kinship rules?

I had not found Abe Jangala, the old rain-maker. He had definitely gone to town, upset for almost nobody had visited his wife, Annie, when she was dying in hospital. However, Abe and Annie, faithful lovers who had no children of their own, had brought up several who had since married. I established that more and more Warlpiri balked at taking care of the very old.

In the same way, they stigmatized with far too much insistence those kids of ten or twelve whose parents attracted by the booze in town, had left them in Lajamanu. In the past, they would have been adopted without any comment. Of course, a few years ago, women did not drink. It was common for children to be raised by older sisters, grandmothers or co-spouses. Nowadays, their relatives said they did not have the money to take care of them for it was the *non-caring* parents who were cashing the child-benefits. Because of this, the children occasionally had to beg their teachers for food. Nevertheless, some elders went to town for the express purpose of collecting the young grandchildren whom they thought were living in bad surroundings.

Many of the adults' bore faces that were at once incredibly poignant and sad, but they also liked to laugh and joke. A kind of philosophy for the moment seemed to animate them, as if moments of happiness were more important than their fate. And yet, this fate could seem disturbing. After the baby boom of the Sixties and Seventies, there were only a dozen births annually for a community of 500 people. A lot of pregnancies were difficult and did not reach term. The newborn babies were nevertheless superb. Coddled by adults and children alike, who like before, learned to move around in groups as soon as they could walk. They were incredibly alive and joyful. What would life for them be like?

IS GOD A DREAM(ING)?

Missionaries only arrived in New South Wales and Western Australia in 1821. Twenty years later they settled in Victoria, Queensland, and South Australia. In the beginning, having been met with the indifference of the Aboriginal people, many missions were abandoned, and it was only around 1940 that they succeeded in gaining a foothold in the Northern Territory.

Toward the end of the Forties a scandal broke out in the Phillip Creek Reserve where some Warlpiri lived. A Protestant missionary was sexually abusing the Aboriginal girls he took away from their families to place in dormitories. Similar to the other missions, every child of *mixed ancestry,* called *half-caste,* child, as opposed to *full blood Aborigine*, was systematically taken from their mother to be sent to special facilities all across Australia. Some Warlpiri mothers recalled with pain this theft of the children they never found again.

Today, with the exception of certain Aboriginal communities, like Jigalong in Western Australia which rid itself of its missionaries,[64] most harbor one or another of the Churches represented on the continent. A large portion of Western Australia is under Catholic *monopoly*. But in the South, North, and East of the Warlpiri, the Churches are Lutheran, Methodist, Anglican,

---

64. Tonkinson, R. *The Jigalong Mob: Aboriginal Victors of the Desert Crusade.* London: Cummings Publishing Company, 1974.

Presbyterian or are dependents of the fundamentalist Evangelical or Pentecostal movements.

In Lajamanu, as in Yuendumu, the mission was Baptist. According to the principles of that Church, one needed to be an adult to be baptized and become a member. Around eighty men and women from Lajamanu have made that choice. The missionary couple settled there with their children for fifteen years and had trained a Warlpiri pastor endowed with a certain charisma as much through his intelligence as his presence.

That Christian leader, Jerry Jangala, a descendant of a family of rain-makers, dreamed at the beginning of his conversion a certain number of songs in Warlpiri respecting the traditional rhythms, but relating to biblical episodes. In 1979, he gathered his relatives once a week to sing them at night in the camp, while on another evening, the missionary made a sermon with a megaphone in the park. At the time I was dead set against those sessions, I could not bear speeches like: "You are *black* with sin, all men *blackened* by sin will be damned."

But the Warlpiri explained that another Baptist missionary living "like the Yapa" died on their land in the past, and as the result of a decision by the elders had been buried in one of their sacred sites. His widow, who departed for Darwin, regularly sent tapes in Warlpiri on the Christian faith. I saw some of them listening to those tapes as if it was a message from the hereafter sent by one of them.

A few years before, the Warlpiri from Lajamanu had worked out a "Christmas *Purlapa*," a performance about the birth of Christ with songs, dances and paintings in the traditional fashion. The Warlpiri from Yuendumu had responded by creating an "Easter *Purlupa*" in the same style. The stage and sound elements of those two entertainments were partially dreamed. Their execution mobilized a large proportion of both communities, including Warlpiri who did not consider themselves as Christians. For them it was a way to incorporate into the ancestral mythology the epic of Christ, Elder of the White people.

In 1984, two of the women who lived with me were regular visitors to the church, but without neglecting the traditional ritual activities. To show I had made peace with the missionaries, although they had taken a year's leave, they asked me to participate in one of their Baptist sessions. On the church lawn, I found myself naked to the waist, two crosses traced with red ochre on my shoulders and my chest painted with a design of traditional inspiration: a big arc representing the Church crowned with little lines symbolizing the divine light and encircling small arcs, the Christians gathered in one single family.

That design to be painted on the bodies of women and men, as well as on wooden dishes displayed in the church, had been developed jointly by the missionary and the Warlpiri leader, Jerry Jangala. The latter, working at the time on the translation of the Bible with a married couple of linguists from the Summer Institute of Linguistics (SIL), had just learned to read and write. Several of the congregation decided to do the same with the help of another missionary linguist. That attempt at teaching the adults to read and write was indeed very laudable but, as supposed by the SIL strategy which sends its missionaries to translate the Bible throughout the world, the fact of making equivalent Indigenous concepts with Christian ones is often the most perverse weapon used to destroy a culture.

My companions, who knew by heart some verses of the Bible already translated into Warlpiri, were perplexed. A word like *Kuruwarri* designated now both the Images of the Dreaming and the sacred text of the Bible. *Wapirra* was both God and the totemic *fathers* of the Dreamings. As for *pirlirrpa*, was the *soul* that left the body to dream different from the Christian soul? In the Book of Genesis they could find neither the reference to the Aboriginal people nor the animals populating Australia. So it was with a great deal of pride they showed me in a Christian booklet, illustrated by the SIL, drawings of Black people and kangaroos springing from God's hand.

I accompanied them to a collective Christening that gathered together for a two day period a hundred Warlpiri and Kurintji on a sacred site belonging to them. A magnificent natural pool stretched for hundreds of meters in the hollow of a valley of sand and rocks. There the Rainbow Serpent was supposed to live, as well as the mermaids with long blond hair, manifestations of *Mungamunga*, the Voice of the Night, which sometimes caught on the hooks of the Aboriginal people who fished there. It was in that water full of mysteries that they plunged the thirty men and women dressed all in white who had decided to be converted. The day after, the newly converted and the older Baptists explained at a session of public confession the reasons for their conversion, a monotonous litany: men because they had understood, thanks to Jesus, that they should not drink any longer, nor beat their wives; women because God had shown them the way to make an example for the men.

Upon returning to Australia in 1988, I witnessed an even greater syncretism. With Bertrand, we had met the Warlpiri at the sports meeting in Yuendumu where the women were preparing to paint themselves with their Dreamings to dance the *yawulyu*. Informed by mail of my arrival, Nakakut and Beryl had been awaiting me for several days.

It was real bliss to meet them again, as well as the *businesswomen* present, Betty Napanangka the Kajirri *boss*, Rosie Napurrurla the dreamer of the Possum ritual, Peggy Napaljarri and the other Napaljarri mother of the deceased Chairman, the two Nangala spouses of the old bespectacled man, the old Nakamarra whom I had taken care of, the Napangardi star of the video recorded at The Granites, and some others too. More than half of these *businesswomen* informed me that they were going to dance that evening, but this time the "Family *Purlapa*," a new Baptist show.

At nightfall we were invited to sit among the Warlpiri men and women in the audience. With the exception of two Japaljarri, Tony and Paddy, Peter Japanangka and their spouses, most of the elders were present to sing along to the rhythm of clapping boomerangs. In front of us stood the *actors*. On one side women in red skirts, their chests painted with the design of the Church, on the other men, equally painted, but their bodies and faces covered with down in the traditional fashion.

A young Warlpiri explained at the microphone that "through *Wapirra*, God, all the *Kuruwarri* (the Images of the Dreaming) have come." A few months ago the Warlpiri had danced the "Family *Purlapa*" in Sydney during the festivities of the Bicentenary of the arrival of the Europeans in Australia. They had created that spectacle to show their solidarity with the other

Yapa of the continent and the Kardiya of the government who considered the signature of the first Treaty between the Aboriginal Australians and Europeans.

Contrary to the Native American Indians, Aboriginal people have never signed a treaty validating the occupation of their lands by the settlers. A few years ago some intellectuals launched a movement to prepare such a treaty, but the idea did not suit all Australians, Aboriginal or otherwise. I discovered the Baptists were in favor, the show being their peace manifesto.

Two men began to dance, one coming toward the other. When they came face to face, they embraced and bowed, their hands joined as if in prayer, before venturing together to sit near a fire. The Warlpiri at the microphone announced they represented the reconciliation of the Kardiya and the Yapa, Whites and Blacks. Two other men did the same dance, this time miming the reconciliation of young and old. Two female dancers took their place, one carrying a bag, the other empty-handed, the rich had to give to the poor. Then a woman arrived, her hands shackled in chains and another dancer took them off, the slaves were freed. Then the Baptist leader danced to meet his wife and took her in his arms. The man at the microphone announced that men and women were equal. A final pair of dancers appeared representing those who have the "Law," that is, the Christian faith, and those who are "without Law." They all danced together. The "Family *Purlapa*" was finished and the audience was ecstatic.

I was moved by that attempt, though a bit desperate, to place the Aboriginal people in our world. But I could not help thinking the idea of defining the non-Christians as "without Law" re-echoed that painful trauma of the time when Aboriginal people were not even considered as humans. Had they not insisted across the continent to translate into English their notion of the Dreaming as their Law: "*the Dreaming is our Law*"? Had they not tried for years to define themselves as living with "two Laws," the one of the Whites and their own?

If, on the eve of the 21st Century we were still identifying the Law of the Western World with Christianity, what can we expect for the future of the non-Christians? What about the Muslims, the Jews, the Buddhists, not to mention secularism and all the other religions which, like that of the Aboriginal people, also had the right to exist?

Under the pretext of general reconciliation, it was the most dangerous intolerance that started to emerge. The effects could already be felt. A few years ago a preacher from a non-Baptist Church arrived in Yuendumu and settled in an Outstation whose members, nearly two hundred, were evangelized. On the same evening of the Baptist ritual, in another spot in Yuendumu, a meeting of a rival movement took place, which, with a thundering sound system, made its own show. The members of the two Churches, considering themselves as enemies, accused each other of having "bad" religion.

At the end of the Baptist ritual, the Warlpiri at the microphone announced that the Baptists from Yuendumu were invited to learn the Family *Purlapa* in order to join with the Warlpiri of Lajamanu who were about to tour four Australian towns. A Nungarrayi, still painted with the design of the Dreaming of the afternoon *yawulyu*, proudly told me she will take part in the trip. Her husband, the elder brother of the Christian leader, Jerry Jangala, would not accompany her for he had to take the *businesswomen* to a traditional intertribal gathering planned for Yirrkala in Arnhem Land. A redistribution of roles in order to deal with the two Laws?

It was not easy to reconcile all of this. On the way back to Lajamanu after the sporting event, I saw the Christians had been seized by a frenzy of painting. They had hoped to take advantage of their tour by selling paintings that represented their Dreamings. They calmed down after a week, once they discovered that they would not be authorized to *sell* their Dreamings but, on the contrary, they had to paint the designs of the Church on panels so that they could be *given* to the Christians they met.

The Warlpiri Baptists also planned to go to Israel to present their Family *Purlurpa*. They wanted, they said, to see the land of Jesus, the desert where he accomplished so many miracles. What would they see? The conflicts of the Jews and Palestinians? Or the perpetuation of a world of legendary wars recounted in the Book of Judges?

In the past, it was not rare for Aboriginal people, denied the recognition of a religion and a culture, to be relegated to the level of animals dancing under Satan's influence. Today, no official speech dares to call the celebration of the Dreamings non-Christian, a more subtle way of not recognizing a statute of religion to those practices. The actual ideology of several missionaries nevertheless censures different aspects of Aboriginal culture as well as our own. On one hand, it challenges alcohol, which determines the majority of Aboriginal conversions, but also cards and sometimes Rock music and sports competitions, which is far from reconciling the converted. On the other, pre-arranged marriages, polygamy, mutilations during mournings, and traditional avoidance behaviors are frowned upon.

A fine theologian, the Christian leader tried to systematically revise all Warlpiri customs. Curiously it was in the Old Testament which essentially struck the final blow to the Aboriginal culture. Indeed in Leviticus one can find the interdiction to mutilate oneself during mourning, as well as that of eating lizards or wild animals like ostriches, the African *sisters* of the emus. Would the repulsion the first settlers had toward the food offered by the Australian land have derived from here, and which stays vivid for so many contemporaries?

Reading the Bible after my first stay in Australia, I was shocked by the fact that, in its own way, Leviticus normalizes the passage from a life of nomadic hunters to that of sedentary agriculturists. The prohibited foods are all wild resources which allowed people — in the Middle East as elsewhere — to survive without having to cultivate the land or rear animals. To forbid access to those resources can be considered as *a posteriori* justification of the cultivation of the land and a certain sedentarization.

The Warlpiri appeared to me to be sensitive to the fact that their life has certain things in common with that described in the Old Testament, like circumcision or the crossing of the desert. But the parallel is ambiguous for the Epistles of the New Testament no longer suppose that Christians are circumcised. And the crossing of the desert under the aegis of Moses is a punishment from God who made Man *regress* into a temporary survival similar to that of nomad-collectors: they had no village

271

but *wander* and feed on the manna that the earth provides for them every day. To be specific, it is with the word *manna* that one translates the famous seeds of wild plants that Aboriginal people traditionally molded on a stone to make dampers.

If one has in mind the mythical references of the Aboriginal people, the Old Testament takes on a curious color. The story of Eve giving Adam the fruit of knowledge as well as love certainly reminds us of the story of the Digging-Stick women who revealed their sexuality to the men and gave them their knowledge about initiations and hunting. The story of Noah is reminiscent of the myths of the Deluge of the Rain Dreaming. Abraham's sacrifice can echo the ritual death of the Aboriginal novices who are *reborn* at the end of their initiation. Finally, the Ten Commandments carved on the stone tablets given to Moses by God evoke that other Aboriginal Law carefully preserved by the signs of the Dreaming engraved on the secret stone boards, known in the Western world as *churinga*.

When I had come across Aboriginal people in books, two things had fascinated me, their relationship to walking and the absence of houses. Apparent wandering, in perpetual search of a home, continually recreated, left and found again by the return to the sacred sites. Sites which are not made to live in but to dream in, sites for singing, painting, and dancing. Sites for love, regret, and sites to keep in one's heart as a land of exile and nostalgia. For, in a certain way, I too was living in exile and my family was scattered all over the world. During my childhood, I had lived with the nostalgia of a mythical homeland on the other side of the Berlin Wall.

At fourteen, I had borrowed a parka from a friend covered with signs in felt tip, including a Jewish star. My mother froze in terror when she noticed it and asked me to get rid of it straightaway. That is how I learned that her own mother was the daughter of a rabbi who had been baptized in order to marry my grandfather. She had never talked about it for the memory of the war and persecutions was too painful. I discovered later that old Aboriginal people had a similar attitude toward the traumas of their first encounters with the Whites.

Questioning my Jewish or Catholic roots, I have always been disturbed by the notion of a unique God. And it is precisely the apparent absence of that monotheism which attracted me to Aboriginal people. The religious question is unclear. If the first observers refused to recognize any kind of religion with the Aboriginal people, most anthropologists defined it as immanent, without deities but with supreme figures present throughout the entirety of the terrestrial and cosmic environment. Others tried, on the other hand, to identify some ceremonies of the South-Eastern tribes with a monotheistic cult.

Destroyed or dismantled, the ancestors of those tribes are no longer here to testify to their beliefs and the status of that so-called sky God, Baiame for some, Bunjil for others. Reading the disparate ethnography left to us, I would rather think it was not a divine notion but an extremely complex concept which crossed several aspects of cosmology and society.[65] But, after all, what is God? If one takes it literally as the Word, could it not as well be designated as the Dreaming?

Aboriginal people say they are both spiritually and carnally bound to the landscape, and to the animals, plants, and stars. They are always looking out for signs in the universe which talk about their individual mortality and their eternity in the cosmic forces of the Dreamings. Such a relationship with the cosmos, if it respects the individual singularity of everyone, has nothing in common with the individualism that the relationship of the Christian or the Jew with his God supposes. It is to reinforce the vital and emotional forces that traverse them in order to take part in the reproduction of the world that Aboriginal people practice rituals. It is in the circulation of goods, paintings, dances, and songs between people and not in offerings, sacrifices or prayers addressed to a superior authority that they celebrate their heroes of the Dreaming.

Their traditional answers to the mysteries of life and death seem sufficient for the Aboriginal people to carry on finding meaning in their place on this earth. How does one understand the conversion of some of the Aboriginal people to Christianity? Do they find in the Bible a symbolic justification for their sedentarization? Or are we the ones forcing them to do it so that they can communicate with our logic? Have they subjugated their

---

65. Howitt, A.W. *The Native Tribes of South-East Australia.* London: Macmillan, 1904; Van Gennep, A. *Mythes et légendes d'Australie.* Paris: E.Guilmoto, 1905.

Dreamings to one unique God or only incorporated Christ into the span of the Dreamings?

THE HYPERCUBE

Retuning to the Warlpiri after years of theoretical speculations about their society, I wanted to confront them with my conclusions. It was not easy. I brought a copy of my new thesis[66] to the literary center in Lajamanu, but it was in French, and, in any case, most of the elders could not read. Nor was it easy to make a summary of its six hundred pages. With the exception of Nakakut, I had never managed to talk with a Warlpiri for more than an hour. They always had something else to do or think about.

Nevertheless I gave it a try. First I presented my manuscript to the Chairman. Intrigued, he agreed to listen to the main ideas, the time it took to drink an orangeade at the door of the shop. I showed him the transcriptions in French of the stories of the myths and the oneiric revelations that several Warlpiri had given me. Being literate, he took pleasure in recognizing the names of the narrators, the toponyms and the Warlpiri terms.

When I opened a page where a strange diagram of kinship was located, other Warlpiri edged closer. I explained it was about skin names. By considering several rules of Warlpiri kinship, I had been led to split those eight names into sixteen numbers that I had transferred onto a figure which combined eight intricated

66. Glowczewski, B. "La Loi du Rêve — Approche topologique de l'organisation sociale et des cosmologies des Aborigènes australiens." université Paris-I, Panthéon-Sorbonne, thèse de doctorat d'Etat ès lettres et sciences humaines, 1988.

cubes. The figure challenged all forms of normal perspective since the eight cubes are presented under angles of different projection. It was a way to flatten the fourth mathematical dimension which passes from a normal cube to the hypercube.

On that hypercube, the lines represent, as on the cube, the classificatory relations *fathers-children* (father's sisters — brother's children) and *mothers-children* (mother's brothers — sister's children) between the skin names. When I had pointed to three numbers of the figure, I had given the corresponding skin names, which were not written on the page of the thesis. Suddenly I hesitated before continuing. Immediately the Chairman gave me the missing name and, following the circuit I was making on the lines, he confirmed the correspondences between the numbers and names. The Warlpiri standing around enjoyed it enormously, finding the hypercube a "good game."

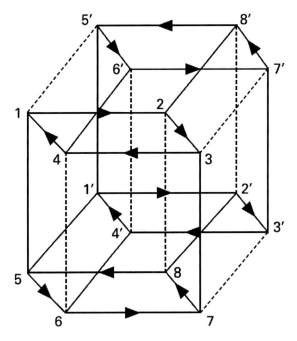

Hypercube with eight skin names multiplied by two

276

1 and 1': Japanangka/Napanangka	5 and 5': Japangardi/Napangardi
2 and 2': Jakamarra/Nakamarra	6 and 6': Jangala/Nangala
3 and 3': Jungarrayi/Nungarrayi	7 and 7': Japaljarri/Napaljarri
4 and 4': Jampijinpa/Nampijinpa	8 and 8': Jupurrurla/Napurrurla

Four cycles *mothers-children* :	Eight cycles	*fathers-children* :
1 2 3 4	1-5	1'-5'
1' 2' 3' 4'	3-7	3'-7'
5 6 7 8	2-8'	2'-8
5' 6' 7' 8'	4-6'	4'-6

Marriages:

men = women	m = w	m = w	men = women
1 = 8	8 = 1'	1' = 8'	8' = 1
2 = 7'	7'= 2'	2' = 7	7 = 2
3 = 6	6 = 3'	3' = 6'	6' = 3
4 = 5'	5' = 4'	4' = 5	5 = 4

I was overwhelmed, even if, secretly, I had hoped for such a reaction. Before leaving France, Lévi-Strauss, to whom I had given a copy of the thesis, had told me: "It would be interesting to know what the Warlpiri think of your hypercube." He has always defended the idea that structures drawn by anthropologists in the studied societies are unconscious for the members of the society concerned.[67] Now, in direct contact with the Warlpiri, I was struck by their stupefying cultural concern to formalize the articulation of their society.

That those Warlpiri men consider the hypercube as a "good game" was even less surprising when one recalls that they are used to thinking complex mental maps, those of their Dreaming trails. In the same way, they play in the space with the kinship by distributing in the course of rituals, people according to their respective skin names. However, the graphics we need to

---

67. In 1989 Lévi-Strauss sent me a nice hand-written letter complimenting *Les Rêveurs du désert* but he asked me to consider, if the book was reprinted, to add the following pages in his work about this issue: C. Lévi-Strauss, *The Savage Mind*. London: Weidenfeld & Nicolson, 1966, 265 (*La Pensée sauvage*, Librairie Plon, 1962, 332-333), and *Structural Anthropology*. London: Allen Lane, 1968, 302-304 (*Anthropologie Structurale*, Librairie Plon, 1958, 308-310).

understand the complex relations, which govern the kinship or the mythical cartography, do not have the same role of representation for the Warlpiri. Their body paintings or paintings on canvas *speak,* but what they are emblematic of is emotionally loaded for those who know their meanings.

The elders sometimes represented on the sand the real or classificatory relationships between people by dots or lines. Using exactly the same technique as that to recount, scene by scene, stories on the sand, they superimposed those connections one on top of the other along with their oral commentary without ever bringing it, at least publicly, to a *total* figure.

Did they have an idea of that *totality* to be able to master the local articulations? I thought so. This was surely much more complex than the hypercube.

Something was clear: Aboriginal people from the desert read time in space. On the one hand with their trails, and on the other by identifying the memory of the past and the virtual with the world *below (kanunju),* that of the subterranean and interstellar space, the present manifestations of that memory defining the terrestrial world of the *above (kankarlu).* In their rituals, the Warlpiri ancestralize what happens and make *become* the traces of the past, for the two dimensions are conceived as being in a relation of constant feedback.

While I was beginning to explain to the Chairman the way I had analyzed the relationships between the taboos and the Aboriginal people, I felt an uneasiness on his part and mine. By saying a word like initiation, I was suggesting something secret, restricted to men. That was not my intention. The Warlpiri do not manipulate their concepts in that abstract way. For them, to enunciate a word supposes concrete situations and thus everything those situations can generate. That is precisely why women never pronounce the word circumcision. Although they know that that practice exists and that the initiation of boys involves several taboos, they are not allowed to talk about it publicly.

I hastened to add to the Chairman that in my thesis I only talked about things accessible to women. I admitted that I mentioned old practices that perhaps had been secret, but that I had read about these in books on other tribes. The discussion was closed. It was out of the question to go any further. Anyway the Chairman had had enough. I still asked him to organize a meeting of the elders at the Council so that I could explain my work. He agreed in a vague way.

The month passed without the possibility of a meeting taking place. In truth there were many meetings and concerns preoccupying the people. One member of the Council did ask me to show him the manuscript. The Chairman had talked to him about it. Occasionally I showed it to other Warlpiri. One Nungarrayi thought the hypercube was "easy." While I was reading the distribution between the skin names of some hundred Dreamings, her old blind father-in-law laughed in his corner, repeating each word in an approving manner. Later, while I was resuming a trail of the Rain Dreaming related to me by a Warlpiri, her husband corrected me. I had made a mistake in a toponym.

When I opened the page on the photos, the Nungarrayi turned away abruptly, asking me to close the manuscript. Somebody in a photo had died.

"I can look, but you shouldn't show that to the Napaljarri and Napanangka," she stated, recovering quickly.

She asked me to open the thesis once again to the page of the photos, and, sweeping the tips of her fingers across the silhouette of the deceased, a Jakamarra, told me to blacken it. I did so. I already had to erase the name of another deceased.

Of course I showed the thesis to Nakakut and her sister Beryl. They too found the hypercube amusing. But I had the impression they were ashamed of the fact that the Warlpiri were reduced to words on paper. Not being literate, writing disturbed them. I shared their feeling a little, having myself a relationship of both fascination and distrust toward writing. While I was reading to Nakakut her name and that of other narrators who had given me their testimonies she said quite seriously that I had to be extremely careful with those signatures. The stories narrated by each person do not belong to them as such, and I should not forget to mention those collective belongings.

Confronted by the Warlpiri deontology, I decided that, once back in Paris, in contrast to the thesis, in this book I was going to change all the forenames of the people I was talking about, citing instead in the acknowledgements the names of all the Warlpiri families who had helped me discover their universe.[68]

---

68. Things changed at the turn of the 21st century. Most of the people appearing in this book, have become, like many other Warlpiri, famous artists. As the young generations are eager to find any written information about their elders, I was asked to give the codes for the names, so in the published English translation I have reinstated everybody's names.

HOW TO SAY AFTERWARDS

It has been ten years since my first fieldwork with the Warlpiri and almost as many years that I have been writing on Aboriginal people. Year after year, stages both emotional and intellectual have transformed the meaning of an encounter I did not know how to *actualize*, namely, to find a way to share it with people from here. A paradox of expression. To bring the Warlpiri people close to here, I had to put a distance between here and my experience there. A painful operation, yet vital in order to not confuse life with the image of its memory.

During my first stay, the Warlpiri had made me discover the importance of women in their social and ritual life, but also the ambiguous games of love and strength in the co-habitation of the sexes. I had been sent back to my own femininity in a collective symbiosis in which I had lost all notion of myself. Separated from that universe, I had seen the emergence of an urgency, finding connections here, in my own culture, and not there, on those desert lands, which speak to the senses and provoke multiple reminiscences.

At home in Paris, I attempted to seek out the existence of mythical trails which, like the paths in the desert, would make my town a territory. I thought I had found them in a network of 300 kilometers of galleries of old quarries which ran beneath the Métro and across the southern districts of Paris. With a media sociologist, an ethnologist and a historian of the quarries, we *studied* those strange secret people, the cataphiles, who run through the night across the underground network forbidden to the public.

The genuine hidden lining of the streets of the surface, those galleries, cut into the limestone, without light, sometimes flooded or plugged with injections of concrete during foundation laying for buildings, tell a curious urban story. They were planned after the Revolution, when the Parisians noticed that the old quarry holes, which for centuries had given stone for constructing the city, threatened the collapse of the houses and streets. They also took the opportunity to empty all the cemeteries and throw the bones of some six millions Parisian ancestors into what has become the ossuary of the catacombs of the Denfert-Rochereau square, the part of the network accessible to the public.

Strange that this sweeping aside of the past and the threat of physical collapse coincided with the social collapse of 1789. I noticed, by delving in the archives of the library of the Villa de Paris, that this fear of instability of urban foundations re-appeared at every social crisis. The newspapers grew uneasy with the Parisian substratum of *gruyere* during the Commune, the First and Second World Wars, the Algerian War, May '68 and after the first election to the presidency of Mitterand, the time when we started that research. That continued after, at the time of the student strikes in 1987, radio and newspapers talked once again about the quarries visited by very innocent urban speleologists.

My friends made fun of me for passing from the Australian desert to the underground network of Paris where a few fallout shelters were found. I gave the impression I was preparing a shelter in case of a nuclear war. Admittedly, at the time I was obsessed by scenarios of survival, admiring the precarious life of Aboriginal people, and moving home unrelentingly, refusing to be burdened with objects! As soon as our research on cataphilic ramblers was published,[69] I responded once again to the call of the desert.

The Warlpiri still haunted me as a personal myth that I had to *deconstruct* in order to grasp the people behind their image. That work of deconstruction began as soon as I once again encountered the uncompromising and often critical look of the inhabitants of Lajamanu. I discovered, not *the Warlpiri*, but individuals with whom one develops affinities or not. As the image of a Warlpiri homogeneity disintegrated, a passionate friendship drew me closer to my privileged *informant*, Nakakut Nakamarra.

When I came back after that long fieldwork of 1984 I threw myself into the project of this book. There was a malaise. Those men and women lived their lives while I wrote. Some had asked me to return, to apply for a job which would have led me to work for them. I hesitated for a long time. On the one hand I felt I was committed to them. On the other, to manage Outstations or to organize tours for the dancers was not ethnology, and I was not sure I desired to permanently live in Lajamanu. Perhaps I would have accepted if I had had a partner ready to follow me, or children. My departure for Australia had provoked another break-up in my love life and I did not want to embark once again alone into exile.

I would have liked to travel backwards along the path of a personal quest to restore, in their entirety, those who had contributed to it. But I could not separate that part of subjectivity from the real life of those who inhabited my dreams. I reached an impasse, a radical powerlessness. A year later, I finished a manuscript without having succeeded in saying what I felt I had wanted to say. I put it aside and waited.

Meanwhile I had met Bertrand. He urged me to go back to more *scientific* work. I analyzed my Warlpiri data, comparing it with archives on other Aboriginal societies. Throwing my

---

69. Glowczewski, B. Matteudi, J.F. with Carrère-Leconte, V. & Viré, M. *La cité des cataphiles*, 1983. Republished (Paris: ACP, 2008) with a new foreword by R. Peirazeau and a 75 pages appendix from a 1982 report for the Mission patrimoine of the French Ministry of Culture. Both editions have a foreword by Félix Guattari, republished in his book *Les Années d'hiver (1980-1985)*. Paris: Les Prairies ordinaires, 2009. http://truth-out.org/archive/component/k2/item/86895:guattaris-relevance.

self recklessly into the quest of formalization, I plunged into a magical figure, a topological figure: the hypercube.

Topology is one of the tools of artificial intelligence. In the field while reading *Gödel, Escher and Bach*, the book of one of the most ingenious thinkers of artificial intelligence, I had not really understood why this reading brought me back to the Warlpiri. Later I realized that it was normal for an ancestral way of thinking to illustrate the problematics of the science which studied the activity of thinking in general. It was the union of physics and metaphysics which had seduced me with the Aboriginal people, and it was the human spirit I sought across society. It was only in this sense that I was interested in anthropology

With the hypercube, all aspects observed with the Warlpiri — kinship, taboos, myths, rituals — were articulated in an astounding logic. Everything made sense while defining a universe totally different from our own. But I also rediscovered the phantasms which had given me that feeling of strange familiarity while reading stories on Aboriginal people before meeting them. It was not an image of the primitive man I was catching a glimpse of, but that of the man of the future. The one who does not think of the universe as limited and men as elected but who examines thought in infinite cosmological paradoxes.

Return to square one. In order to better understand the Warlpiri, I had had to dissect them, and what god-like surgery was going to bring them to life on the paper? By constantly talking about Aboriginal people on the radio, in seminars and workshops, and by answering people's questions, I had acquired new ammunition.

When the Warlpiri had come to Paris, their presence in the flesh, their dance and their painting on sand presented "to form an alliance with the French" had been met with misunderstanding by numerous journalists and spectators. Why, when rushing to see the last *savages*, did not most of the people want to know about their actual living conditions? Perhaps they preferred myth to reality? Confronted by that contemporary reality of the Aboriginal people, I had a great deal of trouble demystifying it. Too many things undoubtedly push us to praise the image of people untouched by our civilization and to refuse that today they are part of our history as we are part of theirs.

Going back to Lajamanu in July 1988, I wanted to drop everything. Faced with changes, the book seemed to have lost its meaning, and ethnology seemed to have become a completely vain project. Anthropologists were, after all, continually condemned to be gravediggers, parasitic mushrooms on dead trees, as one tribe of Paupua New-Guinea call them. That morbid discourse about *ethnologized* populations already existed for last century observers and runs through Lévi-Strauss' postwar publication *Tristes Tropiques*. But the announcement of the *end* of those cultures did not prevent new generations of ethnologists from travelling far away to find populations culturally rich despite the contact. During my previous stays, I had rejected any defeatist perspective, and working with my friends and other minorities across the world, we defended their survival.

So why that discouragement? I had to admit that, at the moment, I no longer held my place alongside the Warlpiri. If I had a place with them in the past, it was only within the limits of a tacit contract I had made with them. I had recorded certain aspects of their culture to make it public and I had gained a professional specialization. Leaving Lajamanu, I admitted the Warlpiri continued living, even if I did not know how to capture them any longer. I had to take up, in that changing world, the place of the Aboriginal people as well as my place and that of anthropology. It remained for me to write about what I had just witnessed.

Each new day spent writing alleviated me, as if I was finally managing to relieve myself from the emotional weight that until then had tied me in a double nostalgia: nostalgia of those desert dreamers whose faces and words mixed with the musky smell of the bush infiltrated my thoughts by surprise; nostalgia of losing myself in a tribal solidarity which having been my experience there, made me vulnerable here.

To accept living with nostalgia was at the heart of the Aboriginal way of life. Thanks to the Warlpiri I was in the process of accepting not only the nostalgia of my time spent with them but also that of Poland. I began to mourn both my Slav and Warlpiri myths. I always felt the past as crossing

285

perpendicularly to the present. Now I finally understood that any past is a dream which only exists in the present through the traces it leaves. It had taken me ten years to understand this ultimate lesson from the Warlpiri!

Finishing this book, I can say that my meeting with the people of the Australian desert has transformed my desperate search for an elsewhere detached from reality into a necessity to learn to walk on the ground. Surveyors of the imaginary, the Warlpiri had taught me that dreams are not a refuge but a mirror of desires that only exist on the condition that individuals and collectivities grasp with all their might the paths full of traps and unpredictable events that they have traced for themselves.

POSTFACE TO POCKET EDITION, ACTES SUD (1996)

Clutching the telephone in the Alice Springs Post Office, I closed my eyes. Would I be the right candidate? Yes, finally, my thesis published,[70] I was admitted as a researcher in anthropology at the CNRS, becoming a tenure member of the Laboratoire d'Anthropologie sociale in Paris. My wandering finished, life took on a new turn. A wage in France, a man in Australia and soon, a child. I went back to Lajamanu to prepare an exhibition of paintings. It was 1991 and there were no longer any camps, everybody lived in houses. The non-Aboriginal population was reduced. The Council aimed at self-determination and had just decided on the creation of an art co-operative to manage the sale of the paintings. I was to be its first customer. A pre-sale from the place of the exhibition in France allowed me to buy a dozen paintings. The choice was difficult but I was guided by the Dreamings I wanted to see figured in the catalog. For example, the fantastic story of the Possums and Plums transformed into rocks and black tide that Nakakut had told me before. A superb painting signed by her illustrated that story, but Nakakut was not in Lajamanu. She lived in Kununurra with her new husband. We were bound to meet again, I thought, because like her, life had led me into the north of Western Australia.

---

70. *Du Rêve à la Loi chez les Aborigènes — mythes, rites et organisation sociale en Australie*. Paris: PUF, 1991.

Wayne, my future husband, whom I had met in Paris, lived on the North-West Coast, in the land of his ancestors, Yawuru and Jabirr Jabirr.

In the meantime I once again found the Warlpiri stories of the *ngarrka* Initiated man and Star Dreaming painted by Lily Hargraves Nungarrayi surrounded, as always, by a pack of dogs. And the *ngurlu* Seeds Dreaming painted by Rosie Tasman Napurrurla who became the *boss* of the *businesswomen*. I also chose a painting of the *ngapa* Rain Dreaming by Linda Hector Nangala and two paintings of the *wirntiki* Curlew Dreaming by my healer Janjiya Liddy Herbert Nakamarra and her niece Jean Birrel Napurrurla. There were also four paintings by men.[71] Having collected a few stories related to the paintings, I reread to the painters the stories of the Dreamings I had recorded with them some years before. Emotion ran high, mixed with pride at the idea of those words of yesterday still being so alive on paper. Rosie and her companions decided that a young Warlpiri trained in video, Francis Kelly Jupurrurla, would record them while they danced so that the film could be shown in France.[72] I left with twenty women to camp for two days a few kilometers away from the community on a Wallaby Dreaming place. They painted their sacred boards and their bodies, then they danced. In front of the camera, an elder confirmed the importance of their *yawulyu* ritual. Then, Lily and Rosie, seated before their respective paintings, explained their meaning in Warlpiri. As it was night, the young Jupurrurla switched on the headlights of his car in order to film. The dancers could not stop. Happy, they danced until morning. I rediscovered the feeling of happiness

71. The catalog of the exhibition that toured in France, *Yapa — peintres aborigènes de Balgo et Lajamanu,* Paris, Baudoin Lebon éditeur, 1991 (in French and English) displayed paintings by Abe Jangala, Jimmy Robertson Jampijinpa, Teddy Morris(s) on Jupurrurla, Tingkiyarri Jacko Gordon Jakamarra, together with paintings by the 5 mentioned women and also, by Nakakut Barbara Gibson and her sister Beryl Puyurrpa Gibson Nakamarra, Ijaturru Liddy Nelson, Nikiriya Maisie Rennie Napaljarri, Pupiya Louisa Lawson Nakamarra, Pampiriya Margaret Martin Nungarrayi, Nampiya Judy Jigili Napangardi, Ijaturru Liddy Nelson and Yulyulu Lorna Fencer Napurrurla; the Lajamanu paintings were presented with art from twelve Balgo artists who refer to similar Dreamings.

72. The Warlpiri filmmaker, Francis Kelly Jupurrurla, has become famous for the work he initiated with American anthropologist, Eric Michaels, *Bad Aboriginal Art* (1994, Ed. by Paul Foss, University of Minnesota Press); he was one of the five Warlpiri artists who came to the Paris exhibition *Magiciens de la Terre* in 1989.

which inhabited me years ago on such nights dedicated to the spirits of the land.

I settled down at Wayne's in Broome, the town where ten years before, I had come to look for the origin of a secret cult observed in Lajamanu.[73] The history and life of the Aboriginal people from the West Coast was very different from those of the desert. Most ancestors had children with either European farmers, Chinese shopkeepers, Japanese divers and, above all, Malayan, Indonesian and Filipino indentured laborers who, from the last century to the Forties, were often brought there forcefully by the pearl industry. The children born of those mixed unions, the Yawuru or local Djugun, forbidden by law, had been deported to reserves or missions and thus very few people still spoke the Yawuru language. During the Second World War, as a result of the Japanese bombings, the whole town had been evacuated and the Aboriginal people were prohibited from staying there. Then there was the curfew which forbade them to stay in town after six in the evening. They had to wait until the end of the Sixties for their life to be less controlled. At the time, the town experienced an influx of Aboriginal people from other regions, thrown out of work by the stock breeders who refused to pay them the wage required by law after the 1967 referendum granting them new rights.

Because of urban development, several young people like Wayne, had been initiated by neighboring tribes. Their initiations were carried out, however, on the local ceremonial ground. Broome is imprinted by important Dreaming trails, one of which is the Two-Men Dreaming that runs through the entire Kimberley country coming from the central desert. The Two-Men Dreaming has even brought to the coast some species of trees. In short, I was following a Dreaming trail!

I discovered the militant actions and the difficulties of daily survival of the town's Aboriginal people. The coordinator of a group of Yawuru women, Theresa Barker, Wayne's mother, invited me to continue an oral history project she had undertaken. I accepted. Some years later that piece of research would

---

73. Glowczewski, B. "Manifestations symboliques d'une transition économique: le 'juluru', cult intertribal du 'cargo' (Australie occidentale et centrale)." *L'Homme* 23 (2), 1983, 7-35.

result in a book of testimonies.[74] Milari, my first daughter, bears the Aboriginal name of one of her Jabirri Jabirr ancestors. She was four months old when her grandmother, Theresa, accompanied us to a big gathering of women in the desert. More than four hundred women from twenty communities met at the well of Yukawala to dance their Law for a few days. The Minister of Aboriginal Affairs for Western Australia also spent a day there, for she was invited to see the women's Law, and listen to their claims and propositions, such as the creation of a *patrol* of *businesswomen* to prevent the abuse of alcohol in the communities. We camped in a circle around the vast ceremonial ring where the dances were performed. Some cars went back and forth to fetch water in Billiluna, the community inhabited by the Kukatja who hosted that gathering.

There I met twenty women from Lajamanu, Rosie at their head. They passed Milari around from hand to hand calling her Nampid, short for Nampijinpa, used for little girls. In the evening I left Milari with her grandmother and went dancing with the *lawwomen* of Lajamanu. Everywhere else in Australia, the term *lawwomen* tended to replace that of *businesswomen*. The day after they did a sand painting. All the communities danced giving each other presents in the form of clothes and blankets: the usual payment — as before in Docker River — in exchange for dances and sacred objects they revealed to each other. On the third day in the morning, a few women played at mimicking the disputes between mothers-in-law who were jealous of the meat their sons-in-law gave to others. The entire camp roared with laughter. On the last morning we were awoken before daybreak and asked to sit down on the ground. While I was holding Milari tightly against my breast, in the cold and early June morning mist, someone whispered to me that the Dreaming women were there. A strange silence surrounded us. The apparition was magic. All the women moved to the other side of the ground. They smeared their faces, hair, arms and legs with ochre. Milari was taken from my arms to be smeared with red too. She did not complain.

---

74. *Liyan — Story of a living culture*: *Jarndu Yawuru Oral History Project*, Broome, Magabala Books. This book was due to print when I was writing this afterword, but it was seized by the State for a Native title tribunal, see B. Glowczewski, *Rêves en colère*, 2004, Ibid.

Soon after, all the women ran toward their vehicles. In a few moments, the camp was entirely taken apart, everybody seated in their cars, buses or trucks. We had to move in a line. At the exit of the campground, each car was daubed with a red liquid: an ochre which would indicate to the Aboriginal people we would meet during the day that we were coming back from a women's *business* and they must not come closer unless they wished to risk becoming ill. The convoy of vehicles splashed with color advanced slowly for twenty kilometers as far as the Billiluna community. There, the leaders of the convoy told us to get out of our vehicles. All the women quickly tore a thin branch from the bushes around. I did the same and was pushed to take my place in the column of two single files which meandered like a serpent in front of the shop where a group of men sat. We were guided so as to turn around those men who lowered their heads without uttering a word. All the women shook their branches above the men as if to cast out something. It was explained to me later that we were cleansing these men in danger of getting a sickness which threatened them, for the women had had their gathering in that country.

Back in Broome, Theresa made me tour the house with a bucket of water so that I could wet the ground and chase away the spirits. Her son was not allowed to touch me either until the following day. A few days later, in front of a small group of men, women and children gathered on the outskirts of the town, we were subjected to a ritual aimed at cleansing us from our journey. I was invited to sit down beside a fire with Milari, her grandmother and two other women. A third woman gave us a thread of red wool to tie around our forehead and, with a branch, she tapped gently on our backs. Arms stretched out onto our neighbors' shoulders, we had to breathe the smoke. The smell penetrated me like a breath of fresh air. Milari seemed to appreciate it a lot.

One day, I took out two friends to show them the coast south of Broome. We ran across the vast swampy plain just after the high tides had flooded it. On the way back, the sun was setting and the car veered off violently to one side. The passengers screamed. For a split second I thought we were going to turn over, mud covered the wheels. We were sinking. I held Milari, still sleeping, tightly against me, saying to myself: nothing can happen to her. She did not even wake up, and after a struggle we regained the track. Later I had a dream. I saw myself in the same spot in my mother-in-law's car with her at the wheel and Milari still a baby but speaking. She said to me: "Mummy, Mummy, look!" while pointing toward the front. We were moving on the water and, in front of us, under the water, I saw a path of stones, but stones painted with extraordinary designs and shining as if they were made of an unknown material. "Mummy, mummy, look!" Milari shouted, this time pointing her hand to the right. I saw a very beautiful group of men and women walking, floating on the water. They were splendid, bodies and faces shining with red, all, men and women, with very long hair down to their feet.

I related that dream later on to an elder from Broome and he told me, amused, that in the dreams, the plain is a lake visited by the *Copper People* who test the dreamers before letting them cross. I was ready to believe that something had protected the car. I also told my dream to a group of women from Balgo who came to visit us in Broome. Wayne and I had spent sometime in Balgo to make a short film on acrylic paintings. Some women artists, including Jemma Napanangka and Bridget Mudjidell, had taken us camping to visit a few sacred sites on the traces of the Pleiades, the Digging-Stick women and the Two-Men Dreaming. Those Western desert women, who knew Broome as a Dreaming place for the Two-Men and the Juluru ceremony, asked me if I dreamed before or after the women's gathering. I answered after. They took counsel together for a moment and told me the message came from the ancestral heroines, the Wanji, who were with us in the desert but came from the sea here.

One night, I had a second strange vision. Lying in our bed, Milari sleeping on a cot at our side, suddenly I saw a tiny black silhouette behind the sliding glass doors. The face was empty and I was terrified. I tried to wake up Wayne with my right arm but he remained motionless. Meanwhile Milari seemed to levitate above her cot and a very thin rope appeared which bound her to the silhouette behind the glass. A double of myself seemed to leave my body and start to dance and sing to my great surprise. All the Aboriginal people I told about the vision gave me the same interpretation: the silhouette was the spirit-child of Milari, her *rayi*. From the Eagle Dreaming according to her father and grandmother.

I accompanied Wayne and his team for the shoot of a documentary on the Aboriginal people of Kimberley.[75] After two weeks on the road in the table lands and forests of the North in search of cave paintings, we came down to Kununurra where I spent the day with Nakakut and her husband. She was happy to finally see Milari, then six months old, whom she called *jaja*, a term used by the Warlpiri women to designate the children of their daughters, those also calling *jaja* their grandmother. Milari was meeting her Warlpiri *jaja* while at the same time we had just lost her Polish *babcia*. My mother had once told me that she would die when I had a child. Like her own mother who died at the time of my birth.

Two years later, our second daughter was born. I found her Aboriginal name, Nidala, in the list of the first baptized of the mission at Beagle Bay set up in 1890 by French trappers. Her grandmother dreamed that the spirit-child bit her hand: the *rayi* of Nidala is a black Snake. Nakakut, who came to visit us in Broome, *smoked* her according to custom to make the baby strong. For two days she sought for the right tree whose leaves would emit a proper smell. It was standing near the site of the Dreaming of the Sisters who had disappeared into the sea. Nakakut dug a little hole and placed bits of wood in it. Then she cut some fragrant branches and covered the hole. She lit the wood underneath and the leaves started to burn. I held out Nidala. She supported her above the smoke and hugged her before presenting another part of her body to the smoke. She turned her several times, also exposing her head. Coiled in her arm, Nidala smiled at her then talked in that baby babble that perhaps belongs to the spirits.

January 1996. I came back from Lajamanu where I found a ritual mobilization close to those of seventeen years earlier. Following the death of a Jangala rain-maker, several families camped outdoors, protected from the sun by shelters made from branches

75. *Milli Milli* by Wayne Barker, 53', funded by ABC, Screen Australia. It won several awards and was broadcasted on many channels.

and canvas. Twenty or so houses had been abandoned because of the taboo compelling everyone to leave the place of a death. Divided into *skin* groups, men and women, faces and chests covered with white clay, hugged and kissed each other as they cried. They moved from one side of the ground to the other, some trying to hurt themselves in their grief, others trying to stop them. They all sat down against each other and a Nangala, sister of the deceased, passed a parcel among the women. The *skin* brothers of the deceased passed it among the men, holding it against them:

"*Jukurrpa*," whispered my companion touching her head lightly.

The hair of the deceased, supposed to retain his vital strength, is always ritually cut and circulated among the kin men and women. It is also used to find an eventual culprit. In the middle of the camp, cans of flour and new blankets were piled up in perfect rows. The distribution of those funeral presents to the uncles of the deceased lifted the taboo of silence of the Nungarrayi widows and Napangardi mothers. The next day, they swept the community with branches purifying the main road to open it for people to pass along.

Two painted poles linked by the sacred hairstring occupied a place of honor in the camp of the *businesswomen* who looked after the *ring* night and day, sometimes while singing. The day after the funerals, a crowd of children and women of all ages gathered there to see the dances of the young mothers of the newly initiated who had to be transferred from a camp on the East side of the camp to another on the West. Some men arrived. A Jangala, whose torso and back were painted, let out the ritual cry while waving his hand before his mouth. All the women and children had to lower their heads. My neighbor signaled that I could watch. I saw thirty or so boys covered with branches pass, boys between the ages of twelve and twenty-five, some already with families of their own.

"They have to stay in a Kajirri initiatory reclusion for four months. This is to punish the youngest ones who broke the school's windows. They will know our Law."

That Law I continue to discover with the *businesswomen*, who wonder why, at nearly forty, I am only the mother of two little girls and not a grandmother like themselves. They sang and narrated new episodes to connect to the cartography of the Dreamings, which, year after year, has been impressed in my memory like a sparkling network that I grasp in fragments of meaning, fragments that are always shifting. An elder insisted I record a long cycle of songs. I was delighted to hear the story of a people of birds whose men fought over the future of a young boy while the women argued over that of a young girl.

"It was like that in the Dreaming, the men wanted the boys and the women wanted the girls. It was the Dreaming and we follow it."

The old Warlpiri laughed, so did I.

Abe Jangala, rainmaker and artist, prepares to march for NADOC (the National Aborigine Observance Committee) in Katherine, 1984; it later became a National day for all Aust... Aboriginal and Islander Peoples (NAIDOC).

ANNEX

(2013)

WE HAVE A DREAMING: HOW TO TRANSLATE TOTEMIC EXISTENTIAL TERRITORIES THROUGH DIGITAL TOOLS[76]

At the closing plenary session of the 2010 Information Technologies and Indigenous Communities (ITIC) Symposium in Canberra, delegates decided to write a series of recommendations for improving Indigenous community access to digital technologies.[77] A young Martu filmmaker, Curtis Taylor, from Parnngurr (Cotton Creek), came to the microphone and said, "We have a Dreaming like our elders: in the mind; digital technologies."[78] This chapter shows some analogies between the cognitive mapping of desert Dreamings, the rhizomatic structure of the web, and the cultural and political contexts of the use of digital technologies.

---

76. Reprint from Glowczewski B. *Information Technology and Indigenous Communities*, Canberra. Eds. Aaron Corn, Sandy O'Sullivan, Lyndon Ormond-Parker, Kazuko Obata. AIATSIS Research Publications, 2013: free download http://aiatsis.gov.au/sites/default/files/products/monograph/information-technology-indigenous-communities-ebook.pdf.

77. This plenary session identified key issues relating to information technologies and Indigenous communities: *Statement on Key Issues Identified at the Information Technology and Indigenous Communities (ITIC) Symposium, Canberra, 13–15 July*, AIATSIS, Canberra, in Corn & al, Ibid.

78. This emerging multimedia artist was a member of the team that produced the video art installation *Yiwarra Kuju: The Canning Stock Route* at the National Museum of Australia in 2010-2011: http://www.nma.gov.au/exhibitions/yiwarra_kuju. Since 2013 the project has an iPhone application: *The Road*.

Aboriginal reticularity and the agency of transformative networks

In a volume on Actor Network Theory, Bruno Latour writes, "Now that the World Wide Web exists, everyone believes they understand what a network is," but before the web came into being:

> the word network, like Deleuze and Guattari's term rhizome, clearly meant a series of *transformations* — translations, transductions — which could not be captured by any of the traditional terms of social theory. With the new popularization of the word "network," it now means transport *without* deformation, an instantaneous, unmediated access to every piece of information. That is exactly the opposite of what we meant.[79]

Another word he criticizes in Actor Network Theory is "actor," for it too is often confused in debates about agency. In computer language, but also for some social scientists,[80] the notion of agency, agent or "actor" only refers to "action," says Latour, and does not necessarily imply an actual empowerment in the sense that was put forward by the work of Deleuze and Guattari, or Foucault, which was all inspired by Spinoza's philosophical notion of *puissance d'agir* (the power of acting) in the sense of being able to transform things and perceptions. I postulate that the way Aboriginal people, and many Indigenous peoples across the world, use the web today is an attempt to transform the perception we have constructed of them through social sciences and other discourses that precisely deny them agency by not taking into account their voice, social practices and desires. My work as an anthropologist over 30 years has been motivated by the search for ways to translate and enhance Aboriginal agency as a dynamic, flexible way of reproducing their social organization, cosmological perception and ritual practice, but also in their struggles for social justice. With all

79. Latour, Bruno. "On recalling ANT." *Actor Network Theory and After*. Eds. John Law and John Hassard. Oxford: Blackwell Publishers, 1999. 15–25: 15.
80. On Agency debates, see Sherry B. Ortner, 2006 *Anthropology and Social Theory: Culture, power, and the acting subject*, Durham: Duke University Press; Eds. Ton Otto, *Tradition and Agency:Tracing cultural continuity and invention*. Aarhus: Aarhus University Press, 2005.

the historical changes and pressures that the Warlpiri and their neighbors have experienced, especially over the past decade, the web has become a new platform to express this political agency, with cinema being another.[81]

When I went into the field in Central Australia in 1979 and 1980, I was struck to find a dynamic transformative reticularity (network structure) in the Warlpiri conception of space and time: "The Dreaming appeared to me not like a mythical time of reference but as a parallel time-space, a permanency in movement, with which the Warlpiri have a relation of feedback."[82] Indeed, I was lucky to record then, and over later years in Lajamanu, many rituals and a creative use of dream revelations for new ritual songs, dances and body paintings relating to stories that connect places through totemic mythical hybrid ancestors and spirits of children to be born. The result of these geographical connections — which are flexible according to narratives, songs and contexts of new alliances, mourning or dream revelations — is an open network of hundreds of virtual pathways or totemic trails. My rhizomatic description of Warlpiri individual and collective subjectivity projected onto a cartographed environment fascinated Félix Guattari in 1983.[83] Our discussions over the years contributed a little to the elaboration of his *Schizoanalytic Cartographies*, a matrix combining four poles traversed by arrows of time: the "virtually real" (Existential Territories), the "actually real" (Economy of Flows: libido, signifier, capital, labor), the "virtually possible" (Incorporeal Universes) and the "actually possible" (Machinic Phylums). The Aboriginal cartography of desire was one example he gives of an active production of "existential territories," which connect people with memory and senses in a dynamic process of emplacement both actual and virtual.[84]

---

81. See, for instance, the world success of the Warlpiri-language film, *Samson and Delilah* (2009), by Aboriginal filmmaker Warwick Thornton: www.samsonanddelilah.com.au.

82. Quote translated by Deborah Rose "The Power of Place." *The Oxford Companion to Aboriginal Art and Culture*. Eds. S Kleinert and M. Neale Oxford: University Press, Melbourne, 2000. (40–4: 41) from B. Glowczewski *Du Rêve à la Loi chez les Aborigènes*, 1991.

83. Glowczewski, B. "Guattari and Anthropology." *The Guattari Effect*, Eds. Alliez, E. & Goffey A., New York: Continuum, 2011.

84. Guattari, Félix *Chaosmosis: An Ethico-aesthetic paradigm*, Trans. Paul Bains and

In the late 1980s I proposed to translate the cosmological relation between the Warlpiri concepts of *kankarlu* (above, on the surface, outside, public, manifest) and *kanunju* (underneath, under the surface, inside, secret, latent) as actual versus virtual; not just as a dual opposition, but as a topological device playing with continuities and discontinuities where the "above" realm reflects the process of "actualization" while the "underneath" realm reflects the process of virtualization.[85] This process is understood here in the way that Deleuze and Guattari[86] defined their concepts of actual, virtual and *devenirs* (becomings), that is, a constant transformative process that questions the dual opposition between reality and the imaginary. I defined totemism as a process of multiple *devenirs*, and the Aboriginal struggle for the recognition of these cosmological links with the land as a form of resistance to capitalistic flows. Guattari's own writings — especially his concept of ecosophy, which simultaneously articulates the ecologies of the mind, of the environment (including all technologies) and the social as a political and ethico-aesthetic paradigm — are currently rediscovered, translated and discussed in several disciplines, even though he died in 1992 before the emergence of the web and its social networks. For instance, the philosopher Brian Holmes writes:

> Guattari took the perspective of an artist and an activist, seeking an ethico-aesthetic paradigm. He explored all the technologies of his day and laid the theoretical and practical basis for the wildest media experiments of the 1990s, even while carrying out a fundamental critique of information science and its applications in the capitalist societies. His aim was to appropriate the powers previously ascribed to myth, in order to reconfigure the articulation of bodies and machines (the relations of biosphere and noosphere). This was the desire of the *Schizoanalytic Cartographies*: to provoke

Julian Pefanis. Bloomington, and Indianapolis: Indiana UP, 1995 (Editions Galilee, Paris, 1992).

85. Glowczewski, B. "A topological approach to Australian cosmology and social organisation." *Mankind* 19(3), 1989: 227–40, synthesis of PhD *La Loi du Rêve: Approche topologique de l'organisation sociale et des cosmologies des Aborigènes australiens*, Thèse d'Etat, Université Paris 1, Panthéon-Sorbonne, 1988 (published as *Du Rêve à la Loi chez les Aborigènes*, 1991, reviewed by Laughren, Mary, *Australian Aboriginal Studies* 1993/2, 1993: 74–80.

86. Deleuze, Gilles and Félix Guattari. *A Thousand Plateaus*. Trans. Brian Massumi. Minneapolis: University of Minnesota Press, 1987.

fresh intersections of artistic constellations, existential territories, social flows and abstract ideas. Not a map of positions and probabilities, but a set of vectors whereby the virtual and the actual come to meet. A cartography of escape routes leading beyond the black holes of neoliberal control, toward the possibility of collective speech.[87]

When multimedia technologies became popular in the mid-1990s, I thought it ideal and challenging to design an experimental cognitive mapping, a hypermedia connecting machine, to try to "translate" with hyperlinks the traditionally reticular model of the desert people who connect sacred sites with mythical stories that are ritually sung, danced and painted. The analogy with hyperlinks was twofold. Aboriginal people have different media, including stories, songs, dances, body paintings, sand stories, canvas paintings and kinship rules, which are related. I had recorded these forms of Warlpiri media in Lajamanu since 1979 with my own media: audio tapes, photographs, films and notebooks, whose contents and my interpretations needed to be reconnected with each other to return the proper ritual meanings. But I was also seeking to enhance the understanding of the principle of these connections through the use of the digital system itself. I wanted to show that the Warlpiri principle of connections was visually resonating with this new technology in its own reticularity: a network of hundreds of named places that could be linked through thousands of different songs that produced songlines or pathways for different Dreaming heroes. The important point was that, instead of being a classificatory closed system, these "story lines" — not actual paths, but virtual tracks expressed though myth, songs, drawings and dancing — were intertwined with each other in a way that was partially open, according to specific cultural protocols, to new interpretations and connections that were often revealed through dreams.

---

87. Holmes, Brian. *Guattari's Schizoanalytic Cartographies or, the Pathic Core at the Heart of Cybernetics.* http://brianholmes.wordpress.com/2009/02/27/guattaris-schizoanalytic- cartographies.

Cultural protocols for making an Aboriginal hypermedia

I designed a menu, which was an interactive map of 14 superimposed constellations of different Dreaming (Tjukurrpa) pathways that connected a selection of approximately 80 named places chosen in Warlpiri land. The selected places—out of some 1000 Warlpiri-named sacred sites, which included rock holes, springs, hills and so on—were the ones most often painted by the Warlpiri women and men in Lajamanu when they started to use acrylics to paint their Dreaming stories and related places on canvas in 1986. This was an adaptation of the Dreaming totemic designs they were painting with ochres on the body and sacred objects, or drawing on the sand. The data that I had collected earlier during rituals in 1979 and 1984, before the start of the Lajamanu art movement, were related to the Dreamings they were now painting on canvas. So I used a sample of their knowledge, organized into 14 constellations of Dreamings, that they had chosen to make public by using them in paintings to be circulated all over the world. Thanks to hyperlinks, I was able to connect my old data with paintings of the places and Dreamings they were painting on canvas in the mid-1990s. The digital result was thus inspired by the cognitive mapping of the Warlpiri themselves, whose reticular ways of organizing knowledge about places, and Tjukurrpa (Dreaming) stories and songlines, seemed to reflect the network and hyperlink principles of multi-media and the web.[88] In 1995 I worked with a very knowledgeable Warlpiri lady in her late forties, Barbara Gibson Nakamarra, to check the trans-lations of a sample of songs and stories from my 1984 recordings.[89]

The original version was designed as an HTML digital program and was tested on the intranet during a Qantum Indigenet workshop at the Lajamanu school in 1997. At the time the community did not use the Internet, so the Lajamanu artists and council members were told that they should be careful

88. Glowczewski, B. "Lines and criss-crossings: Hyperlinks in Australian Indigenous narratives." *Media International Australia* 116:24–35 (*Digital Anthropology* issue, Eds. H. Cohen and J. Salazar, 2005).

89. Glowczewski, B. and Nakamarra Gibson, Barbara. "Rêver pour chanter: Apprentissage et création onirique dans le désert australien." *Cahiers de Littérature orale 51, Récits de rêves*: 153–68, 2002.

about how their knowledge appeared online. Everywhere in the world Indigenous peoples were beginning to think about how to protect their intellectual property. The artists, mostly elders, were very happy that I had respected the taboo on the images of the dead by developing a digital tool to mask images of people who had passed away. The graphic chart followed the colors of the Aboriginal flag: black for the background, all text in yellow, and words in red wherever there was a hyperlink to another section of the digital program. For instance, a lexicon window would appear as a rollover to explain any Warlpiri word, and a change of pathway was proposed for every place name that was common to two different Dreaming tracks. The students and adults involved were invited to choose one of the 14 constellations of Dreaming tracks that they were custodians for as *kirda* (owners) or *kurdungurlu* (managers) through Warlpiri kinship. Each constellation included about an hour of data: films and photos of rituals and places, photos of body and canvas paintings, and related Tjukurrpa (Dreaming) stories, songlines, images or geographical marks called *kuruwarri*.

My challenge was to enable Warlpiri elders in the community, who could not read and write, to check the content of the links, and to also make it possible for children to navigate through the images and sounds. I designed smaller icons so Dreamings could be recognized without having to read the attached English or Warlpiri titles and texts. For instance, a little vine for the *ngalyipi* (Vine) and *ngarrka* (Initiated Man) Dreaming constellation, or a grinding stone for the *ngurlu* (Acacia Seed) and *wampana* (Wallaby) Dreaming. The review process to check this digital resource in Lajamanu was very well received. All the generations were navigating together on the ten Mac computers in the school computer room. The program also featured QuickTime films, including two films made by the Warlpiri filmmaker Francis Kelly Jupurrurla.[90] He was living in Lajamanu when he filmed the women's *yawulyu* (dancing) for an exhibition I had organized in France with art from Lajamanu and Balgo, a community in Western Australia with which Lajamanu

---

90. See his work with Eric Michaels, *For a Cultural Future: Francis Jupurrurla makes TV at Yuendumu*, Artspace, Malvern,Vic., 1987, (Arts and Criticism Monograph Series 3) and his website at www.bushmechanics.com.

holds ritual exchanges.[91] The navigation available for testing combined information about Dreaming tracks that connect Warlpiri people from Lajamanu and other groups from Balgo.

The Lajamanu elders and council asked for the program to be based only on data gathered in Lajamanu and they did not want to make it available on the Internet. They were interested in it being made available to help their art to be properly contextualized to outsiders, but only on the condition that they would have control over what content would be included the program. I was asked to record new songs with men to add to the 1984 songs that I mostly recorded with women. Back in France, to respect the Warlpiri desire to protect their data from the Internet, I decided to reprogram everything using the Macromedia Director proprietary software for making CD-ROMs. This meant that the amount of data used had to be reduced to the 600 megabytes available on a CD-ROM. I managed to compress photos, films and sounds so as to allow for 14 hours of navigable materials, a sample of three hours of sound containing Warlpiri stories and songs, half an hour of films including silent 16-millimeter footage I had shot in 1979 with a post-edited soundtrack, and short videos from the 1990s demonstrating various hand signs. In the following year, 1998, I went back to Lajamanu to check this new format.

To contextualize the Dreaming constellations interactive map, a section called "the notebook" offered 20 thematic entries including art, contact history, hand sign language, deaths, the church with images, and texts extracted from my French publications and translated into English. The "fieldwork and anthropology" entry described the process of making the CD-ROM with a photo of the Qantum Indigenet 1997 workshop. The "multimedia" entry presented the Tanami Network, which then connected (via satellite) the Broadcasting for Remote Aboriginal Communities Scheme (BRACS) facilities at Lajamanu to other Warlpiri settlements and the hospital and jail in Darwin. It also showed the photo of Paddy Patrick Jangala filming a long line of women at The Granites in 1984 during the making of the first Lajamanu video. The elders had decided to make a film for the mining company to explain the

<hr>

91. Glowczewski, B. (Ed.), *Yapa, Aboriginal Painters from Balgo and Lajamanu*, exhibition catalog in English and French, Paris: Editions Baudoin Lebon, 1991.

importance of this sacred site in the Tanami Desert so as to protect it from gold exploration. This site was later fenced off for protection. At the time, unfortunately, people filmed over the original tapes, and there is no archive of this video other than my photographs of the different scenes when the Lajamanu *lawwomen* performed each of the many Dreaming places, the springs, rock holes and rocks that are significant within this vast sacred site of huge granite boulders.

The Warlpiri elders in Lajamanu were delighted that this experimental digital resource and device enabled us to illuminate and put into practice an insight into the reticularity required for navigating through the Aboriginal knowledge encrypted within places and songlines. Children were excited about having a computer "talking in Warlpiri" with photos of their families. The beta version of the CD-ROM called *Yapa*, meaning "People" in Warlpiri, received the special prize from the jury at the international multimedia Moebius competition in France. This allowed me to approach UNESCO to develop a version compatible on PCs, as the first version of the CD-ROM that was installed at the Lajamanu school in 1998 was only for Macs. We developed a special protocol with UNESCO Publishing that allowed for one-quarter of license sales to museums, universities and individuals to go back to the 50 contributing Lajamanu artists who would hold joint copyright.[92] The 50 artists were represented by the Warnayaka Art Centre, the Lajamanu art co-operative that was then managed by the famous Warlpiri artist Jimmy Robertson Jampijinpa. He was one of the 12 Warlpiri men who had been in Paris in 1983 to create a big sand painting of *Pirtina* (Python) Dreaming for the sacred site of *Jurntu* at the Museum of Modern Art, and to dance a dreamed *purlapa* (public ceremony) based in this same law in the Peter Brook Theatre.[93] The final agreement to publicly

---

92. Glowczewski, B. "Returning Indigenous knowledge: This CD-ROM brings everybody to the mind." *The Power of Knowledge, the Resonance of Tradition* (electronic publication of papers from the AIATSIS Indigenous Studies Conference, September 2001). Eds. GK Ward and A Muckle. AIATSIS, Canberra, 2005, 139–54, free e-book on www.aiatsis.gov.au/ research/docs/Indigenous_studies_conf_2001.pdf.

93. This marked the entry of Aboriginal art onto the international contemporary art stage. The 12 Warlpiri men were guests of the exhibition *D'un autre continent, L'Australie: Du rêve et du réel* (From Another Continent, Australia: Dream and Real) at the Museum of Modern Art, 1983, in Paris, which showed a large selection of

release this CD-ROM with UNESCO was reached in August 2000 at a Lajamanu Council meeting organized with John Stanton, Director of the Berndt Museum, as part of a collaboration established with my institution in France, the National Scientific Research Centre (CNRS).[94]

The Aboriginal appropriation of ITIC and YouTube

Jimmy Robertson Jampijinpa came to Paris in May 2001 to launch the *Dream Trackers* CD-ROM[95] at a symposium on Indigenous identity and new technologies organized at UNESCO with CNRS. Over the span of four days Indigenous writers, publishers, curators, scholars and artists from all over the world spoke with anthropologists and linguists about the use of new technologies, protocols and partnerships in different Indigenous projects. One of the 64 Indigenous guests was Marcia Langton, who gave a keynote address and also read a presentation by Helena Gulash on the pilot of the Ara Irititja digital archive project. Jimmy Jampijinpa talked about his first contact with white men as a child and sang a song about funeral paybacks.[96] Many Indigenous representatives asked him to demonstrate the use of the *Dream Trackers* CD-ROM and recommendations were made to UNESCO to support the

contemporary Australian art; at the theatre of Peter Brook, 17 dancers from Arnhem Land performed before the Warlpiri dance (see the exhibition catalog, B. Glowczewski, "Ritual and political networks among Aborigines in Northern Australia: Ancestral pathways across the seas" in *DreamTraces:Australian Aboriginal Bark Paintings*, Geneva: Infolio, Gollion/Musée d'ethnographie, 2010. 131–40); see the chapter "The Warlpiri in Paris" in the present publication.

94. Our collaboration followed from John Stanton's own involvement in contributing to the making of the *Moorditj* CD-ROM, an encyclopaedia of 100 Aboriginal artists, which was freely distributed to hundreds of schools around 2000.

95. Glowczewski, B. *Dream Trackers: Yapa art and knowledge of the Australian desert (Pistes de Rêves: Art et savoir des Aborigènes du désert australien)*. Paris: UNESCO Publishing, CD-ROM. (Joint copyright with 50 artists from Warnayaka Art): http://portal. unesco.org/science/en/ev.php-URL_ID=3540&URL_DO=DO_TOPIC&URL_SECTION=201.html.

96. His testimony is recorded in proceedings released on a CD-ROM with the United Nations Charter to promote Cultural Diversity; *Cultural Diversity and Indigenous Peoples: Oral, written expressions and new technologies*. Eds. Glowczewski B., Laurence Pourchez, Joëlle Rotkowski, John Stanton and the Division of Cultural Policies and Intercultural Dialogue. Paris: UNESCO Publishing, 2004. CD-ROM.

production of similar digital tools with other communities. When interviewed by a reporter for the UNESCO journal (*Source*, June 2001), Jimmy Robertson Jampijinpa said, "This CD-ROM brings people to the mind."

A big question in the 1990s was the secrecy surrounding knowledge that justifies its restriction in terms of public access in writing or in multimedia. The issue in Lajamanu was not necessarily about the content of knowledge, but the way and scope in which different kinds of knowledge are linked. It is the power of making connections that gives the power of understanding. Elders become wise and influential through alliances formed all their lives that allow them to build different links through a network of people who carry very different knowledge. Some Lajamanu men of my generation, who were in their forties during the making of the CD-ROM, have experimented with a different life of power influence. They did not go through the same stages of initiation as their elders, or to so many ceremonies or other events, to expand their alliances. Yet they gained other types of knowledge in their discussions with mining companies, government officials, lawyers for land rights claims and so on. They were bitter about the scope of their own traditional knowledge and would say things like, "Why should this power of connection be given to an outsider [through the CD-ROM], when it takes us so much time of hard work and rituals, travelling the land and all that, to acquire such knowledge."[97] However, older people, who knew that the CD-ROM was only presenting a very small sample of their knowledge, did not feel threatened. On the contrary, they wanted to demonstrate how their knowledge works, because, as Jimmy Jampijinpa said, "It brings people to the mind" by showing these principles of connection that help others to understand their relation to the land and the importance of their Dreaming law.

In 1979 I was allowed to film Warlpiri women dancing, on the condition that I screen this footage only to women in my own country, France. This was secret women's business connected with the *Kajirri* initiation of 22 young men. According to Mervyn Meggit,[98] women were excluded from this initiation

97. Glowczewski, B. Ibid.
98. Meggitt, Mervyn. Ibid.

ceremonial cycle, which he spelled "Gadgeri" 30 years earlier. During my fieldwork experience in Lajamanu in 1979 and 1984, I witnessed a daily negotiation between "businesswomen" and "businessmen," as the Warlpiri call people in charge of rituals. Each day over weeks, each gender would stage a process of exchange between the kin involved in this *Kajirri* ceremony for transforming young men into *Malyarra* initiates. The production of the individual value embodied by each initiate was conditioned by the secret value of the dancing, singing and painting of sacred objects in separate spaces by men and women. Between 1995 and 2000, during the process of returning my films and other data for the *Dream Trackers* CD-ROM, the 50 custodians of Warlpiri law, who were involved in this project through their recorded rituals and recent acrylic paintings on canvas, agreed to include for general viewing some women's-only footage from 1979 on the condition that they were paid for this intellectual property and that it was not put on the Internet. This negotiable aspect of value — of what is "dear" or "cheap" in the public performance of women's rituals and how the boundaries of what can be shown or not can shift over time — has been highlighted by other anthropologists.[99] One way of expressing the value of the Dreaming knowledge stored on the CD-ROM was to make users recognize the individual copyright of individual artists when seeking to reproduce their works, and to have them pay for software licenses to access related information.

From 2001 to 2004 a teacher who was looking after the information technology room for several years in the Lajamanu school facilitated access to the *Dream Trackers* CD-ROM for all generations, so that children, young people, literacy workers and older kin were all welcome at the school. In September 2005 I went to Lajamanu to bring copyright payments from a publisher for the reproduction of paintings in a photo book that compared art and rituals from Lajamanu and Galiwin'ku.[100]

99. Dussart, Françoise. *The Politics of Ritual in an Aboriginal Settlement: Kinship, gender and the currency of knowledge*. Washington, DC: Smithsonian Institution Press, 2000; Sylvie Poirier, *A World of Relationships: Itineraries, dreams, and events in the Australian desert*, Toronto: University of Toronto Press, 2005; Kimberley Christen, *Aboriginal Business: Alliances in a remote Australian town*, Santa Fe, NM: School for Advanced Research Press, Global Indigenous Politics Series, 2008.
100. Glowczewski B. and J. De Largy Healy. *Pistes de Rêve: Voyage en terres aborigènes*.

The CD-ROM was accessible to the community, not only in the school, but also in a special room set up next to the Lajamanu Council office, where three PCs were installed for Internet access. A constant flow of people of all ages, including young mothers with babies on their laps, were using these facilities and browsing through various Aboriginal websites. I was then asked why our *Yapa* CD-ROM was only on these hard disks and not on the web. With digital technologies entering the economic and political life of Indigenous people in Australia, either to promote their art or convey social messages, many Warlpiri users started to think that it was important to use the Internet to explain to their young ones the knowledge connections of their Dreaming law and culture. A similar shift was then taking place in other places like Arnhem Land, for instance, with the Galiwin'ku Knowledge Centre, where a digital archive was being developed with materials returned from different collections in museums and elsewhere.[101]

In 2006 a young Warlpiri literacy worker from Lajamanu, Steve Patrick, known by his Aboriginal name Wanta Jampijinpa,[102] elaborated on a complex cognitive system that encompassed the concept of *ngurra-kurlu* (belonging to land), which he promotes as a teaching tool and a strategy "to work with Warlpiri" language and people in many ways. On YouTube, we

---

Paris: Editions du Chêne, 2005.

101. This project is documented by Joe Neparrnga Gumbula, "Exploring the Gupapuynga legacy: Strategies for developing the Galiwin'ku Indigenous Knowledge Centre" *Australian Indigenous Knowledge and Libraries*, Eds. M. Nakata and M. Langton. Sydney: UTSePress, 2005. http://hdl.handle. net/2100/835 accessed October 25, 2012; Also see Jessica De Largy Healy who has worked with him since 2003 when she volunteered for the Galiwin'ku Knowledge Centre while researching her thesis: *The spirit of emancipation and the struggle with modernity: Land, art, ritual and a digital documentation project in a Yolŋu community, Galiwin'ku, Northern Territory of Australia*, doctoral thesis (co-supervised by M. Langton and B. Glowczewski), Paris: the University of Melbourne and EHESS, 2008; "The genealogy of dialogue: fieldwork stories from Arnhem Land." *The Challenge of Indigenous Peoples. Spectacle or Politics?* Eds. B. Glowczewski and R. Henry, Oxford: Bardwell Press, 2011. 47–70; On Yolŋu reappropriation of knowledge, see the film by Barker and Glowczewski, 2002. *Spirit of Anchor* (*L'Esprit de l'Ancre*), 53 min. documentary, CNRS Images, free viewing online http://videotheque.cnrs.fr/index. php?urlaction=doc&id_doc=980&langue=EN.

102. Jampijinpa, Wanta. *Ngurra-kurlu*, YouTube, www.youtube.com/watch?v=iFZq7A-duGrc&feature=related, 2006; Wanta Jampijinpa Pawu-Kurlpurlurnu (Steven Jampijinpa Patrick), Miles Holmes, (Lance) Alan Box, *Ngurra-kurlu: A way of working with Warlpiri people*, Desert knowledge CRC (Report 41), 2008.

hear his voice in Warlpiri and see subtitles and his hand drawing a sand design in which five circles represent Warlpiri cosmo-sociological concepts he translates in English: *ngurra* (land) in the center, and around this, *kuruwarri* (law), ceremonies including *purlapa* and *jarda-wanpa*, *jaru* (language) and family structures that comprise four interrelated father–son "skin" groups. These five concept circles are connected by lines as an expression of interconnections that hold together this Warlpiri system of knowledge. Wanta Jampijinpa explains that, if a link between any two of these concepts is broken, or if any concept does not hold strongly, everything collapses; for example, if language is not taught, if family is dislocated, if ceremonies are not performed, if land is not looked after and so on.

After that, we see him in a schoolroom with papers on the pin boards. He explains the meaning of an acrylic painting, which is standing on a couch, and like his sand drawing also has a five-circle structure. This time around the central circle is for the land; the other four show the complementarity of the four skin groups: *Yarriki* designates the patrifilial group of the speaker's mother; *Wurruru*, the patrifilial group of the speaker's mother's mother (also man's mother-in-law, woman's son-in-law); *Kirda*, the patrifilial group of a spouse (woman's children or wife's father); and *Wapirra-jarra*, the speaker's patrifilial group. A color is allocated to each of these four skin group circles. Blue is for owners of the Water and Emu Dreamings, like Wanta himself, and is represented by an emu footprint painted in a blue circle. Green is for owners of the Yam Dreaming, with a yam rhizome painted in a green circle. Red is for owners of the Wallaby Dreaming, with a wallaby footprint painted in a red circle, and yellow is for owners of the Bush Turkey Dreaming, with a bush turkey footprint painted in a yellow circle.[103] These painted footprints are not explained on the video, yet are like icons for all the other Dreaming constellations under the care of each of the four Warlpiri skin groups. They visually summarize a Warlpiri conception of the cosmos, and people's

---

103. See *Lesson Drawn in Sand* by Wanta Jampijinpa. *Ngurra-kurlu*, YouTube, Ibid. About Wanta Jampijinpa see also B. Glowczewski, J. De Largy Healy and A. Morvan, 2008; "Aux sources de la création." *Aborigènes-La collection australienne du Musée des Confluences de Lyon*. Lyon: Fage Editions, 2006. 20–37.

place and duty for maintaining the balance within their land and society.

Wanta Patrick Jampijinpa established, with Tracks Theatre Company, the Milpirri "Raincloud" Festival to promote these concepts through local events at which young people wear these four colors and dance in their skin groups with elders. He also developed guidelines for Indigenous Protected Areas of land. In May 2009 he was invited to France by the Musée des Confluences in Lyon for a meeting called *Paroles Autochtones* "Indigenous Voices," along with another young Indigenous Australian from Queensland who authored a book on his language[104] and five Indigenous students from a United Nations training program. They spoke with different audiences in the city, where two Aboriginal exhibitions were also organized, and a film was produced with all the Indigenous guests.[105] Wanta Patrick Jampijinpa said in one of these meetings, like Jimmy Robertson Jampijinpa nine years earlier, that the purpose of his Milpirri Festival project was "to bring people to the mind."

This Warlpiri interpretation of the analogy between social, ritual, and mental or cognitive networks also relates to digital networks as tools to "bring people to the mind": that is, to understand how meaningful and emotional connections work, and how thinking can act as a propeller for action. Such a vision is a challenge to anthropologists to construct more than simple databases with Aboriginal knowledge. Our work is to do some kind of interpretation, and not only to limit ourselves to classifying raw data into our Western categories. That is to say, data speak if they are connected with different kinds of meanings that go with them. Nowadays, on the Internet, you can use any search engine, like Google, to interrogate a word, a name or a concept, and you will have thousands of web links that are proposed. Yet this information is not organized, only prioritized by number of visits to each website in descending order. In other words, it is the websites that are mostly visited that are returned as top choices, like Wikipedia, and not the most relevant to finding first-hand data. Organization of data, through research currently developed by

104. Sullivan, Lance. *Ngiaka Yalarrnga*. Cannington Press, 2005.
105. Galindo, Cesar. *La terre est notre vie (Land is our life)*. 30 min. DVD, produced by the Musée des Confluences, Lyon: France, 2010.

some anthropologists and ITIC specialists in other disciplines, is about trying to develop a semantics of interpretation and create specific ontologies that allow for searched concepts to be returned with links to their various meaningful connections and the stories they carry; with the links these imply for related concepts; and, at the same time, there are some restrictions to implement so that ethical Indigenous protocols are respected in relation to the circulation of knowledge.

Transmission of knowledge and cultural creativity

By 2007 half of the elders involved with the *Dream Trackers* CD-ROM had passed away, so I went to Lajamanu for a big meeting to find out who were the inheritors of those 25 elders. The money owed to each of the 50 copyright holders was only $200 — "lollies," as some Warlpiri say. I proposed to put all the money in a collective fund to restart the Warnayaka Art Centre, which was in a process of re-registration as a business after requests from many artists and the Lajamanu Council. The program was already in its seventh year and there were not as many sales of licenses as there had been during the first years, when thousands of dollars from CD-ROM sales were transferred from UNESCO Publishing to Warnayaka Art. The centre was closed in 2002 after the death of its chairman, Jimmy Robertson Jampijinpa. Following various attempts to find a caretaker for the UNESCO contract, the Warlukurlangu Art Centre in Yuendumu agreed to hold it for the Lajamanu artists from their CD-ROM royalties until their own art centre was re-opened. The collective discussion with the families of the 50 original artists revealed that it was symbolically extremely important to distribute 50 checks so as to confirm the copyright of the contributors. There were 10 old men and some 15 women at this meeting, which was filmed. For most of the deceased artists, they collectively designated an heir who was not a son or a daughter, but a grandson or a granddaughter living in Lajamanu or in another Warlpiri community like Yuendumu or Willowra, or in towns like Katherine, Tennant Creek, Alice Springs or Darwin. This was very moving for me, because I had seen these young people as babies or children in camps in 1979, and some came to me to express their own emotions: "You grew us up living in the camp with our old people, and we are carrying that thing now...."

Why did these elders decided to "skip" a generation? One reason was to give the responsibility to young people aged between 20 and 25 because they can read, are used to travel, are parents themselves, teach at the school, and know how to use new technologies or have other skills. One was even training to be a policeman. It was important for the elders to recognize these young people as caretakers by officially telling them, "You have to carry the law. You are responsible." This is interesting, because this choice to recognize young people shows an adaptation of the current priorities at Lajamanu to saving Warlpiri culture. In 1979 the law leaders were upset that some young people who wanted to learn the law were spending a lot of time doing other things, such as training for jobs, and going to many meetings to negotiate land and mining deals, and would not spend enough time learning their own hereditary knowledge in the camps during rituals and in the bush.

With time, the Warlpiri have adapted a lot of things, for instance, regarding marriage. Until recently, during a boy's initiation, *kurdiji*, a girl of his age was betrothed as his future mother-in-law, and from that day he could not speak to her or any women having the same skin name as her. Since the 1980s lots of teenagers have had love affairs and children at an early age without respecting the kinship principles that forbid them to marry and have children with somebody carrying the same skin name as oneself, one's mother, or a male's mother-in-law or a female's son-in-law. Wanta Patrick Jampijinpa, with his concept of the Milpirri Festival, has iconized the four colors in an attempt to teach and protect the complexity of the traditional cosmological classification of the four skin name groupings:

The skin names have been color coded so that they relate to the dreamings that are owned by each group. N/Jakamarra + Na/Jupurrurla are red because they are custodians for the red kangaroo and many other land animals. N/Jampijinpa + N/Jangala are blue because of the primary importance of the rain dreaming. N/Napaljarri + N/Jungarrayi are yellow because they have many bird stories and star stories. N/Japangardi + N/Japanangka are green because they have many plant stories like the bush potato, which is very important and has very green leaves. In Lajamanu it is common now to hear kids refer to skin as the green group, yellow group, etc. This is a modern interpretation of an old system. As Wanta says, *"The color coding gets them started, then they can learn the other relationships."*[106]

The colors of costumes that dancers wear at the Milpirri Festival are determined by their own skin names, much like the colors of uniforms in sport teams. Wanta Patrick Jampijinpa has also produced plastic bracelets, which are given to children and adults according to their skin names as a way of helping them to identify the traditional rules that organize the whole cosmos. Skin names are attached to all animals and plants, and other things like rain or fire that identify Dreamings and places. Interestingly, plastic bracelets, popular in the Western youth cultures, were forbidden in Brazilian schools because some children, not knowing the color code, were wearing bracelets with a color that identified them as "free for sex" (pers. comm. from Brazilian friends). In the Lajamanu case, the four skin colors also carry a message in terms of courtship and potential sex, but only as an attempt to prevent the wrong choices, as the traditional skin name classification determines from which group one can find a spouse, while it is forbidden to even have love affairs with the other three groups. People who carry the same skin name are considered as skin brothers and sisters, and cannot flirt because this is considered incest. The colored bracelets thus remind children which member of the opposite sex is or is not allowed to be a potential spouse, or even boyfriend or girlfriend. For Warlpiri, therefore, the way people marry preserves the balance among all the Dreamings, the fertility of related species, and the general wellbeing of the society and the land.

On January 18, 2008 a group of *lawmen* from Lajamanu recorded and posted on YouTube a protest against police who had interrupted a boy's initiation that they were organising on a restricted ceremonial ground. The video in English and Warlpiri, with subtitles in English, provides strong statements by

---

106. Wanta Jampijinpa Pawu-Kurlpurlurnu (Steven Jampijinpa Patrick), Miles Holmes, (Lance) Alan Box, Ibid.

lawmen asking why police cannot accept the sanctity of their sacred sites and law. It also provides an explanation of why the entry of a policewoman onto the initiation ground was a transgression of their law: the men's ground is forbidden to women precisely because it is the place where boys learn how to respect women.[107] It took two years of discussion for the police to finally make an official apology to the Lajamanu community for their intrusion on this sacred ground. This event, like many others resulting from the Northern Territory Emergency Response or other discriminatory experiences, has provoked a mixture of anger, mistrust and despair among old and young generations alike. This potential for new ways of civil expression that call for responses and contribute to conflict resolution is an important aspect of the Internet, especially when such initiatives are grassroots.

Experimenting with digital reticularity to change perceptions

When I went back to Lajamanu in August 2010, the Warnayaka Art Centre was run by four staff members, with lots of artists painting every day and workshops for children and young people.[108] It had several computers and one with a huge screen. I transferred onto this computer 90 hours of my 1984 Lajamanu recordings, which the linguist Mary Laughren at the University of Queensland had digitized as part of the Warlpiri Songlines project she was undertaking with Nic Peterson and Stephen Wild at the Australian National University. I also reinstalled the *Dream Trackers* CD-ROM in the school where PCs had replaced Macs, in the Council office, and in the new library jointly funded by Northern Territory Library and mining royalties to Lajamanu families.[109] Lajamanu was then hosting a Warlpiri

---

107. *Lajamanu and the Law*, www.youtube.com/watch?v=aU4m3bRyRqU& feature=related, 2008.

108. *Lajamanu Keeps Culture Alive and Builds Business*. https://www.youtube.com/watch?v=XnYzNxxY, 2010

109. The CD-ROM is still readable on PCs, but not on Mac OS X. The French Musée des Confluences in Lyon funded an attempt to automatically convert the programming of the CD-ROM with Director software to its latest version working on Mac OS X, but it did not work properly. Many CD-ROMs are in this situation and the only solution is

Triangle meeting, which was also partly funded through mining royalties in an initiative to promote Warlpiri teaching in the three communities of Lajamanu, Yuendumu and Willowra. All of the delegates were Warlpiri teaching assistants and literacy workers who were very affected by the recent reduction of the bilingual schooling program to half-an-hour a week per class. Many were proposing to use more digital technologies to promote and teach their language to young ones. Teachers and other participants asked for the *Dream Trackers* CD-ROM to be put on the Northern Territory education server and found it to be an exemplary model for organising data. More than ever, I felt compelled to provide for students and teachers access to this Warlpiri knowledge via an easy web interface.

After several projects presented to UNESCO, which required important funding, I was invited to put my digital Warlpiri audio-visual material on the Online Digital Sources and Annotation System for the Social Sciences (ODSAS), which was conceived by French anthropologist Laurent Dousset as a participative platform to safeguard online collections from Oceania, including his Western Desert collection, Karel Kupka's field notes from Arnhem Land, and data from some 30 other French researchers working in the Pacific. On July 2011, with Mary Laughren, I organized a workshop in Lajamanu to show the Warlpiri a sample of my online data and how they could use the system to annotate their photos (200 from 1984) and films (three hours from 1979), or transcribe stories and songs (90 hours from 1984). The photo set was made accessible to the public, while other sets required the use of a password. I photographed and filmed the annotation process, which met with enthusiasm from different generations. Back in France this audio-visual documentation was put online as a public set.[110] It demonstrated young people writing names of the relatives that they recognised on the photographs; Elisabeth Ross Nungarrayi transcribing in Warlpiri a myth told by a deceased ancestor; Jerry Jangala dictating to Mary Laughren the

---

to reprogram in another format, preferably open source, so there is no risk to prevent safeguarding again. The issue of saving our data and programs of linkages in formats that can be easily converted has inclined most of the research community, and archive and academic institutions, to push for this development of open sources.

110. Available at http://www.odsas.net/scan_sets.php?set_id=752&doc=78219&step=5.

transcription and translation of a ritual song; or Henry Cook Jakamarra, more than 80 years of age, singing a 1984 ceremony he had not practiced for years with striking concentration and animated gestures — and continuing to sing the cycle once the recording stopped.

In 2012 I was able to add a thousand photos and link to some Warlpiri songs and stories English transcriptions and texts I had used on the *Dream Trackers* CD-ROM. Another trip to Lajamanu allowed Mary Laughren and me to test again the ODSAS system so as to improve the interface (Figures 1 and 2). Many Warlpiri people gave us USB flash drives to upload photos so they could view them at home on their PlayStations as very few have computers at home to access the Internet.

Figure 1: Warnayaka Art centre, Lajamanu, August 2012: Shannon Nampijin-pa annotates a photo of her father, Joe Long Jangala, during a *Kajirri* trip in Docker River, 1984.

Internet access in Lajamanu is a problem: each collective service (Northern Territory Library, school, council, shop, hospital, art centre etc.) pays providers for its Internet connection but Warlpiri households are asked to pay a $250 subscription per month or to buy connection on credit through Telstra. This is contrary to the whole idea of free access to knowledge and the reappropriation of their archival material. An Aboriginal community of less than a thousand inhabitants should have free WiFi for all, instead of multiple subscriptions. Another problem is access to computers, maintenance and training. Many young people — and even children — are very good at using computers (they also use Facebook on their mobile telephones) but with the reduction of the bilingual Warlpiri curriculum, teenagers and some young parents are unable to write in Warlpiri and many cannot properly write in English either. In 2011 The Northern Territory Library was very interested to use the Warlpiri collection on ODSAS as a tool for computer training but it has not been organized yet because of a lack of staff, which — like in many other communities of the Northern Territory — does not allow for someone to even open the Library and let the Warlpiri use the community computers, which are partly funded by their own royalties. The situation is not due to a real lack of money but to the disempowerment of communities through the Northern Territory intervention and the new shire system that does not allow them to manage their community as they would like to (for instance, by employing two or more part-time staff members to share the same job rather than one full-time position that no Warlpiri can really assume when there are so many meetings (mining, funerals etc.) to attend all the time).

Transmission of Indigenous knowledge, digital and other forms of cultural education,[111] and the digital anthropology I engage with[112] are not about mapping heritage and strategic data onto a Google map, but, rather, about allowing new social

111. Martin Nakata. *Disciplining the Savages: Savaging the disciplines.* Canberra: Aboriginal Studies Press: 2007.
112. Michael Wesch, (uploaded March 8th 2007) "Web 2.0...The Machine is Us/ing Us (final version)", https://www.youtube.com/watch?v=EAVmB5dKZZ8, *An Anthropological Introduction to YouTube,* presented at the Library of Congress, June 23, 2008. www.youtube.com/watch?v=TPAO-lZ4_hU.

practices of sharing, as advocated by Guattari, that empower the people involved. It is collective intelligence that is at stake, which is understood as a collaboration between actors at the intersection of cultures and disciplines. This is a "connected intelligence" according to the ethics of De Kerckhove and Pierre Lévy's pioneering insights.[113]

Figure 2: Lajamanu Library, August 2012. Warlpiri digital archives (from left to right): Juddy Napangardi is watching a DVD of her tour in Europe (with Denise Napangardi, Rebecca Napanangka and Agnes Napanangka for exhibitions in Paris, Berlin, and the Brave Festival in Poland, June 2012); Julieanne Ross Nampijinpa is documenting the ODSAS Lajamanu collections (1979–2011); Rebecca Napanangka is watching the *Dream Trackers* CD-ROM (2001) produced with 50 artists from Warnayaka Art. See also Louw 2013.

113. Derrick De Kerckhove, *Connected Intelligence.* Ed. Wade Rowland, London: Kogan Page, 1997; Pierre Lévy, *Collective Intelligence: Mankind's emerging world in cyberspace.* Trans. Robert Bononno. New York: Basic Books, Perseus Books, 1994.

This ideal echoes Curtis Taylor's visionary statement at the 2010 ITIC Symposium: "We have a dreaming like our elders: in the mind; digital technologies." The "we" he puts forward here in representing his generation echoes both Martin Luther King's speech of August 28, 1963, "I have a dream,"[114] and the title of Stanner's 1979 collection of essays, *White Man Got No Dreaming.*[115] This progressive rise of black consciousness across such discourse, and international recognition for transnational Indigenous solidarity, has opened new "Dreaming networks" that can inform the use of digital technologies in ways that can foster new forms of dialogue and a better future, including a better form of social justice.[116]

---

114. Film *Martin Luther King I Have a Dream 1963 Part 1.* www.youtube.com/watch?v=wYUCLMjUcbk, 1963.

115. Stanner,WEH. *White Man Got No Dreaming: Essays, 1938–1973.* Canberra: ANU Press, 1979.

116. Following the violent death in custody of Cameron Doomadgee or Mulrunji in November 2004 on Palm Island, the acquittal in June 2007 of Senior Sergeant Hurley, who had been charged for this death, and Lex Wotton's trial in November 2009, as the leader of the ensuing riot, a campaign of support spread across Australia. Some protests were filmed and posted on YouTube. In July 2010 Lex Wotton was released, but with no right to speak to the media or in public meetings: Vernon Ah Kee, an Aboriginal artist of international renown, produced an art installation in support of Lex Wotton at the Milani Gallery in Brisbane. It included film footage shot by the police during the 2004 Palm Island riot that followed the death of Mulrunji. A month after the closing of the exhibition, the artist was interviewed on the *7.30 Report*, and this footage was presented on the ABC as the first publicly available police footage of the incident. This footage, which I analysed in *Guerriers pour la Paix: La condition politique des Aborigènes vue de Palm Island* (Glowczewski 2008, with two chapters by Lex Wotton), Indigène Editions, Montpellier (free download of the English translation *Warriors for Peace:The political condition of the Aboriginal people as viewed from Palm Island* on http://researchonline. jcu.edu.au/7286, with foreword by B. Glowczewski and postword by Lise Garond, June 2010), was shown publicly in the Courthouse of Townsville during the committal hearing of the rioters, where many journalists were sitting to report. They commented on some of it at the time in local and national newspapers, but it is as if the meaning of these images was suddenly making another impact when exhibited by a famous artist known for his critical approach to colonial history and social injustice.

Univocal Publishing
123 North 3rd Street, #202
Minneapolis, MN 55401
www.univocalpublishing.com

ISBN 9781937561963

Jason Wagner, Drew S. Burk
(Editors)
All materials were printed and bound
in January 2016 at Univocal's atelier
in Minneapolis, USA.

This work was composed in Garamond
The paper is Hammermill 98.
The letterpress cover was printed
on Crane's Lettra Ecru.
Both are archival quality and acid-free.